A Program Guide For

CIM Implementation

Second Edition

A Project of the

CASA/SME
Technical Council

Editors, Second Edition

Dr. Leonard Bertain
Lee Hales

Published by

Society of Manufacturing Engineers
Publications Development Department
One SME Drive
P.O. Box 930
Dearborn, Michigan 48121

D1249442

A Program Guide For
CIM Implementation

Copyright © 1987
Society of Manufacturing Engineers
Dearborn, Michigan 48121

Second Edition

First Printing

Library of Congress Catalog Card Number: 87-62381

International Standard Book Number: 0-87263-295-4

Manufactured in the United States of America

Introduction

Computer Integrated Manufacturing (CIM) is a strategic response to changing business conditions. It is a more flexible and more effective way of doing business in today's globally/competitive environment. The integration of computer and automated systems helps us to make more extensive and more timely use of information, which in turn, can have dramatic impact on cost, quality, cycle times, and asset utilization.

In 1984, NASA asked the National Research Council (NRC) to study the impact of integration efforts at McDonnell Aircraft Co., Deere and Co., Westinghouse Defense and Electronics Center, General Motors, and Ingersoll Milling Machine Co. The NRC's committee on the CAD/CAM interface checked the results carefully before printing them. The committee found that these companies had already received significant benefits, even though they were only partially into their 10 to 20-year integration efforts. The figure below summarizes these benefits.

Reduction in engineering design cost	15-30%
Reduction in overall lead time	30-60%
Increased productivity of production operations (complete assemblies)	40-70%
Reduction of work in process	30-60%
Increased product quality as measured by yield of acceptable product	2-5 times
Increased capability of engineers as measured by extent and depth of analysis in same or less time	3-35 times
Increased productivity (operating time) of capital equipment	2-3 times

The focus of CIM technology is the shared use of information by marketing, engineering, production, and other major operations of the manufacturing firm.

However, CIM is more than technology.

It is the corporate strategy for survival. It is an overall strategy that *includes manufacturing*. For CIM to succeed it requires strategy, tactics, and implementation. This *Program Guide* covers all three.

When the first edition of this book was published in 1985, most companies were still in need of the motivation for CIM. The "what and why" of Computer Integrated Manufacturing were major issues of the day. Since then, the CASA Technical Council has observed much progress, from motivation to action, and a resulting interest in the "how to" of planning and implementing a CIM program. The challenge for this second edition of the *Program Guide* has been to organize our observations and experiences, and to put forth a framework or path that will guide the reader toward the achievement of CIM. To this end, the second edition contains four parts, each representing a major phase in the process of planning and implementation. We have given each part its own brief introduction, to help weave a thread through individually contributed readings. The consistency of conclusions among independent authors is at times remarkable, and will hopefully add to your confidence that we have charted a pragramtic course and covered the appropriate issues. An Appendix section presents other selected readings from the first edition.

Part One—Strategic Thinking, recaps the first edition's focus on motivation. It discusses the need to get organized and to establish baseline conditions. It also discusses the identification of competitive issues that will be addressed by the CIM program and focuses attention on the importance of people in the CIM planning process.

Part Two—Conceptual Planning, shows by example what CIM is all about. It describes the kinds of leading-edge planning and integration that is showing results today. This part of the book also covers the issues of standards and justifications that are central to a conceptual plan.

Part Three—Systems Design, is about tools and techniques. It covers the important issues to consider as individual projects are defined and specific systems are built.

Part Four—Installation, illustrates many of the unique issues and concerns that emerge when integrated systems are brought on-line.

There is a certain "bulge" to the content in Part 2. This is deliberate and reflects our belief that good conceptual planning is critical to the ultimate success of CIM, and therefore worthy of extra attention.

This *Program Guide For CIM Implementation* is a unique collective effort of the CASA Technical Council. Those who have contributed are recognized below. Vic Muglia is kindly acknowledged for his help in organizing this edition. We acknowledge our debt to Dr. Charles Savage, Editor of the First Edition, for showing us the way. We also wish to thank the dedicated staff at SME—Cheri Willetts, James Warren, and Bob King—for their efforts in producing this book.

Dr. Leonard Bertain
Editor

Mr. Lee Hales, CMC
Editor

The following persons have contributed their time and knowledge to help develop this CIM guide.

Edward J. Adlard, Litton ITS; Daniel S. Appleton, DACOM; Gregory J. Barcklow, Eastman Kodak; Edward L. Barnett, E.L. Barnett & Co.; Ralph G. Bennett, Arthur D. Little Inc.; Dr. Ralph R. Bravoco, Texas Tech University; Gary K. Conkol, Picker International; H. Lee Hales, SysteCon; George Hess, Ingersoll Milling Machine; Ernest H. Kahn, General Electric; Jerry Kaser, Rockwell International; Anil Kumar, Hewlett Packard; Guy Little, Varian; Dr. Jack R. Meredith, University of Cincinnati; Ronald J. Meyer, Rockwell International; William Muir, Price Waterhouse; Dennis J. Mykols, Digital Equipment; Rex L. Nelson, IBM; Wade L. Ogburn, AT&T Technologies; Stephen J. Orth, University of Minnesota; Larry Phillips, AT&T Technologies; Peter K. Punwami, Price Waterhouse; William G. Rankin, Deere & Company; Oscar G. Rhudy, Rust International Corp.; Jack R. Schneider, Digital Equipment; David C. Scott, Deere & Company; George W. Sibbald, Genovation; M. Syamak Shafi-Nia, Micro Media Controls; Warren L. Shrensker, General Electric; Dr. Craig Skevington, Rensselaer Polytechnic Institute; John F. Snyder, General Electric; Mark H. Stern, IBM; Paul M. Trotta, Cummins Engine; and Madden T. Works, Aeroject Electro System.

about CASA/SME

The Computer and Automated Systems Association of the Society of Manufacturing Engineers (CASA/SME) was founded in 1975 to provide comprehensive and integrated coverage of the field of computers and automation for the advancement of manufacturing.

As an educational and scientific association, CASA/SME has become "home" for engineers, managers and other professionals involved in computer-based technologies and automated systems. CASA/SME is applications oriented and addresses all phases of research, design, installation, operation and maintenance of the total manufacturing enterprise. This book is one example of its wide-ranging activities.

Specific CASA/SME goals are: to provide professionals with a focus for the many aspects of manufacturing which utilize computer systems automation; to provide liaison among industry, government and education in identifying areas of further technology development; and to encourage the development of the totally integrated manufacturing facility.

The CIM Enterprise Wheel

The purpose of the CASA/SME Wheel is to provide industry with a common vision of Computer Integrated Manufacturing (CIM). Originally published in 1980, the Wheel became the centerpiece of many corporate programs focused on the objective of implementing Computer Integrated Manufacturing. However, as time marched on, the original vision of CIM began to change. It became clear to the CASA/SME Technical Council that the purpose of CIM was not simply to bring automation to bear on the problem of integrating traditional manufacturing processes, it was to improve the productivity of the total manufacturing enterprise through integrating all of its processes.

This is a top-down perspective of CIM—a view from the office of the business executive rather than the manufacturing technologist. It is the only view of integration that makes sense, because integrating is more of an imperative to those who must derive economic benefit from it—that is, to the integrators—than it is to those who must submit to its rules and controls—integratees.

Computer Integrated Manufacturing is a goal. The mission of the Computer and Automated Systems Association of the Society of Manufacturing Engineers (CASA/SME) is to provide industry with a means of visualizing that goal, and, further, with the education and training necessary to achieve that goal and measure progress toward it. The job of the CASA/SME Technical Council is to particulate the goal and the path to the goal. Through the CASA/SME Wheel, we have provided a vision of the goal. Through the CIM Planning Guide, AUTOFACT, and our CASA/SME Technical Programs, we are providing some of the stepping stones in the path toward it. And, through our CASA/SME LEAD Awards, we are monitoring progress along that path, enterprise by enterprise.*

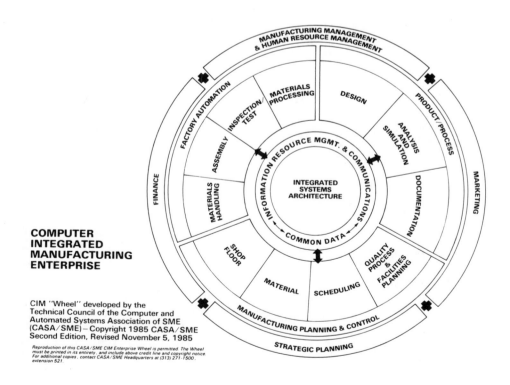

COMPUTER INTEGRATED MANUFACTURING ENTERPRISE

CIM "Wheel" developed by the Technical Council of the Computer and Automated Systems Association of SME (CASA/SME) – Copyright 1985 CASA/SME Second Edition, Revised November 5, 1985

Reproduction of this CASA/SME CIM Enterprise Wheel is permitted. The Wheel must be printed in its entirety, and include above credit line and copyright notice. For additional copies, contact CASA/SME Headquarters at (313) 271-1500, extension 521.

*By Daniel S. Appleton from the booklet: *Introducing the New CIM Enterprise Wheel* (1985).

Table of Contents

PART THREE--SYSTEMS DESIGN

PART FOUR--INSTALLATION

Editorial Overview of Part One

This part of the *Program Guide* is about the motivation and strategic thinking that must precede sound plans for CIM. It is about getting organized and defining the roles of the top management, as well as those of specialists in computer and automated systems.

In the lead paper, Mr. Dan Appleton gives us a valuable definition of CIM, and a perspective on the kinds of funding required to put a sound CIM program in place. Next, Dr. Charles Savage outlines top management's role in setting the direction and policies that will guide the CIM program. The third paper, by Dr. Leonard Bertain, suggests that "Reculturing for CIM" is a critical part of the CIM program and can have dramatic impacts on the bottom line before investment in large computer systems. Lastly, Peter Punwani suggests step-by step approach to assessing business needs, and setting the specific objectives to be addressed by the CIM effort.

STRATEGIC THINKING

CONCEPTUAL PLANNING

SYSTEMS DESIGN

INSTALLATION

Part 1

Strategic Thinking

Building
a CIM Program

by Daniel S. Appleton
D. Appleton Company, Incorporated

INTRODUCTION

What does Computer Integrated Manufacturing (CIM) have in common with Zero Defects, quality, productivity, safety, and asset management?

These words and phrases define more than just abstract concepts, principles, or philosophies. They describe distinct management programs which either have been or are operating in your enterprise. You know what a Zero Defects Program is, and what types of projects are executed under the umbrella of a Quality Program, a Productivity Program, a Safety Program, or an Asset Management Program. "Programs" are familiar techniques which are employed to effect specific changes in the style, attitude, approach, or philosophy of the people in an enterprise.

A program is an umbrella, under which you plan, finance, validate, manage, and implement specific projects. The objective of a program is to focus individual projects toward a common, well-defined goal. Programs do not die. They fade away, giving way (hopefully) to fundamental changes in the day-to-day operating style of the organization. However, while they are alive, they are managed, marketed, ballyhooed, funded, and monitored by all levels of management. They are taken very seriously.

Integration is achieved through a program, not a project. The objective of an integration program is to achieve integration of various independent "islands of automation" projects. You must accept that any automation project executed under an integration program will be integrated with the others. Integration is accomplished through specific integration methods and tools for planning and executing integrated projects.

WHY INTEGRATION?

The need for integration has evolved in response to a set of specific problems which arise as a result of the traditional process of industrial automation. These problems were articulated in a special study done for the United States Air Force Integrated Computer-Aided Manufacturing (ICAM) program. This study of the state of industrial automaton in 1983 found five crucial problems:

1. users cannot control information,
2. change is too costly,
3. systems are not integrated,
4. data quality is poor, and
5. systems take too long to change.

These problems arise from a job shop approach to automation. This approach takes specific sets of user requirements and discovers special technical solutions for each of them, creating what have come to be called "islands of automation" and "islands of data."

These islands can sometimes be interfaced (cross referenced) after the fact, but they can never be fully integrated. Interfacing is accomplished by wiring independent islands of automation together. Integration is accomplished by creating individual solutions which share common parts, such as data.

The job shop methodology which created islands of automation looks for specific vendor technical solutions to specific user requirements. Each solution has its own unique input, output, storage, and processing structure. Each may also have its own hardware, data management, programming, and communications structure.

The problem is that while user requirements tend to change rapidly in response to market, political, social, and managerial forces, technical solutions do not. Technical solutions respond to whatever forces are driving individual vendors. The islands of automation approach not only places individual user requirements at the mercy of specific vendor solutions (often holding them hostage); it allows for individual vendor solutions to be inconsistent, incompatible, and generally not shareable.

WHAT IS CIM?

CIM is a new enterprise-wide management process for industrial automation. It appears as a special program under which industrial automation projects are planned, executed, and integrated.

What is new about CIM? Well, it is the introduction of a third perspective on industrial automation as a complement to the user and technical perspectives. It is this enterprise perspective which provides the common ground for integration and sharing, and which ensures quality, consistency and flexibility in the total automated structure of the enterprise.

The keys to the enterprise perspective of CIM are the standards, procedures, and performance measures which are established. These must be employed on all projects, to ensure integration where it is required. These standards and procedures affect the planning and financing of industrial automation projects, and they control project justification, selection, prioritization, and management.

Standards are critical to ensure integration in a CIM program. But, before dealing with what kind of standards are needed, there should be a discussion of standards in general. Standards are not permanent. To be effective, standards must be changed. They must be kept up to date. They must respond to user needs. The critical issue is how standards change--not that the standards are inflexible. People will accept and use standards if they believe there is an effective mechanism for changing them. This mechanism must be responsive, and it must ensure backward compatibility between implementation under the new standards and implementation under the old standards.

THE CIM PROGRAM STRUCTURE

A CIM program, to be successful, must be structured around new concepts in:

1. Planning.
2. Finance.
3. Project selection.
4. Project management.
5. Standards.

These five areas must cooperate to create and maintain an integrated, automated environment for manufacturing.

Planning

The traditional management process calls for deterministic planning--also called "top-down planning." This kind of planning treats the organization as if it were a closed system--a system which is rational, efficient, predictable, effective, nondynamic, and understandable.

CIM planning treats the organization as if it were a free market within which some computing requirements are known and predictable, but many are ad hoc random and dynamic.

Free market planning can only be accomplished by planning both market demand (user) profiles and asset (data and computing) structures. The key to handling dynamic demand is in building products (outputs) which maximally leverage assets.

Thus, CIM planning must focus on forecasting market demand (user requirements) for all types of information (for example, operational control, management, and strategic planning), and on defining asset structures (hardware, system software, databases, application programs, and communication facilities) which have the maximum leverage in servicing the market demand.

CIM planning requires the development of three basic architectures: an information architecture; a computer systems architecture, and a data architecture. The information architecture defines information demand in terms of business, engineering and manufacturing processes and decision problems. The computer systems architecture defines technical standards for controlling technology procurements. The data architecture defines data standards (business rules) for applications procurement and the development of shared databases. Each architecture is developed using structured methods. CIM plans also must reflect a concept of migration from the realities of the existing environment to the ideals of a future environment.

Finance

The traditional financing strategy for automation is a "bootstrapping" concept. Dollars are spent on islands of automation from departmental budgets. However, there is rarely any significant money invested in building assets which are to be shared. Capital is spent on fixed assets, i.e., hardware systems, software, and communications.

CIM financing strategies make capital investments in shared, value-added assets, such as databases and data architectures. These assets cannot be bought; they must be built. Unlike current strategies, CIM financial strategies do not allow common assets to be bootstrapped. These assets are "owned" by the enterprise, not an individual user group. Nonshared resources are locally funded, but much of the money spent on the care feeding of highly valuable, shared enterprise assets.

Project Selection

Currently, project selection techniques are random and fairly arbitrary. Projects can be as big, take as long, and impact as many organizations as the power structure will allow. Also, projects are selected based on local functional imperatives, not business imperatives.

CIM project selection strategies keep projects small (under six months) and they keep costs down. Projects are mixed between those needed to build assets, such as product definition databases, and those which deploy those assets to service specific user requirements, such as a manufacturing bill of material. Projects are prioritized based on asset leverage, not on arbitrary political needs, because asset leverage is an enterprise concept, not a functional or technical concept.

Project Management

Project mangement today is a black art. Most project managers do what feels good, even if they have been trained in project management techniques. The outcome is project results of widely varying quality. These results are not integrated.

CIM projects are managed consistently across the board, because consistency is the key to both quality and integration. CIM projects use structured approaches to define requirements and implement solutions. They operate by employing the same (enterprise defined) standards for computer technology and shared data. CIM projects require heavy user involvement because users are the only ones who understand their requirements.

Standards

Two classes of standards are crucial to integration of the enterprise: technical and data. Technical standards are used to manage and to integrate the hardware, operating systems, data management systems, programming language, communications technology, and more (see this guide's standards chapter). Data standards are necessary to manage what is stored on the machines.

The difference between technical and data standards can be illustrated with the analogy of the mind and the brain. The brain is physical. The mind is logical. Experiments have proven that the body can be manipulated by the brain without cooperation from the mind, and the mind can observe the brain at work.

Technical standards are necessary to control the CIM brain structure. Such standards as the International Graphics Exchange Specification (IGES) and the General Motors Manufacturing Automation Protocol (MAP) are needed to control and integrate the machines.

Data standards are needed to control the CIM mind. What is a part? What is configuration management? What are drawings? How do all of those "data concepts" relate to one another. How are they changed? The mind is controlled through concepts like business rules, or an agreed upon set of definitions for key information entities and the relationships between them.

The difference between these two kinds of standards is very real. Having an IBM computer, for example, does not mean that your managers will have good cost data or that the cost data will be accurately reflected in estimates or product pricing. The latter issues are mind issues. They cannot be delegated to vendors--unless you intend to have them control your business ghost. That is an enterprise-level issue, not a vendor technical issue.

Integration is separately accomplished for both the mind and the brain. Machine integration alone will not hack it. Mind integration (the integration of various databases and data architectures into a logical resource for the entire enterprise) is not a vendor technology issue. But, mind integration has more to do with overall productivity than does brain integration. The mind should never be hostage to the brain.

WHAT TO DO

No one can buy integration--even from IBM. Integration is a management process, not a set of technologies, a system, a product, or a project. To get integration, you must build and manage a CIM program in much the same way as you (should have) executed a Zero Defects Program or a Safety Program.

The first task is to establish an enterprise perspective of CIM. This is done by building a CIM control structure, which includes financing, project selection, project management, and standards setting. Organizational issues also must be addressed.

Under the control structure several projects can be initiated simultaneously.

1. Build a CIM Plan.
2. Define CIM Standards.
3. Define CIM Financial Management Concepts.

Based on these three directives, industrial automation projects can be defined, selected, prioritized, and executed.

Many companies have tried to bootstrap in the CIM program without committing the time and resources to create the context for success. There is a great deal of work to be done by key people in the company to set the right context. It is a mistake to underestimate the cost and significance of this undertaking.

A CIM program control structure will cost the average 500-employee manufacturing enterprise $100,000-$200,000. Once the CIM program control architecture has been established, plans must be built and standards must be set. The plan (using a consultant to support) could cost about $100,000. Setting technology standards may cost about $100,000. And the setting of data standards will range in cost from $150,000 to $250,000. This is exclusive of the hardware and software which may be chosen as a result of the CIM program strategy.

Thus, the total CIM program setup cost may be around $500,000. Now you have the structure to define, manage, and integrate automation projects, on an ongoing basis. These setup costs usually will be recovered within two years, as automation projects provide reductions in business costs, product development leadtime, inventories, and so on.

IN CONCLUSION

Integration is not a destination. It is a direction. If you examine your annual rates of expenditure in industrial automation, you will see that you are already in motion, and accelerating rapidly. (IBM expects that the total market for industrial computing will reach $26 billion in 1989, up from 1983's level of $6.2 billion.) Without a CIM program to manage and integrate your projects, who knows where you will end up.

CIM and Management Policy a Word to the President

by Dr. Charles M. Savage
D. Appleton Company, Incorporated

INTRODUCTION

The development of a CIM program involves not only the technology but also the organization and it is essential that the CEO gives quality leadership in the transition process.

Traditionally, manufacturing organizations have divided the flow of work into functions and coordinated the various activities in a serial manner. This logic worked well at one point of time but it is now out of date.

There is another logic in the computer systems designed to support CIM. Increasingly, it is necessary to develop a parallel and networked environment with much more interaction between the various functions. Therefore, as executives develop their CIM strategy and implementation programs, they are going to have to pay as much attention to the political dimension as to the technology.

As we have observed companies working towards CIM, we find there are three levels which need to be addressed. They are outlined in Figure 1.

Levels	Goal	Need to Manage
Level I	Integration	Policy, Information Architecture
Level II	Interfaces	Network, Standards and Protocols
Level III	Isolated Islands	Build Network Linkages

Figure 1. Three levels of CIM.

There are approximately 55,000 manufacturing companies in the United States with more than 100 employees. If we were to divide these into the three levels, a rough estimate indicates that Level III contains about 97% of them, Level II 2%, and Level I well less than 1%.

Levels of CIM

Levels III and II are technical. Level III involves a company in the creation of coordinated work cells which may combine machine tools with automated feed systems. The challenge of Level II is to interface dissimilar systems, such as that being done in the GM-inspired MAP (Manufacturing Automation Protocol) effort supported by CASA/SME and the development of the

IGES (Initial Graphic Exchange System) guided by the National Bureau of Standards (NBS) and others. There are also other efforts to tie various systems together, from CAE and CAM to DNC and shop floor control. Others are tying the mainframe with the micro, the central database with distributed processors and the like.

Level I is both technical and political. Without strong leadership from the CEO or the division general manager, it is going to be hard to put CIM in place. In Level III and II efforts, the best software and hardware are put into existing functional departments. But as these become networked together around a common database resource, the traditional power balance in the enterprise is challenged. It is no longer possible to maintain isolated fiefdoms, be they in marketing, engineering, manufacturing, or finance. The technology of CIM challenges these departments to work in a more integrative and interactive manner.

And it is unwise to continue to put third, fourth and fifth-generation computer technology in second-generation organizations. We need to struggle together to understand how to network not only the technology but the people, the management and knowledge workers, into an effective, flexible and responsive organization.

In the past, the best MRP, the best DNC, the best shop floor control, and the best Local Area Network system were chosen as isolated solutions.

This is no longer an adequate approach.

Those companies which have begun the move into Level I have had the strong support from the top executives. These executives have established CIM strategy and implementation programs and chartered their top executives to lead this effort. We have found that it is essential to establish a context in which CIM can develop. This context is defined by management policy. This is why Level I must involve top management in the CIM effort.

POLICIES: FORMING THE CONTEXT FOR CIM

Charlie Knox, President of Knox Associates, says, "If policies do not come from the top down, politics will come from the bottom up." These "politics" can hamstring an organization. The style of foxhole management in many companies is testimony to the role of politics as a driving force. But this is a short-sighted approach.

One major hardware vendor has discovered the importance of clear and direct policies as a way of lessening company politics. It has articulated for itself a series of corporate policies which are having a profound impact on the interaction pattern of its internal resources. For example, this corporation is now saying that any new product must be as reliable when introduced to the market as the product it is replacing. Gone are the days in which it was ready to introduce a product and spend 18 months field tweaking it up to a proper level of performance. This policy forces engineering and manufacturing to work much closer together on a new product at a very early stage. This is a good example of how the serial approach to manufacturing is being changed to a networked approach which encourages much more interaction between the various functions.

This corporation also is demanding that new products must be designed for automated assembly and testability. This forces the engineers to understand the manufacturing and assemble constraints and opportunities. It also forces engineering and manufacturing engineering to work hand in glove.

Also at this corporation, marketing is not left off the hook. When a new product comes off the line, it is carried on marketing's books (marketing is responsible for the finance charges for the goods not sold). This forces marketing to be much more observant of the market. Moreover, marketing realizes how important it is for engineering and manufacturing to build a great deal more flexibility into their production capabilities. Only in this way will marketing have the flexibility to respond quickly to changes in the market.

This corporation is certainly not alone in setting policies which are helping them move towards CIM. A farm implements manufacturer has recognized the need to rethink its manufacturing process from the ground up. It has dedicated itself to a program of total waste elimination, now called Value Centered Manufacturing. It does not want to computerize its complexity, contradictions and confusions, but rather is striving to simplify the manufacturing environment while adding computer-aided systems to help manage key information.

New terms are being developed to describe the changes in policy and approach: "Design for Manufacturing," "Design for Assembly," and Design for Quality." These concepts are forcing a closer working together of the various functions. A nodal relationship is evolving. Certainly as we build on the lessons we have learned from the Japanese about material flow, simplify our manufacturing processes and continually strive to improve processes, we are laying the foundation for an interactive and integrative environment necessary for CIM.

As these companies have clearly recognized, there is no option but to work together to find new ways to coordinate efforts, share resources, and formulate cross-functional assignments on a product basis. There will be a constantly changing pattern of relationships around our various products and services. We will have to use a variety of means to keep track of these initiatives, from good project management and simulation tools, to electronic mail and computer teleconferencing.

As the company begins to articulate its policy relating to CIM, it may want to consider the following steps.

THE CIM STRATEGY AND IMPLEMENTATION PROGRAM

Some top management groups have taken a couple of days off-site to explore the range of issues which needs to be addressed in formulating and launching a CIM program.

Information Architecture

One of the key steps is going to be to think through the way the company presently does its business, and how it would like to streamline and simplify this process. Jim Lardner of Deere and Co. made in his Autofact 84 presentation a strong case for reducing the "complexity index," It makes little sense to just computerize existing methods and procedures. Present methods are often a result of political accommodations and jerry-rigged solutions. Certainly it is important to understand existing procedures as a starting point.

But this is only the beginning.

It is necessary to build a more conscious architecture in leverage the power of computer-aided systems.

Dan Appleton refers to this process as the development of information architecture. Ralph Bravoco gives a brief introduction to a method of developing an activity and information model of the company so that the key executives and middle managers can agree upon the appropriate architecture.

By developing activity and information models, these executives will be able, as a group, to more clearly see the efficiencies and inefficiencies in their company. They may choose, as some companies have, to use these models to aid in the capital budgeting process and in the setting of priorities of additional information system modules, not to mention the aid given to new business development.

They may then wish to develop some simulation modeling to see where investments or improvements in their processes or products would have the highest return.

In addition, they can begin to identify the data entities, the items of information, which the different departments need to draw on. Most companies identify from 300 to 500 such items, such as vendors, part numbers, drawing, processes, contracts, and so forth. By developing common-recognized definitions for these key entities and building a data architecture, it is possible for knowledge professionals in each department to access a sharable database with their specific questions and needs. Moreover, it is possible to save thousands, if not millions of dollars in preventing duplication of effort, maintaining data security and integrity, updating and adding information.

Even though it is possible to work with vendors and consultants to architect the overall system of hardware and software, there is still a great deal of hard work, time and money needed to reach an agreement across the various functions as to the meaning of the common data elements.

Those companies which are able to get their hands around their own data needs will have a strong competitive advantage in the 1990s. Just as the "experience curve" was the darling of the 1970s, "information integration" will be the test of survival for the next decade.

Critical Success Factors

Once the corporation has built an activity model of itself, and understands its architecture (or lack thereof), it can step back and ask what it will take in its industry over the next few years for market success. Is it to provide leading-edge technology, items with style and design, energy efficiency, reliability, or quick market responsiveness?

Each department might then take a look at the agreed list for the industry and the corporation or division and then develop its own three to six Critical Success Factors (CSF), the ones which will most contribute to the overall success of the company.

These CSFs can then be mapped onto the activity model of the company, discussed between the functions and agreed upon. Then each department can define its own CSFs within the larger context. In and of itself, the process of reaching an agreement on the CSFs between the levels and across functions will bring more clarity and direction into the entire company.

This process will quickly point out where there are deficiencies or opportunities in their plant and equipment, their information systems and other resources. And this will help to build an agreed on set of priorities for the further development of the company. In fact, it will help them realign their various assets, their technology, management systems, and information systems with their markets.

Brick and Mortar Concepts

Identifying Critical Success Factors by themselves is not enough. To achieve CIM, it is necessary to introduce a growing variety of techniques and approaches which provide the "brick and mortar" for CIM.

It is a new experience for most to think in terms of the "digital thread." But as marketing, engineering, manufacturing, and service begin to share the same data, it is going to become increasingly common to find the digital thread woven throughout the corporation. Efforts at product data definition, such as McDonnell Douglas' "Product Data Definition Interface" effort sponsored by the U.S. Air Force, and "Product Data Exchange Standard" (PDES) which is a follow-on effort from the Initial Graphic Exchange System (IGES) work, are two examples of trends towards the digital thread.

Many pioneers in CIM are finding "group technology" to be an essential ingredient in the CIM equation. It makes it possible to sort out families of parts and processes in a much more rational manner.

Likewise, more and more companies are turning to a just-in-time (JIT) approach not just because they want to cut inventory, but because of the philosophy implicit in JIT. The key is to expose the inefficiencies in their present processes and practices and eliminate those steps which do not "add value" to the product.

After many years of work, the efforts of two University of Massachusetts professors, Boothroyd and Dewhurst, are being recognized. "Design for Assembly" is a system they have developed which helps engineers recognize the manufacturing and assembly constraints they must consider, especially as more robotic assembly systems are being introduced.

The recognition that it is necessary to "Design for Assembly" has lead a number of executives to say they also want to understand the processes of "Design for Manufacturing," "Design for Test," "Design for Service" and "Design for Logistics Support." More of these concepts will be seen in the near future.

As quality grows in importance, there is a growing interest in statistical process control. It is critical to get control not only of the design of the product in its various phases, but the process as well. In fact, it is likely in the future that the process itself will be designed with as much care as the product presently receives.

There are a variety of other concepts which can only be mentioned at this time They include: Cube Assembly, CADMAT (Computer-Aided Design, Manufacturing, Assembly and Test), Parametric Design, and Single Product Definition. Certainly these represent serious efforts at redefining the production process to take advantage of the power of the computer and microprocessor, while simplifying the overall processes. Certainly, as these and other concepts are introduced, their manufacturing organization will have an opportunity to realign itself.

CIM Organizational Architecture

As companies are defining their information architectures, identifying their CSFs, and building in a number of newer concepts, it is not surprising if they begin to act more as a nodal network.

This is already happening.

As the various functions better understand how their activities impact other departments, they are getting out of their functional foxholes. Instead of jealously guarding their turf, they realize that with a little more effort, they can make life easier for the other parts of the corporation or division. They begin to realize how costly their mistakes and shortsightedness are as they ripple through other departments. For example, most companies do not have a good handle as to the true cost of marketing or engineering change orders, but their impact is usually of a magnitude several times higher than anyone expects.

As the company becomes more interactive, departmental charters will be changing. The boundaries between functions are more open-ended. Each department will be expected to ask for more information from the other departments. Manufacturing will assist engineering in understanding the standards for "design for manufacturability." Marketing will describe the range of likely products so assembly can design its processes to be more accommodating and flexible.

The reward systems will need adjusting. Individual executives, managers and knowledge professionals will be rewarded not for hard-nosed independence, but in accordance with their cooperativeness and support for one another. Have they assumed joint responsibility for particular projects? Have they been open and receptive to ideas from other departments? Have they made quality suggestions for improvement not only in their own departments, but in others? Have they overcome the NIH (not invented here) syndrome? The annual review process is going to take on a whole new dimension. And it is up to the chief executive officer to set the tone and climate for these changes to take place.

Too many integration issues have been shipwrecked, not on islands and reefs of automation, but on reward systems which perpetuate old modes of behavior more attuned to the traditional mode of serial hand-offs.

Top executives, using the conveniences of electronic mail and computer teleconferencing need to become more accessible and interactive with the knowledge professionals. I expect that there will be a shift from the use of "directives" from on top to the use of well-chosen questions. A good question is a much more powerful motivator than an order. And knowledge professionals, with their own sense of worth, will respond more effectively to a probing question than an arbitrary order.

The real task in a nodal network is to keep a strong sense of business focus and direction, as the key functions work more in a parallel and interactive fashion than in the conventional serial manner. Top management can no longer afford to remain out of touch with the fast-moving abilities of their key professionals. A vigorous dialogue is necessary. To set the context, it is essential that a good set of policies be articulated to give everyone a sense of direction and vision.

Policies to set the Context for CIM

There are a whole range of policies which need to be established to achieve the information integration, critical success factors and organizational integration. They will have to deal with market responsiveness, inventory turn, product reliability, process flexibility, quality, personal growth, financial objectives and team work.

Policies need to be articulated which will bring marketing, engineering and manufacturing into a closer working relationship. The corporation which redefined its expectations for a newly introduced product influenced the way engineering and manufacturing interact. Likewise, when it made marketing responsibility, financially, for the carrying costs of finished goods in inventory, it set a policy which is causing marketing and manufacturing to work together like hand and glove.

Policies which set internal standards and project an image to the marketplace are essential.

Does the company wish to turn its inventory 25, 50 or even 100 times a year? Does it wish to be the high-volume, low-cost producer? Should it be able to produce effectively in lot sizes of one? Should its cycle time from initial contract to delivery be measured in days instead of weeks or months?

There are companies which are making these policy decisions right now, and it is likely that they will be the survivors in an increasingly competitive world.

It should be clear by now that a CIM strategy and implementation program is much more than just introducing computer hardware and software into the enterprise. A CIM program is primarily one aimed at overhauling the functions of the enterprise into a more dynamic and responsive business. CIM has as much, if not more, to do with managerial leadership than it does with computers. Perhaps we should drop the "C" from CIM and talk of "IM," "Integrative Management" as the key task. This will help top executives lead their companies to Level I more quickly.

In short, the President and top executives have an absolutely vital role to play in achieving CIM. Their primary task is the redefining corporate policy to facilitate greater networked interaction between the various functions.

Reculturing for CIM

by Dr. Leonard Bertain
Business Spectrum Associates

INTRODUCTION

Everyone by now has heard of CIM. "Computer Integrated Manufacturing, the solution to our manufacturing malaise." However, lest you hook your career to the CIM bandwagon, <u>just before it goes over the cliff</u>, remember that CIM is more than just technology.

CIM is a corporate strategy for survival. It is an overall strategy that <u>includes manufacturing</u>.

Above all, CIM involves the people in the factory: managers, executives and blue-collar workers alike. Because the strategy effects a significant change in the business, it is natural that the people are affected as a consequence.

People matter everywhere in the business, especially in the factory. Their positive participation is the key to the cash generation of the business. The environment of the factory and its culture affects quality and production.

Profitable implementation of CIM involves the people. If CIM doesn't contribute significantly to the bottom line, the change is hardly worth it.

The reculturing process of CIM discussed in this paper involves phenomenal returns on the investment.

Although it initially involves people, the return on the time and capital expenditures can generate returns of over 800%. The performance improvement in reduction in WIP is frequently in excess of 50%. The cash generated by "Phase 0" performance improvements is intended to create enough bottom line contribution for a pay-as-you-go, self-funding program.

This article is intended to briefly address some of the key issues of CIM, as it relates to the change in the factory culture. The "reculturing for CIM" is "Phase 0". It sets the stage for an effective CIM implementation.

THE GOAL OF CIM

The world is constantly in a state of economic warfare. The current battlefield has found the United States manufacturing industrial base taking it on the chin from Japan, Korea, Germany and other Pacific Rim countries.

Are we waiting for the knockout punch?

Probably not. However, we seem to have reached a point of almost desperation in groping for help in the technology arena. MRP, JIT, TQC and Quality Circles have all fallen short of the mark as quick fix solutions to the malady. The new "quick fix salve" CIM, when applied to the manufacturing "wound", would make the pain and the problem go away. It didn't. The question is why?

Joe Harrington, the father of CIM, never said that CIM was technology. He defined it as a strategy. In his words, "CIM is a policy decision not an investment decision." And as Dan Appleton rightly noted, "CIM is a strategy for the whole enterprise, not just manufacturing."

The goal of CIM is to make effective and efficient use of our enterprise resources (including management) "to deliver the right product, right features, at the right price and at the right time."(1) An effective CIM strategy must be supported by the wholehearted commitment of all involved, machine operators, foremen, managers and executives because it affects the whole enterprise.

WHY THE FAILURES? -OR- BETTER YET, WHY THE SUCCESSES?

It is a given fact that we all believe in revitalizing the American manufacturing base. The generally accepted proposition is that the first thing to do is immediately start on a project to show management that progress is being made. Wrong!! Such a course utilizing CIM is now recognized as an almost automatic predisposition to failure.

A careful look at the past Lead Award winners reveals they have one thing in common. They didn't rush the results. They involved all aspects of the organization, they trained people and formed teams. Without exception, they all recognized the importance of involvement of all affected people. But for this very significant common action, they would probably have failed like most other unsuccessful projects.

Part of the initial frustration with CIM is that it can easily become another MIS attempt to meddle in the affairs of manufacturing. Or muddle it up as some would have it. It involves planning meetings, review meetings, and meeting meetings. Usually, however, these meetings do not invite or involve active participation of the one person or group which can contribute most significantly to the success of the CIM program. The blue-collar worker, actively participating in and supporting the program, is the missing player. He makes the difference.

Unlike every other person in the planning meetings, he has the greatest ability to directly increase profits. All the other meeting participants can reduce costs of manufacturing by their actions, he can increase profits and margins by his direct contribution at the work station.

People are important. In CIM, the worker is very important.

The natural impact of the CIM program with its "NEW VISION" is on the environment of the employees. A major result of an effective CIM program is that a whole new workplace is necessary to effectively implement a program.

The changes must be gradual. They must be absorbed by the employees in small doses until the system responds.

The Sibbald Open Systems Antithesis Theorem (1) draws the parallel of the factory culture to the Petri dish cell experiment. If the acid of the dish is changed dramatically, the cell dies. But, if the acid concentration is changed gradually the cell adjusts and survives. Sibbald maintains that the objective of the reculturing process is to elicit a change gradually, but control the direction of the change. Change the PH but use it to direct the response of the cell. So it is, at the factory level in a CIM program. The environment is changed. But it must be a slow, gradual process.

The objective of successful implementation is improvement, but we want to direct the results of the reculturing process. We want to start the mechanisms for "perpetual improvement." In order to exist in this new environment a gradual educational program is necessary, an employee reculturing for the CIM environment.

Why is "Reculturing for CIM" so important?

STAGES OF CIM

The bottom line is that the reculturing process serves as the foundation upon which the successful CIM program is developed. Reculturing must be implemented <u>before automation and integration.</u>

CIM has given us an opportunity to re-examine and rethink the management lessons of the past. It provides a wonderful opportunity to get back to the basics of business management. The Buckminster Fuller "less is more" philosophy, while not universally applicable, is certainly worth reconsidering. In a survival environment, do we really need all that overhead?

Sibbald has noted (1) that the four phases of CIM start with Phase 0: Preparation for change. The preparation for change is a reculturing process. It involves restructuring of the enterprise for motivation and reculturing for innovation and creativity. Innovation and motivation come before automation and integration.

In our normal understanding of the problem, and Sibbald's as well, Phases 1 to 3 involve automation, integration and emulation (of the management process). In that order.

The interesting part of all the successes in CIM, the Lead Award winners, is that they focused their activities on the process of the factory rather than the operation per se. The famous Japanese manufacturing engineer, Shingeo Shingo, notes (2) that the primary focus of any manufacturing engineer should be toward improving the process of the manufacturing operation. Most American CIM designers seem driven to neglect this step and go directly to the automation of the process and the integration of the "islands of automation."

Therein lies the root of success or disappointment in CIM.

We have all read that phenomenal returns are to be expected from CIM systems and when successful, they are phenomenal. However, are they attributable to the process improvement or the operation improvement? Can they be separated?

Yes, they can be separated. And, yes, I believe, that the process improvement is responsible for 80% of the measured return. A recent experience with a small manufacturer in California, AMOT Controls, showed a work cycle reduction of one product from 10 days to 6 minutes. There were no computers involved. There was no integration involved. But people were involved.

The people were educated about Just-In-Time. (Note the choice of prepositions.) They were made to feel the importance of their contribution as part of a team. The craft culture within a union shop began to return.

In the reculturing process, the team met and decided the direction of the program. The management participated but basically stood back and provided, as needed, support. The team generated the results.

THE FORMATION OF A TEAM

One of the exciting moments of my career was meeting John Wooden, the famous coach of the UCLA basketball team. During his 27 years as coach, his teams never had a losing season. In his last 12 years at UCLA, they won ten national championships, seven of those in succession, and still hold the world's record for the longest winning streak in any major sport--88 games bridging four seasons.

His coaching philosophy was non-pareil. His was the best. It stressed the team over winning. It emphasized character but not ego and it demanded improvement and steady performance. Success was measured with the peace of mind that comes from self-satisfaction in knowing you had done your best.

Wooden emphasized character versus reputation. "Your reputation is only what others think you are, whereas, your character is what you really are."

The factory team is very similar. It has a goal: To improve manufacturing quality, productivity and costs for a specific area of the factory. The difference is that the factory manager, unlike Coach Wooden, cannot give scholarships. He is usually given an assortment of players from different ethnic backgrounds, religions, interests, etc. In fact, many managers feel that they are given a scrub team to go against the NBA champions (Japan, Inc.).

However, there are always winners in any game. As Bum Phillips, the former coach of the New Orleans Saints Football team said of Don Shula, Coach of the Miami Dolphins: "He can take his'n and beat your'n, then take your'n and beat his'n."

The factory manager has the same situation. He plays the only hand he has, the one he's dealt.

In a successful project, the plant manager starts the process small. The small team is important. It is a first step. He identifies a project that isn't too big. One that is sure to succeed. Top management must provide all the support necessary to make the first team successful. It cannot be allowed to fail.

There will be doubting Thomases and they will wait on the wings hoping for the failure that's sure to come. Management's commitment is necessary to insure that the program will be successful.

Reculturing for CIM can seem to be an agonizingly slow process. The conversion process must be paced to obtain a stated objective. The leap of understanding which will encourage rapid acceptance by succeeding teams will only occur after the solid demonstration of results achieved by the first team. Phase 0 for Team 1 is a patient process. In many cases, the concepts of CIM--single part processing versus batch, elimination of waste, focus only on value added processes, etc.--are hard for people to understand. They will comprehend in time but management must show a willingness to wait.

The process of opening up to the blue-collar worker is difficult for most managers. The reculturing process involves a quest for ideas. New ideas. Yes, even dumb ideas. The manager must guide that first team through the development of the program for process improvement. The objective of the reculturing process is to open up the restrained resource of the factory worker's idea stream. The ideas for improvement are there. Patience, understanding, time, and trust of the motives will set them free.

CASE STUDY

AMOT Controls manufactures about 20 different models of thermostatic control valves with over 75,000 permutations of possible deliverable products. The permutations arise with all the fittings and thread sizes possible. The company knew from its 40 years of manufacturing experience that batch manufacturing was the right way to manufacture. If someone needed 20 valves today, then 480 valves of the 500 part batch would go to inventory.

The Plant Manager was convinced that the concepts of Value Added Manufacturing present in the Toyota Production System would work at AMOT Controls. Batch manufacturing was choking its opportunity to grow and he wanted to make AMOT Controls an intermittent manufacturer. He wanted to be able to make parts one at a time. Instead of manufacturing batches of 500, he would make batches of 1. With this idea and a new twist added to create the Value Added Manufacturing System (VAMS), a new program was started. A small team was formed to develop the concepts and ideas for a work cell. This occured only after extensive education had occured for management and blue-collar workers.

The objective of the first team was to address a new priority; to reallocate monetary and human resources. The waste of human potential was identified as the first of eight correctable wastes of the Value Added Manufacturing System. A determination was made that the money allocated to be spent on expensive computer systems was better spent on people. The indicated return on the investment was greater. The eight wastes are noted on the next page.

1. Waste of Human Potential.
2. Waste of Over Production.
3. Waste of Waiting.
4. Waste of Transportation.
5. Waste of Process.
6. Waste of Motion.
7. Waste of Stock.
8. Waste of Making Defective Parts.

The transfer of the understanding of the eight wastes of VAMS was nontrivial. It was hard work and needed constant overview and reinforcement. But it paid off handsomely.

Innovation was encouraged by handing out "AMOT Idea Pins" to any person who suggested an idea, good or bad. It was important to get ideas, but it was more important to recognize the "process of change". The use of the Idea Pin to recognize the process, not the results, was a deliberate act of reinforcement of active participation at every level. The Vice President and General Manager handed out the pins. Initially, they were given freely to start the ideas flowing. As time has evolved, the pins are now given to those ideas which directly address one of the eight wastes.

The measure of the success of this program, in effect for less than a year, is seen in two major areas.

First, the quality of the ideas coming in daily and hourly are almost staggering. The manager can no longer track all the improvements. It is now part of the culture ingrained in the work force as a vital part of being a member of an important team, and the reinforcement of the team now flows from all sectors within the factory. Each new cell is encouraged by the predecessor cell members and they constantly interact with each other. The walls of separation between workers are being torn down by the workers through the encouraged interchange of constructive ideas between team members and between teams and management.

And second, the success is seen in bottom line improvements. The cells are now able to process a new product in minutes versus days. Overhead has been thinned, WIP has been reduced and quality has improved. The system is responsive to the customer demands, more space is available in the factory, and more improvements are on the way.

These are returns directly resulting from the reculturing process. They have generated a very significant, measurable and enduring cash flow return, prior to the addition of the computer. Replication of this "Phase 0" achievement is possibly one of the most significant objectives of anyone seeking to salvage a present installation. Most certainly, anyone contemplating such an undertaking would do well to thoroughly investigate this phenomenon.

CONCLUSION

Significant reculturing activity is required for the CIM program as a major part of the overall CIM strategy. It provides a time for motivation and innovation of the workers. It is through the reculturing activity that you examine the current processes of the factory and determine improvements which can be made and goals which can be achieved.

Process improvements preceed those of the operation. The CIM phases 1 to 3 address the improvements of the operation by first creating the islands of automation and then linking them together. By achieving the extensive reculturing program, the simplicity of the final integrated system solution is insured. The payback is phenomenal in "Phase 0". It provides a source of funds to assist Phases 1, 2, and 3 to become self-funded.

The reculturing process needs to reward the process of change. People need to feel that they are being rewarded for changing the system. The reward system encourages that process and directs the factory personnel toward perpetual improvement.

If the factory workers are involved in the program from the beginning, the overall chances of success of your CIM program are greatly increased.

The basic objective of CIM is to revitalize the company. The improvements afforded the enterprise by the development and implementation of your CIM plan are phenomenal. The ultimate objective of all these programs is to make:

MADE IN THE USA

THE
SIGNATURE
OF
EXCELLENCE.

REFERENCES

1. Sibbald, George. "Roadblocks to CIM", CIM Review, October 1987.
2. Shingeo, Shingo. Revolution in Manufacturing--SMED, Productivity Press, 1986.

CIM Business Strategy Case Study for an Aerospace Organization

by Peter K. Punwani
Price Waterhouse

TOO IMPORTANT

"Technology is too important a resource to be ignored in our strategic business planning!" Bob Adams, President of Aerospace Products, stated at his Board meeting.

Aerospace Products, a pseudonym for a medium-sized aerospace subcontractor, had an international reputation for providing quality, engineered products. However, like most industries, the company was experiencing significant cost pressures from competitors. At the same time, commercial and military customers were demanding shorter lead times, better product reliability and lower unit costs. While the company was investing millions of dollars annually in new technologies, these investments lacked a clear, integrated direction. As one executive termed it, "we're creating too many islands of technology." Also, lacking a clear picture of the financial returns from such investments, management was reluctant to invest in technology for "technology's sake."

Upon further discussion at the Board of Director's meeting, the need for a well-designed business strategy for implementing Computer-Integrated Manufacturing (CIM) technologies became readily apparent. There was no doubt in anyone's mind that the harnessing of the right material, process and information technologies would provide Aerospace Products with a significant competitive edge. However, the central issue was one of determining how substantial new technology investments could be put to the most effective use for meeting company goals and long-term objectives.

Some of the strategic questions regarding the implementation of new technologies that management wanted to address were:

- What business functions would benefit most from new technologies?
- How can we ensure an adequate return on our investments in capital-intensive technologies?
- How should we integrate different technologies into a true CIM environment?
- How can we implement short-term improvements for immediate results while we wait for longer-term technology solutions?
- How should we translate a high-level CIM business strategy into a tactical plan for specific actions?
- How can we effectively manage the inherent risks associated with the implementation of new technologies?

To develop a CIM business strategy, Aerospace Products engaged the services of an outside management consultant. The consultant provided the necessary initial and day-to-day project management direction, specialized techniques, education and training to Aerospace Products personnel in the development of this strategy. Company personnel, in turn, were heavily involved in all facets of the project, so that they could effectively implement the tactical plans developed and continue to maintain the CIM business strategy as a living document.

In the remainder of this paper, a synopsis of the approach used for developing the CIM business strategy is presented.

OVERVIEW OF STRATEGY DEVELOPMENT

Figure 1 describes the framework used for developing the CIM business strategy.

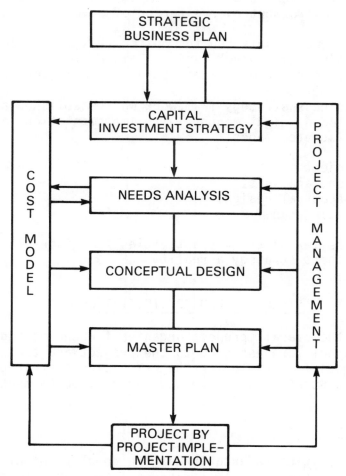

Figure 1. Framework for CIM business strategy.

The company's established Strategic Business Plan was used to provide a long-term outlook at future products, markets and business environments. Based on this outlook, a high-level Capital Investment Strategy was developed to handle the realities of evaluating new technology investments. A well-defined project management approach set the stage for controlling the different activities required to develop the CIM business strategy. Using the Capital Investment Strategy as a guideline, a Needs Analysis was conducted to determine what business functions could most effectively profit from new technologies. A key element of the Needs Analysis was the development of a cost model that defined the "real world" costs associated with different business functions by cost element. This cost model was used in all phases of the strategy.

Once the Needs Analysis was completed and specific company functions defined as the best candidates for technology modernization, the conceptual design activities were initiated. During this stage, alternative technologies were evaluated and selected to overcome major deterrants to productivity in the current business environment. These technologies were evaluated for cost/benefit purposes using the Cost Model. Finally, the individual technology projects were converted into a Master Plan for implementation. This Master Plan would take the company from its current business environment to its required CIM environment over a period of several years.

Finally, mechanisms were established to monitor the implementation of the Master Plan on a project by project basis. This would allow project management to fine tune the CIM business strategy on a continuing basis.

This overall CIM business strategy framework was established at Aerospace Products over a period of eight months. Its implementation can best be described in four discrete stages:

- Stage 1: Project initiation.
- Stage 2: Needs analysis.
- Stage 3: Conceptual design.
- Stage 4: Master plan.

The following is a review of the key activities that took place in each stage to make the CIM business strategy a reality.

STAGE 1: PROJECT INITIATION

During this stage, the overall project organization and methodologies were established. Personnel were assigned to the project and trained in specialized techniques for developing the CIM business strategy. The Corporate Investment Strategy was examined and refined to meet the company's changing needs.

Project Management Plan

One of the first activities undertaken was the development of a Project Management Plan. This plan clearly defined the key tasks to be undertaken for the development of the business strategy. Expected results and deliverables, estimated man hours by specific personnel assigned, and planned completion dates were defined for each key task. The plan formed the basis for allocating resources and managing the project to ensure a timely and quality business strategy.

Project Organization

A high-level steering committee was appointed to provide top management direction and commit resources to the CIM business strategy development project. It consisted of the President and the Vice Presidents in charge of each major organizational function.

A Project Team consisting of selected professionals from industrial engineering, management information systems, design engineering, manufacturing engineering, advanced technologies, finance, materials management, manufacturing, purchasing, and quality assurance was assigned to the project based on the needs expressed in the Project Management Plan.

A project leader was selected to head the project team. Appropriate periodic reporting mechanisms were established to provide sound communications between top management, project team personnel and key middle managers in the organization.

Capital Investment Strategy

An evaluation of the company's investment strategy showed that the direct labor-based cost accounting system used to justify capital expenditures was inadequate for the financial analysis and justification of new technologies. While direct labor costs were very well-defined by specific manufacturing function and product, they represented less than 10% of total manufacturing costs. On the other hand, key costs, such as those associated with carrying inventories, scrap, tooling, computer hardware and software development were typically buried in large overhead pools.

As a result, no common yardstick existed for evaluating the cost/benefit impact of different technologies on significant cost elements within a business function.

With the active involvement of the Steering Committee, a new Capital Investment Strategy was developed to meet the future needs of the organization. The five-year strategic business plan was used as a basis for defining the future products and business environment in which Aerospace Products would operate. The company's critical success factors were then defined. Appropriate performance measures were developed for each critical success factor. These performance measures were classified as financial and nonfinancial. The financial performance measures were organized by significant cost element into a cost model (discussed later). Weightages were assigned to financial and nonfinancial measures for developing a ranking methodology. This methodology formed the basis for comparing the cost/benefit profiles of different technologies, based on top management's critical success factors.

Also, through the Capital Investment Strategy, corporate guidelines were established for defining individual technology projects on a consistent basis; identifying cost/benefits for each project; obtaining technical, financial and management approvals; and determining the minimum returns on investment expected by management for authorizing capital investment.

By participating actively in the development of the Capital Investment

Strategy, the Steering Committee established a meaningful "top-down" commitment to the entire project, as top management got an excellent perspective of the changes in thought processes needed for implementing modern technologies.

Education and Training

As a final step of the project initiation process, a number of seminars were conducted for Aerospace Products personnel. Project plans, resources required, and results anticipated were reviewed with all top management, project team and key middle management personnel throughout the company. Technical seminars on specific techniques were held for project team members to provide them with the necessary tools for conducting the project. These included methodologies for conducting factory analysis, development of a cost model for financial analysis, evaluating different business functions for improvement potential, developing conceptual designs for individual technologies, conducting return on investment analysis utilizing the Capital Investment Strategy guidelines, and the overall project management methodologies for ensuring high-quality results in a timely manner.

Having completed project initiation, the Aerospace Products project team was now ready to start on the Needs Analysis.

STAGE 2: NEEDS ANALYSIS

The Needs Analysis stage was aimed at analyzing the company's business functions to determine where technology could be applied most effectively based on management's objectives, as established in the Capital Investment Strategy.

Factory Model

Using a structured modelling approach, the Aerospace Products organization was analyzed by major business function such as marketing, product design, production, manufacturing engineering, materials control, quality assurance and other administrative support functions. Using smaller study groups within the overall project team, each of these major business functions were decomposed into subfunctions at greater and greater levels of detail. Through this analysis, the organization was subdivided into a total of 416 functions. These functions ranged from shop work-centers, such as a group of vertical broaching machines, to indirect functions, such as master production scheduling.

The result of this analysis was a factory model that clearly showed the decomposition of major functions into well-defined subfunctions. The model also illustrated the interrelationships between the 416 functions.

Cost Model

Using special computerized models, business costs for the current year were analyzed in a top-down manner through the factory model. Fourteen cost elements were defined to be truly significant across the organization based on the Capital Investment Strategy. These cost elements were different from those used in the traditional cost accounting system. For example, they include inventory carrying costs, scrap, rework, energy, tooling, and information systems.

Controllable business costs for each major business function were systematically allocated in a top-down manner to subfunctions in the factory model based on available financial and statistical data. Throughout the process, care was taken to ensure that each function's cost was reasonably allocated and that, when combined, the total cost of all functions was equal to the overall controllable business costs for the organization.

The result of this analysis was a cost model that reasonably depicted the current costs associated with each of the 416 functions comprising the organization. Further, it provided a breakdown of costs across the 14 cost elements for each of the 416 functions.

Improvement Potential Analysis

Using a specially designed structured approach, project team members then assessed the improvement potential for each function. This was based on an evaluation of current materials, methods, processes and information systems. Current performance was analyzed based on quantitative and subjective data. Available technologies were considered. Also, a variety of organizational, training, policy, procedural, methods and system enhancement issues surfaced.

As a result of this analysis, a list of 120 recommendations were made to management for short-term improvements, not requiring major capital investments. Over half these recommendations were implemented within the next six months, resulting in significant improvements in work flow, product reliability and employee morale. In addition, a quantitative improvement potential assessment was made for those functions that could be significantly aided through longer-term material, process or information technologies.

Prioritizing Improvement Opportunities

By applying the results of the improvement potential analysis to the costs associated with each function in the cost model, functions with the best opportunities for utilization of new technologies were identified as illustrated in Figure 2.

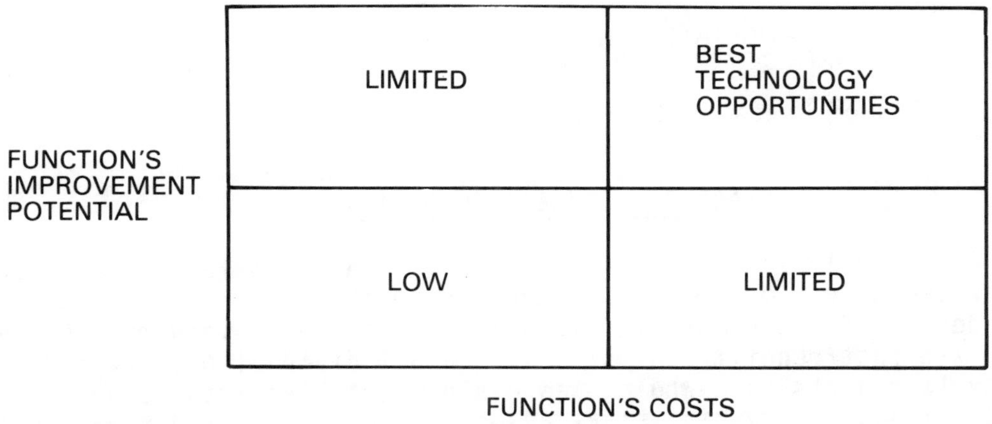

FUNCTION'S IMPROVEMENT POTENTIAL	LIMITED	BEST TECHNOLOGY OPPORTUNITIES
	LOW	LIMITED

FUNCTION'S COSTS

Figure 2. Prioritizing improvement potential.

High-cost improvement functions were then evaluated for integration into technology areas (Tech Areas) based on work cell/center combinations of functions as well as the linking of direct and indirect functions.

Also, nonfinancial criteria were evaluated for each major Tech Area. Tech Areas were then ranked by priority, using the ranking methodology developed as part of the Capital Investment Strategy.

As a result of this process, four Tech Areas were selected by the Steering Committee for further development into specific technology projects for conceptual design.

Figure 3 summarizes the results of the Needs Analysis stage.

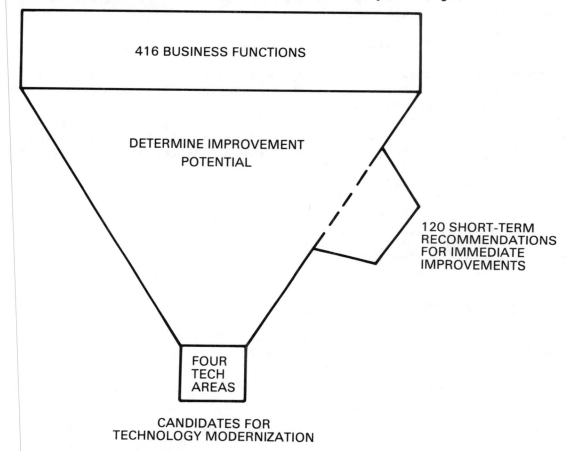

Figure 3. Results of Needs Analysis.

STAGE 3: CONCEPTUAL DESIGN

During the Conceptual Design stage, the four Tech Areas selected were analyzed in depth for technology modernization. Based on the research conducted, conceptual designs for the most feasible integrated technology projects were developed. The cost/benefit analysis, for each individual project and for all the individual projects as a whole, was evaluated taking into account technology, human and financial risks associated with each individual project. The total package of suitable technology projects then was presented to the Steering Committee for review and approval.

Technology Projects Definition

Each Tech Area was carefully analyzed to identify the significant productivity drivers associated with each cost element of the functions included in the Tech Area. For example, the impact of scrap in one fabrication Tech Area was found to be approximately $500,000. An analysis of the factors causing the scrap showed that 50% of the scrap was traceable to defective tooling design, while 30% was traceable to inadequate process control.

Potential technology alternatives were researched by the project team with the assistance of appropriate technical experts. The key objective of the project team was to identify those alternatives that could most significantly remove the deterrants to maximizing cost reduction, product reliability and schedule performance. The cost model was used as a basis for simulating the impact on Tech Area costs associated with each technology alternative.

By eliminating marginal solutions and combining different technology alternatives, a selected few technology projects were identified for each Tech Area. Conceptual designs were prepared for each project.

Implementation Analysis

The detailed design and implementation activities associated with each technology project were defined. A preliminary cost/benefit analysis was prepared using the cost model. Care was taken to ensure that benefits were not duplicated for different technologies applied to the same function.

Assumptions regarding technical considerations and financial analysis were carefully recorded, to support the implementation analysis.

Risk Assessment

At this point, each technology project was presented by the project designer to key users who would be responsible for obtaining the results anticipated. The purpose of these discussions was to obtain constructive criticism regarding technical, human and financial assumptions surrounding the project. Sensitive assumptions were carefully tested by obtaining the viewpoints of those who would have to "live" with the solutions.

As a result of this step, the conceptual designs and their cost/benefit analysis were modified based on new knowledge gained through the meetings. Also a formal "risk management" program was prepared for each project to define how the design and implementation of each technology project would be managed to maximize the real benefits to the company. Besides the significant technical and cost-validation advantages obtained, this step resulted in a very positive acceptance of responsibility by key middle managers to "make the projects happen."

Finalizing Conceptual Designs

Project team members then finalized their conceptual design documents for each project ensuring that besides the technical designs, they also had all relevant data on strategies and costs for detailed design and implementation of the individual technologies along with anticipated benefits. The tracking mechanisms for monitoring schedule, cost and benefit performance also were defined for each project.

Because of the variety of material, process and information technology projects involved, care was taken to ensure that the design documents prepared were consistent with the guidelines established in the Capital Investment Strategy.

Project Economics

A financial analysis was then conducted to identify the return on investment for each project and all the projects as a whole. Based on the Capital Investment Strategy, this included assessments of before and after tax implications, investment tax credit considerations and savings/investment ratios. The return on investment was compared to the company established hurdle rates. The overall package was then sent to management for approval.

As a result of the conceptual design process, 12 technology projects were identified for implementation. Some representative ones included:

- A Flexible Manufacturing System (FMS) for a fabrication area.
- A robotic welding line.
- An Automated Guidance Vehicle System (AGVS).
- An integrated engineering database for CAD/CAM/CAE.
- A process monitoring system.
- A modified cost management system.

STAGE 4:   THE MASTER PLAN

The fourth and final stage in the development of the CIM Business Strategy was the organization of the approved conceptual design projects into a suitable master plan for implementation at Aerospace Products.

Implementation Plan

The individual technology projects were analyzed for logical interdependencies from a CIM environment perspective. Because Aerospace Products desired to move quickly to a flexible manufacturing environment, it was vital that the master plan accommodate the progressive union of the different technology projects into an integral long-term solution. Certain projects, such as the integrated engineering database, had therefore to precede other dependent technology projects, so that a suitable architecture was in place for the longer-term CIM environment. Given the individual cost/benefit assessments by project, as well as the combined picture for all projects, top management was in a better position to make meaningful decisions on the master planning process.

Also, a resource profile was constructed to identify the types and quantities of skills needed for implementing the individual technology projects as well as the capital investments associated with each project. Based on management's willingness to commit annual capital funds to the CIM business strategy, the master plan was finalized. It detailed specific steps, personnel responsibilities, and key time periods for accomplishing results against the overall master plan for technology modernization.

CIM Business Strategy Maintenance

Organizational mechanisms for monitoring progress against the Master Plan were established.

Management recognized the need for tracking costs and benefits at a reasonable level of detail by specific project. For the CIM business strategy to be a "living document," it was essential that actual variances from planned expectations be fed back to the steering committee on a periodic basis. This information, along with an analysis of reasons for variance, could then be used to take appropriate corrective measures by either fixing problem areas or changing the original assumptions for each project.

RESULTS OBTAINED

What were the key results obtained by Aerospace Products through this project?

Five of the most significant results were as follows:

1. Top management was able to answer the strategic questions that it had regarding new technologies. The result: a commitment to invest over $28 million in CIM implementation over a five-year period based on a reasonable projection of return on investment and other competitive advantages.
2. There was a significant consensus of opinion at all management levels that the right technology projects had been selected. Further, key managers and professionals had a strong sense of commitment to a successful implementation of individual projects because of their involvement with the selection and design process.
3. Different professionals with engineering, manufacturing, information systems and financial backgrounds developed a new-found respect for one another's abilities by working to a common goal through the project team approach. This boosted morale and was expected to have a favorable impact on the productivity of these professionals.
4. The cost model provided a useful mechanism for analyzing the impact of all capital investment projects, not just those associated with CIM technologies. Management was particularly impressed with its practical ability to measure indirect costs and benefits, avoid overstatement of benefits and analyze the impact of different cost drivers.
5. Finally, and most importantly, management had successfully incorporated technology integration into its overall strategic business planning process. This gave Aerospace Products a significant competitive edge for increasing corporate return on investment and more effectively serving its customers, while developing a flexible manufacturing environment.

Editorial Overview of Part Two

This part of the *Program Guide* applies the strategic thinking and policies described in Part One. The first three papers are case studies of award-winning CIM implementations. Each company has focused its CIM effort on those applications that will yield clear competitive advantage.

Mr. George Hess, of the Ingersoll Milling Machine company, describes the application of advanced technologies to the design and manufacture of custom machines. Mr. John Snyder, of General Electric, describes the integration of marketing, engineering, and manufacturing system, with a focus on competitive service parts production. The use of group technology is explained and can be seen to play a key role in the overall CIM strategy. Mr. Larry Phillips and Mr. Wade Ogburn, of AT&T's Richmond Works, describe the application of integrated control systems and telecommunications to support high-volume circuit board production.

The last three parts of this section are of a technical and procedural nature. Mr. Lee Hales covers the status and direction of CIM standards which are vital to achieving consistency of the CIM deliverables. The subject of cost justification is addressed at two levels. First, George Sibbald examines the issue of cost justification of a CIM system as it relates to pay-as-you-go philosophy. The final chapter is Gary Conkol's case example of cost/benefit and productivity analysis. This article details the issues needed to fund the various components of a total CIM program.

STRATEGIC THINKING

CONCEPTUAL PLANNING

SYSTEMS DESIGN

INSTALLATION

Part 2

Conceptual Planning

Computer Integrated Flexible Manufacturing—1985 (CIFM – 85)

by George J. Hess
Ingersoll Milling Machine Company

INTRODUCTION

The purpose of this chapter is to share our Computer Integrated Flexible Manufacturing (CIFM) experiences (along with the other three "LEAD" award winners). Although this paper describes a case history of Ingersoll as a user of CIFM, the approach that we use internally is the same as we use with our customers. We consider ourselves a customer, but more than that as a laboratory to develop new concepts in emerging technologies, and then reduce them to practical application for state-of-the-art systems.

You cannot plan an FMS system in isolation from the CIM system anymore than you can plan a CAD system in isolation from the CAM system. You simply must plan the complete CIFM (computer integrated flexible manufacturing) system as one integrated whole. This CIFM system must include places for the introduction of new emerging technologies, and not simply be based on just the present state of the art. For many years, we have built systems based purely on deterministic, or even probabilistic approaches. We are now seeing the emergence of new heuristic, and even "inferistic" approaches. Inferistic systems are emerging very rapidly in the technology, and within a few years, will be reduced to state of the art. These are "expert" systems where a precise answer cannot be determined, but the most practical answer is inferred based upon the knowledge built into the knowledge base accessible by the system.

A fully integrated CIFM system with a natural monolithic flow in and out of the corporate database, and supported by a full range of deterministic to inferistic systems, is where we stand today in the dawn of a fantastic information age. We have certainly not "arrived." We are only in the dim light of the early years of this age, and are developing new tools faster than we can apply them, fueled by a virtual collapse of computer costs. It is up to us to exploit these opportunities, and that is exactly what we are trying to do at the Ingersoll Milling Machine Company.

CORPORATE INTRODUCTION

Before we get into the details of this case history of computer integrated flexible manufacturing, we want to take a minute and introduce you to Ingersoll so that you better understand the setting in which this system was born. Ingersoll is a large privately held group of companies consisting of four operating entities:

- The Ingersoll Milling Machine Company--The American-based special machinery builder.
- Ingersoll Cutting Tool Company--The American-based cutting tool company.
- Ingersoll Maschinen Und Werkzeuge GmbH--The German-based manufacturing company building machinery and cutting tools with its subsidiaries, Waldrich-Siegen and Bohle.
- Ingersoll Engineers Incorporated--The multinational consulting company with offices in four countries.

The information presented here is really a case history related to the first two companies.

We build special machinery systems. We seldom build a duplicate. If the spectrum of normal businesses runs from a job shop on the left to a flow shop on the right, we would be one step to the left of the job shop whose normal jobs have some repetition. We do not have time for models, prototypes, test units, etc., we are always beyond the schedule point of no return, going for broke with a quantity of one. We reuse as much engineering as possible, but that is not much. Our average engineering cycle is five months, and our engineering costs are 5% to 15% of the selling price. You know what this means--the standards program is tougher because we have few parts reused, the manufacturing procedures are tougher because fewer of them are recorded, and the whole manufacturing process is more complex because we are stuck on the worst part of the learning curve--the first experience.

BUSINESS REASONS FOR CIFM

The compelling business reason for venturing into CIFM was obviously to secure the long-term viability of our company. That, however, is an "effect" (a dependent variable), and to achieve that effect, we had to introduce the proper "causes" (the true independent variables) that will bring it about. In our case, the "causes" that we addressed were product innovation, quality, cost, and delivery.

We started our development by an analysis of the work that had to be performed, not only to meet our present demands, but to meet the emerging demands as we say them in our strategic planning effort. We then planned the processes to accomplish this work, followed by the machinery, the fixturing and tooling systems to support that machinery, the necessary automation to serve the machinery, and finally the software system to integrate the entire operation, and assure that all elements operated in concert to accomplish the overall objectives. This software was developed in three distinct phases which is now the same approach that we are using on the commercial systems that we supply. In both 1983 and 1984, we were among the leaders in the machine tool industry in the orders that we received to supply FMS systems.

During the initial planning phases, the "conceptual specifications" were prepared. These presented a conceptual description of the software to be used as a starting point for discussions with our executive office. They described the overall operational concept of the recommended system. The conceptual specifications included a computer hierarchy diagram showing the interconnection of the main hardware elements of the system.

After project approval, the "functional specifications" were written to describe what software modules were required to serve the unique needs of our business. In other words, this became the "systems requirements definition document."

Following a complete management review and approval of the functional specifications, we proceeded to prepare the "programming specifications" to describe in detail the operational database and each of the program modules with all of their features, and how they would function and interact together.

A number of our strategic planning meetings were (and are) devoted exclusive to our systems planning. Although these strategic planning sessions are aimed mainly at our own system, they are attended not only by our Chief Executive Officer, but also by the President and the General Managers of the product divisions that supply FMS systems to our customers. In this way, our planning, although concentrating on our own needs, never forgets that the reason we are in business is to serve our customers.

Our corporate strategy is to help our customers reduce their costs and become more competitive with our primary objective--"to make them the low cost producer of their products--worldwide." Our consulting company, our cutting tool company, and our machinery companies in USA and West Germany all share this common objective. To attain this objective, we are constantly searching for new and better proven ways to do things. Numerical control in itself proved to be a greater opportunity, but we really needed the integrated CAD/CAM system with its single geometric model to make it work for us. NC machines are inherently almost infinitely flexible (within their physical constraints), so they are a logical building block for our next step--a fully computer integrated flexible manufacturing system (CIFM).

CRITICAL STEPS IN PLANNING AND IMPLEMENTATION

Before serious planning can take place for the CIFM system, the overall strategic plan for the business must be developed. This will describe the "general nature and intent" of the business, the "served markets," the products that are in production today, and those that are in the product planning cycle. It will describe the organization and facilities needed to excel in the production, installation, and field support for these products, leading to satisfied and repeat customers. With this as a background, then serious planning for the CIFM system can proceed.

With this general framework constructed, we then progressed through five critical steps in the planning and implementation of our CIFM system:

- The first of these was the decision to pursue the use of numerically controlled machines from the moment they were practically available. This was the beginning of CAM.
- The second was the decision to employ computer-aided design, again from the moment that is was practical for us to start. This was the beginning of CAD.
- The third was the decision to employ computer graphics as a way to

accelerate CAD and build a solid foundation for CAM. This was the beginning of integrated CAD/CAM.

- The fourth was the decision to rewrite all the information system application software programs to install a company-wide database information system. This was the beginning of the management and business information systems integration into computer integrated manufacturing (CIM).
- The fifth was the decision to install a $20 million FMS system to essentially replace our "light" machine shop. The light machine shop manufactured prismatic parts, 1 meter cube and smaller. This was the beginning of the computer integrated flexible manufacturing (CIFM) system.

The CAD/CAM concept is the first critical step in of CIFM, and may be the single most important development in the manufacturing industry in this generation of top management. It is important because of its inherent value to the customer in products with superior performance, features, and up-time--delivered on time and at lower prices. But also because of its value to the supplier, in shorter development cycles, improved quality, lower inventory, reduced costs, fewer marginal people, and real job enrichment for employees who are superior performers.

"CAD/CAM" really means integrated computer-aided design and manufacture in the broadest sense of the word. Too many users today settle for CAD, or worse yet, a small segment of CAD such as computer graphics. Similarly, some see CAM as NC tools, others see it as MRP (manufacturing resource planning, including material requirements). These people need to extend the limits of their thinking beyond CAD/CAM. They are missing the high pay-out from the synergism of an integrated manufacturing system.

CAD by itself generates savings, but the real pay-off is in its solid foundation for CAM. CAD/CAM together directly control one of the two primary competitive elements of the business--"how much the product will cost."

The second critical step in the CIFM system is the management and business information (MIS/BIS) system. This is the system that serves the information needs of the entire business. It controls the second primary competitive element of the business--"how long it will take to deliver the product." The main part of this for manufacturing is the (alphanumeric) "product database" consisting of bills of material, master schedule, MRP, dispatch lists, and shortage lists.

The third critical step in the CIFM system is the database management system. This has been talked about and under development for 20 years, but only in the late 1970s did it become a practical reality. It is a powerful set of software programs that control complex data structures with a practical balance of integrity, security, resource costs, and ease of understanding.

The fourth critical step in the CIFM system is the flexible machining system (FMS) on the shop floor. This is a tightly linked series of processes that are fully automated. These processes include the primary functions of storage transportation, metal cutting/measuring, and administration.

It is very important to understand that the four parts of the CIFM system introduced above and described more fully in subsequent pages operate as one fully integrated monolithic system. They are described as separate parts because it is impossible for the human mind to grasp all aspects of this huge system at once. However, the data flows smoothly through the system, in and out of the database, uninterrupted and uninhibited by man-made interfaces.

SYSTEMS DESCRIPTION

Overview

The main modules in our computer integrated flexible manufacturing system are:
- Master Schedule.
- Engineering Design (Assembly & Piece Part Drawings and Bills of Material).
- Production Planning and Control.
- Inventory Control.
- Purchasing and Accounts Payable.
- Routing and Process Planning.
- Numerical Control Programming and Post Processing.
- Flexible Machining System
- Parts Storage and Retrieval, Automatic Transportation, Part Identification and Tracking, Direct Numerical Control (DNC), Automatic Inspection (QNC), Tool and Fixture Management, and Process Data Management and Report).
- Assembly.
- Job Cost and Management Reports.

CAD/CAM Computer Graphics System

The computer is deeply involved in presale activity. This work generated during the proposal phase is saved in the computer and becomes the basis of design. When we get the order, product design is the first CAD/CAM function. The computer does the complex design calculations and finite element, stability, and strength analyses that help the designer create the optimum design. The results are described graphically in the form of a geometric model in the computer this is used to produce the necessary assembly and piece part drawings using the CADAM system.

We start with the assembly layout drawings, and dissect them to make the individual part details. This is just the opposite of what we had planned. We thought we would draw the parts and fit them together into an assembly, but we find that starting with the assembly is better, the basic shapes of the parts are already drawn. The geometric models of these parts in the computer becomes the driving force for the whole rest of the system, particularly NC programming for the machining and coordinate index measuring machines. We are finding that because of this, the geometric model of the part in the computer must now be designated as the drawing original. A mylar tracing produced by the plotter (if one is required, we try to work from COM produced microfilms and prints therefrom) can no longer be the original because if that is changed, and the computer geometry is not, the part gets made wrong. Thus, a mylar tracing becomes just a reproducible copy for convenience, but it must never be changed.

Each part and subassembly is identified with a unique attribute attached to its identification number on the main assembly layout drawing in the computer graphics file, telling the computer to automatically down load this information to the alphanumeric database. This automatically becomes the Bill of Material for this job, and controls the design integrity of the product from then on.

CAD, even in isolation, is important to design engineering because essentially any product can be designed on CAD, it improves their productivity, produces higher quality drawings, and more importantly higher quality designs. It enriches the jobs of the key people and really multiplies their efforts. However, the real value of CAD is obtained when it is taken out of isolation into full integration with CAM. One example is the very same geometry that the engineer drew is the basis for routing, NC programming, and QNC performance assurance.

The NC program for chip cutting is prepared in the NC Programming Department, using both graphics and other languages. The operation times from this NC program are fed back and added to the routing for machine shop load planning long before the part is machined. The QNC programming for the quality control inspection machine is done in the Quality Control Department. The QNC programing is done either by the QNC programmer writing a program in advance, or by the inspector directing a minicomputer through the necessary steps to inspect the first part. Then if we have subsequent parts, they are inspected automatically by playing back either of these programs.

The NC is done in various ways for different machine tools. Our milling machines and flame-cut torch are programmed using computer graphics where it is necessary only to call in the geometry that the engineer has drawn, and touch the geometric surfaces that you want to cut in the order that you want to cut them. The computer takes over and produces the NC instructions for the machine automatically with no further involvement from the programmer. The programmer must, of course, have made the proper setup, specified the tooling, the coolant, and other nongeometric operations. We are constantly striving to improve our collision checks in our post processors. For our two-dimensional work, we are able to prevent collisions by "clearance planes" around the part, fixture, or any part of the machine, so that we get a software collision, thereby preventing an actual machine collision. For our three-dimensional parts, this is not so easy. Our approach is to prove the tapes at a graphics scope by watching the tool motions in both the plan and elevation view, and thereby allowing the NC programmer to detect any collisions prior to actually running the tape.

Business Information System

Our business information system is a real-time system operating from a single database, allowing multiple concurrent on-line updating. We are told that we have the largest database in the world, not in number of transactions, but in the span of integrated business functions under one database. The entire system described in the following paragraphs is in place and in full production operation.

The day that we receive the order, the delivery date is put in the master schedule, the Accounting Department registers the order as an order received, and the Contracts Department is advised. The order is assigned, and thereafter tracked by a five-digit serial number, like 25575.

The Contracts Department prepares an acknowledgement to the customer the day that the new order is entered. The acknowledgment confirms the customer's delivery date. The Contracts Department is part of our performance planning activity which provides project management from time that the order is received, until the machine is turned over to production in the customer's plant.

The master scheduler enters four key dates into the master schedule system:

1) The shipping date (from the quotation).
2) The engineering completion date.
3) The machine shop completion date.
4) The purchasing completion date.

These dates drive the detail scheduling that is done internally within the individual functions. The master schedule is a computer record that contains and controls all dates in the company related to that job. It directly drives the Engineering, Purchasing, and Manufacturing systems. If we want to reschedule a job, even with several thousand parts in process, we need only to change one demand date via a computer terminal, and it is done. This is a transaction subject to careful security checks, such that only one person (the Vice President of Manufacturing) can change a date in the master schedule--everyone else gets a "security violation" if they try.

Bill of material systems are, of course, the heart of any manufacturing information system. We are in business to serve our customer needs by producing products at a profit. The bill of material defines our product--nothing could be more basic. No other single document approaches the bill of material in importance to our business (except the customer's order).

Purchasing works with the designers early. Purchasing establishes a long lead time report, and updates it monthly. This helps the engineers identify those items that will require early release to meet delivery. By having Engineering release individual items on a "working bill," Purchasing places long lead items on order before the final bill of material is released.

Within the engineering cycle are the functions of design, detail, and check. The checked geometric model and the checked bill of material are released to the manufacturing function at the time that engineering is complete.

The completed bill of material and the completed geometric models generated on CADAM are made available to the downstream functions. For example, the bill of material prepared by Engineering is, in fact, the bill of material that Purchasing uses to buy. The geometry of the engineers designed in CADAM is the geometry that the tape programmers use to program weldments and machined parts.

The bill of material and the master schedule work together to develop dated gross demands on the three supply systems. After these dated gross requirements are passed against the inventory file, the dated net requirements are placed on the other two supply systems--the purchasing system for all those items to be bought, and the manufacturing system for all those items to be manufactured. In our business, very little of the total is in inventory stock. It is typical that Purchasing will run between 40% and 50% of the total cost of the job. The manufactured parts represent the balance with the stock room perhaps supplying only about 1%.

The FMS system is controlled by the dispatch list. This is what allows us to work on parts in the order needed, and this had been a problem for a long time. An old story still lingers that Winthrop Ingersoll, founder of the company, whose office was directly above the employment entrance, one day said to the shop superintendent as the men filed in to work, "If only we could tell each of those men exactly what jobs we wanted them to do today, we could double our output." Seventy-five years later, using bill of material, routing, and master schedule programs, we deliver, every morning at 7 am, to every foreman, a list of parts we want worked on that day in order of priority. There are always more parts on the list than could possibly be finished. Continously, as changes are called for, as parts are spoiled, as customer breakdowns occur, the entire work load is reshuffled in the computer, and at 7 am the next morning, a new correct dispatch list appears.

When the three supply systems complete their functions, they deliver all required parts to the Assembly Stores. At that time, we go back to the Bill of Material and be sure we have all parts specified by the latest Bill of Material. If anything is missing, it is called an assembly shortage. The "latest" Bill of Material that we check is not the one that was originally issued several months ago, but the one that is perpetually updated on-line in real time, including the latest Engineering notice of change and the part that was received on the receiving dock both within the last five minutes. The result is an assembly shortage report that is more up-to-date than any one function could possibly provide. A printed assembly shortage report is prepared for each machine on our assembly floor 7 am every day, and you can get an instantaneous update at any time from any computer terminal.

The assembly operation begins on or about the date of the machine work being complete. There is a scheduling offset for certain machine work and purchase completion dates in advance of the master schedule machine work complete date for items that require longer lead time in assembly. In other words, there are some subassemblies that are begun before the machine work is complete on other parts (parts that require less time to assemble).

We perpetually track and measure our cost performance against a plan for this customer's order. There are major categories within the plan--like, the total engineering cost, the total purchase cost, the total fabrication cost, the machine shop cost, the assembly cost, and the grand total.

The technique used to manage and coordinate work from date of order until the machine is in full production in the customer's plant is called performance planning and it consists of several subphases:

- Manufacturing Planning--a joint effort of engineering and manufacturing for maximizing producibility.
- Assembly Planning--Developing the detailed schedule for the assembly,

and specifing the resources required to do the assembly task.
- Installation Planning--Developing the plan for receiving and installing the machine in the customer's plant, and specifing resources required.

As the machine is being erected on the assembly floor, the Contracts Department is encouraged to bring the customer in to observe the machine and its progress. This gives the customer an opportunity to review progress, and to become more familiar with the machine. After the assembly people finish the construction work, and the electrical people turn the power on, the machine is made ready for our testing.

After our check-out is complete, the customer comes to Rockford for the final run-off of the machine. Here, we cut metal parts that he expects to produce on this machine. The finished piece is sent to Quality Control where a high accuracy coordinate measuring inspection machine measures the actual geometry of the part. This is fed back to the computer where we already have stored in the CADAM file what the geometry should be. What we "have" is compared to what we "should have," and the deviations noted. The computer then proceeds to calculate the exact adjustments that must be made to the machine to produce a part within the promised tolerances.

These adjustments are presented to the assembly floor in the language of the machine adjustments so that the necessary corrections can be made prior to cutting the next customer part. What this has done is to change the old "cut and try" method of final adjustment of a complex machine to a precise computer calculated "deterministic" approach. This means that the adjustment moves are always made right the first time. The results are nothing short of startling. It has taken days and weeks out of the check-out cycle for complex machinery.

The computer-directed inspection machines also check the accuracy of parts made in our FMS system to be sure they are "made to the drawing" before being sent to the assembly floor. This results in the main floor being a real production assembly floor rather than a cut and try fitting department.

Our Field Service organization has a representative close to the machine during the final stages of run-off. The serviceman that is assigned to the re-erection of the machine on the customer's floor stays with the machine while it is being disassembled, boxed, and packed, such that he will be witness to where things go, where things have been, and how the boxes are marked. This makes the erection of the machine at the customer's plant much easier.

Our shipping organization has worked with the customer's traffic department during the last few weeks of the assembly, and has established a plan for getting the job packaged and shipped properly. A typical job will go on several trucks or railroad cars. It is rare that a job is shipped on a single truck; it can go to as many as 40 or 50 trucks, depending upon the size.

The field servicemen go to the customer's plant, and put the machine together. They ultimately perform a run-off to the customer's satisfaction, similar to that we did in Rockford. Our responsibility extends through the warranty period.

FMS System

Our flexible machining system (FMS) will replace 90% of the conventional "light" machine shop (parts that fit into a 1-meter cube). This system was started in 1983, is in operation now, and will be expanded as funds permit over the next several years.

Our first taste of success has already been realized, even though the system is just now being installed. With just the first five machines in operation, we can attest to their flexibility since we have already eliminated 17 old machines, and the next six new machines will release 23 more.

The key to this early success was the strong position that we had achieved in both the integrated database and our CAD/CAM systems. Without those earlier decisions, and the strong corporate commitment to develop them to their fullest, these latest steps would not be possible.

The "problem set" is open-ended. That is, we expect to produce about 25,000 different prismatic parts on this system each year. Seventy percent of these parts are machined in lots of one and 50% will not be manufactured again. These characteristics are very important in a special machinery business like ours.

In addition to the CNC machining centers, the system includes wireguided vehicles, pallet setup stations, coordinate index measuring machines for inspection, wash and debur station, and a complete tool and fixture management system. It is controlled by a Digital Equipment Corporation's VAX-750 cell management computer in constant two-way communications with the corporate host computer which is a National Semiconductor NAS-9060 mainframe. The VAX cell management computer is in constant contact with the Allen-Bradley 8200 CNC controllers via the ABCAM two-way communications interface.

Ingersoll's FMS software is organized around the seven basic resources that must be allocated and controlled in any FMS system. They are:

- Parts.
- Pallets.
- Fixtures.
- Tools.
- Storage (ASRS).
- Transportation (AGVS, robots, etc.).
- Machines (cutting, deburring, washing, measuring).

The monitoring system will track the usage of each tool, as well as the current state and location of each tool. The tool room operator is notified at the time a part is being set up on the setup stands as to what tools will be required to run that part. The automatic guided vehicles move the pallet containing the fixtured part to the incoming table of each machine. Similarily, they retrieve a completed pallet from the outgoing table at each machine. This is all done automatically under computer control.

In the pallet setup area, the parts are mounted in fixtures on specific pallets that are identified to the computer. From there on, only the pallets are tracked throughout the system. The parts and the fixture components are delivered to the pallet setup area from the storage system. There are five setup stands. Each one uses modular fixture components. When the part is completely setup, the operator identifies the pallet, and signals the cell computer that the part is ready to be entered into system. The cart will then pick up the pallet at the setup stand automatically, and deliver it to the machine automatically.

The inspection station will consist of two Zeiss Mauser coordinate measuring machines. These will be operated under full DNC control.

The wash station will be a power wash to completely remove all of the chips prior to inspection. A manual check prior to entering inspection will make sure that there are no burrs to interfere with the automatic inspection machines.

The entire system is served with an under-the-floor chip removal system, which links into the existing system in the rest of the factory.

All of the components of the system, the machines, the carts, the tool setup and transportation system, and the storage system, all communicate with each other through the cell computer. When a warning or emergency situation occurs, the system will try to correct itself, such as with tool compensation. If it is unable to, it will signal a fault condition through the monitoring system to alert the cell manager. The system is being designed to be as nearly automatic as possible, and the software is designed so that it is flexible and very adaptable to change.

One important motivation behind the installation of this new system in our shop is to improve product quality by gaining a whole new level of control over some of the most critical processes in the manufacture of products. The things that make it possible for us to do this are that it also will directly reduce costs and increase production levels.

The FMS system is an integral part of the larger corporate business system. It is just the latest part of the computer integrated manufacturing (CIM) system to be fully automated. This is why we now call our overall system the computer integrated flexible manufacturing (CIFM) system.

The primary communication from the corporate host to the FMS will be the dispatch list from the MRP module. This is a list of "dated net requirements" consisting of a list of lots (work orders) to be produced in specific quantities in a specified sequence.

The primary communications from the FMS back to the host computer will be event driven data, such as:

- An emergency condition.
- A lot completion notice for each lot giving all the cost, production, and quality control data required for each part in the lot.

It will also be periodic management information system (MIS) data, such as:

- Personnel statistics (time reporting, etc.).
- Machine statistics (up-time, etc.).

- Resource statistics (tool inventory, etc.).

KEY POINTS LEARNED

Computer-integrated flexible manufacturing is not generic. There is no "canned" approach that will fit all cases. The success of any system of this nature is dependent not only upon its inherent technical capabilities, but also on the human and organizational environment into which it is implemented. Therefore, there cannot be an absolute best list of tasks, or even principles, to guide the CIFM newcomer. However, if you have a job shop business in a fiercely competitive environment with a very practical but aggressive entrepreneurial management, the following may help.

TEN COMMANDMENTS OF CIFM PLANNING & IMPLEMENTATION

First, thou shalt anticipate emerging technologies. It is going to take you several years to implement your CIFM system, and if you base this on mature technologies, or even state-of-the-art technologies, by the time you get it installed, it will be obsolete and noncompetitive. Therefore, you must look at the emerging technologies that are just beginning to come over the horizon, and try to anticipate which ones of those will reach practicality within your planning time frame. This is not to say that you whole plan should be completely "blue sky" to the point of being impractical, but it does mean that you simply must anticipate the future in this field of very rapidly changing technologies.

Second, thou shalt agree on corporate strategic direction. You must have a clear vision of the future direction of your company if you are going to invest millions of dollars in a system to automate that company. True, the system should be flexible enough to adjust to changes in direction, but nothing can be infinitely flexible, and the cost of your CIFM system will be in direct proportion to the clarity of this vision that you describe. This does not mean that you have to have every single detail of the future business defined, but at least it should incorporate not only the changes that you have presently planned for your business, but considering the emerging technologies and the political environment in which you are operating, you also must plan on the likely changes that other forces in the environment will force upon your business.

Third, thou shalt establish a single systems coordinating organization. No matter how hard you try, there is no way that you will design and implement a successful integrated system with a disintegrated design staff, unless there is a strong coordinating organization to pull it all together. This coordinating organization could be the systems department, or it could be the systems department operating under the umbrella of a corporate steering committee, but this should be an organization bent on really effectively serving the line functions of the business, and not be an ivory tower organization with dictatorial powers and delusions of grandeur.

Fourth, thou shalt explore full business CIFM automation. CIFM is at the very least a mind stretcher. In its fullest form, it is beyond the capability of any one human mind to fully grasp. Therefore, we must be careful that the definition of the task is not cut down in size to fit the capability of the mind describing it. The shop/office dichotomy that has existed in industry for years has led to most CIFM attempts being lopsided toward either the office or the shop. Worse yet, some within the office magnify only one function, such as accounting, engineering design, or manufacturing planning, out of proportion to the other functions. The CIFM approach must truly be a balanced approach. Certainly, all of the design planning and monitoring functions in engineering, manufacturing planning, and accounting are extremely important, but without effective shop operations, they are impotent at best.

Therefore, the FMS system must be planned with every bit as much care as the rest of the system. This is why the other three commandments precede this one. We need a clear vision of where the business is going, a careful look at new technology opportunities, and a balanced approach to our planning. The FMS system must consider the product line requirements in all phases of development. That is, some products will be mature products that are winding down, while others are just emerging from the product planning phase, and are being built in only prototype form, while still others are the main stream of today's business.

The selected machinery must have the rugged repeatability and precision needed for unattended operations for your type of products. You need to plan the fixturing, tooling, material handling, and storage equipment with equal care. The FMS software is one of the real keys to success.

This is the flexible part of your FMS system.

It must fit your factory needs very effectively, and tie back to the corporate host, and thus the corporate database with equal effectiveness.

Fifth, thou shalt establish corporate and departmental objectives. After full exploration of what the total CIFM effort can do for your business, you must reduce that down to the individual departmental objectives which should be prepared by the management of each function, so that they really feel as though they are having a part in this planning effort. Like any other strategic planning effort, this is an interactive process, since when the first objectives are defined, the overall project has not yet been approved, and therefore as we cycle through these steps, these objectives are refined to fit the practicality of the situation.

Sixth, thou shalt force operations management to decide "what." The operations management is the very lifeblood of the organization, and they must be heard and served. Therefore, we organized our effort to make it very much "user-driven" with the operations management being the dominant force to define what they needed to best serve their parts of the business.

Seventh, thou shalt allow systems management to decide "how." Operations management does know the needs of the business, but by the very nature of their assignment, they have a very decentralized viewpoint of the total business. Therefore, our systems department became the coordinating function to insure that these plans fit together using the most advanced hardware and software available to implement them. In other words, they decided "how" it should be implemented. The systems department must be a true service organization, but they are certainly not a servant organization to be subjugated to every strong operating executive's desire. They must lead with the "authority of knowledge."

Eighth, thou shalt develop a comprehensive plan. You must build a series of planning and performance predictive and optimally seeking simulation models to quantify the range of uncertainty of performance of the new system to a practical level of assurance considering all of the risks involved. From this, you must develop a comprehensive plan for your implementation by defining controllable-sized projects with specific goals and target dates. Then, you must track these projects from both a cost and a schedule viewpoint.

You must do these things, but you must not worship the plan.

Indeed, you must be very flexible yourself because new technologies carry with them the very seeds of destruction of the status quo, even to the point of making your whole present business obsolete. You cannot change that, but you can be very alert to the "winds of change," and decide to exploit the new ideas and modify your plan accordingly.

Ninth, thou shalt install one integrated database, however painful that may be. You must accept (graciously if you can) the fact that you will probably have to redesign the thousands of application systems in use today so that they can work from the same high-integrity information in the central corporate database. You cannot get out of it so you might as well get started, because the longer you wait, the more it will cost you in rewriting the new programs that you write between now and then.

Lastly, tenth, thou shalt gain full top management involvement and support. This is not optional. It is an imperative! If you do not have this, you will not succeed. "Support" does not mean blank checks or blind faith. It means understanding and knowledgeable guidance. It means real leadership and involvement by all levels of management. It means courage to learn from your failures (and there will be some), and willingness to opportunistically exploit your successes.

We do not mean to imply that our approach is right for every business, but it worked well for us, and if your business is similar, it will likely work well for you. You can follow these same steps, and wind up with a first-class computer integrated flexible manufacturing system.

RESULTS

The Manufacturing Studies Board of the National Research Council selected five companies that they considered as representative leaders in computer integrated flexible manufacturing systems. Ingersoll Milling Machine Company was one of these five. Although we are both a producer and a user, we were selected based on our experience as a user.

They published a report of their findings in a late 1984 report titled "Computer Integration Of Engineering Design & Production: A National Opportunity."

They reported the following savings as representative of CIFM results in the companies that they visited:

- 5-20% reduction in personnel costs.
- 15-30% reduction in engineering design costs.
- 30-60% reduction in overall lead time.
- 30-60% reduction in work-in-process.
- 40-70% gain in overall production.
- 200-300% gain in capital equipment operating time.
- 200-500% product quality gain.
- 300-3500% gain in engineering productivity.

As a final summary, we would like you to hear what our Chairman and Chief Executive Officer has said about the value of CIFM to Ingersoll:

- "The gains our company is making through computer integrated flexible manufacturing represents our most important immediately available competitive edge.
- "Computer integrated flexible manufacturing, more so than with any other large investment in a manufacturing company, is based on people's brains and imagination. There is nothing at all automatic about the benefits. It simply depends on people and the directions they get.
- "In order to build the skills and gain the experience, one must get started. This is not a technique where you wait for somebody else to perfect the programs or the 21st century version.
- "There is no way one can effectively put in computer integrated manufacturing with an eye on an immediate return on investment. People say American industry suffers because its managers pay too much attention to the short term ROI. Well, if you go at computer integrated flexible manufacturing, incrementally looking to get every penny invested back within a short and definite time scale, this competitive advantage will be lost to you.

When we look back at the good things we achieved along the way, it is no exaggeration to say that the most important improvements were frequently unpredicted or underestimated. We simply did not know enough to see what could be achieved. How is it possible, then, to predict what profit gains will result from the improvements to come?"

Computer Integrated Manufacturing at Steam Turbine-Generator Operation: A Case Study

by John F. Snyder
General Electric Company

OVERVIEW

General Electric (GE) is a highly diversified international corporation with 330,000 employees world-wide and 1984 sales of $28 billion. Its product line ranges from light bulbs to jet engines, from refrigerators to power plant equipment, from insurance and other financial services to natural resources, GE's size, diversity, strong management disciplines, and a balance sheet characterized by high cash reserves, consistent earnings, and low debt, afford it a reputation among the financial community as a "Blue Chip" corporation.

GE's Steam Turbine-Generator business dates back to the turn of the century, supplying the utility industry with the heavy machinery necessary to convert the thermal power of steam into the mechanical power from a turbine then into the electrical power from a generator. A single, large nuclear turbine-generator, for example, can provide over 1,300,000 kilowatts for power--enough to light a major city. GE turbine-generators provide over half the electricity generated in the United States and are used extensively for ship propulsion and industrial applications as well.

Throughout the 1950s and 1960s, electrical consumption in the United States doubled every 10 years. This expansion fueled a commensurate expansion in manufacturing facilities to produce turbine-generators. In the 1970s, demand began to shrink. The oil crises of the decade fostered energy conservation. The regulatory environment and high costs of new power plants forced utilities to cut back on construction, cancel orders for projected equipment, and extend the life of existing power plants. With excess capacity world-wide to manufacture turbine-generators, supply began chasing demand with the result being a classic price/cost squeeze.

New Strategy

This business environment caused the Steam Turbine-Generator business to adopt a strategy of downsizing and reducing costs while maintaining its reputation for high quality and reliability. Computer-Integrated Manufacturing (CIM) systems played a key role in implementing this strategy.

The strategy to downsize and reduce costs placed demands for flexibility and productivity on systems. The parts business, once a side-line, became increasingly important and required the systems to respond flexibly to short cycle orders. The business had to supply just as wide a variety of parts but with a reduced workforce and smaller capacity. The competition engendered by excess capacity placed demands on computers to provide major cost take-outs through productivity gains.

With utilities increasing maintenance activity and up-grading their equipment to last longer, the short cycle parts business became a larger share of the business mix. Unlike the business of providing an entire unit (which took up to three years to produce), the parts business placed demands on systems to integrate all the functions more closely and provide order entry capabilities that could handle less predictable production flows.

Finally, the competitive environment forced attention on providing better customer service. For systems, this implied finding ways for computers to minimize quote and delivery cycles. With less ability to differentiate on price the business sought differentiation through customer service factors, especially for a wide variety of parts which the market viewed almost as commodities with little perception of quality differences among vendors.

CIM TACTICS

The CIM tactics that evolved from the business strategy stressed integration not only of the business' systems but of the functions themselves. Marketing, finance, engineering, manufacturing and relations all had to be closely interwoven to attain the objective of a paper-less factory employing the latest computer technologies in all areas. This coordination was achieved through the development of a computer technology master plan in 1981 that looked out 10 years, identifying the state-of-the-art technologies, projects, schedules, resources, and anticipated results needed to meet the realities of the marketplace. The master plan is up-dated every two years to keep abreast of changes in technologies and shifting business climates. Each year the master plan translates into detailed operational plans which identify monthly milestones for each project and assigns responsibilities for completion.

The organizational structure that has evolved to develop, implement and integrate the efforts drew all functions into a new component called Technical and Management Information Systems (TMIS). Once-separate, information, engineering, and manufacturing systems organizations were brought into this group along with experts in marketing systems, finance, and planning. Such broad representation was crucial to integrate successfully the entire business cycle from quotation to a customer to shipment of a finished product without the use of paper or drawings. Rather than organizing itself along functional lines (e.g. engineering systems, financial systems, etc.), TMIS structured its components cross-functionally in four general areas: those who seek out new technologies, those who develop them, those who install them, and those who provide end-user support once the technology has been implemented.

Major Modules

The 10-year effort focuses on eight major modules operating in an on-line, real time environment:

1. Marketing systems which provide instantaneous quotes and on-line order entry, forecast demand, and manage complex international projects.

2. Business systems employing the latest Manufacturing Resource Planning II concepts.

3. Engineering design systems employing interactive graphics and design programs and generating digital codes that provide complete descriptions of parts for use by other functions, i.e. the basis of an integrated product database.

4. A generative, automated process planning system that captures planning logic in an expert type system to route parts most efficiently through the manufacturing shops.

5. A numerical control (NC) programming system employing the latest techniques to instruct machine tools on how to cut complex parts.

6. A factory management system that provides distributed numerical control, factory communication among the work stations and their support functions, and shop floor control modules that track each piece through the shop and the resources applied to it.

7. "Hard" automation systems employing the latest computer numerically controlled machine tools in flexible manufacturing cells serviced by robots.

8. Professional productivity programs based on broad use of networked personal computers.

Each of these major modules present significant technological challenges in themselves, but the major CIM challenge is integrating these systems into a synergistic whole.

Technically, the CIM system's layered architecture is comprised of a Honeywell mainframe computer, GE's largest interactive graphics facility (CALMA), seven Data General MV8000 and MV10000 minicomputers, and hundreds of microcomputers. They key element in the network has been the creation of a unique part definition database internally called the Part Recognition Code or "PRC." The code serves as a replacement for traditional drawings in terms of digitally defining the product for use by all business systems. The "PRC" is based on Group Technology Family of Parts concepts and provides all of the information, including notational data, normally provided by the engineering drawing.

PART RECOGNITION CODE

The basic concept which allows the Part Recognition Code to work is simple recognition that although a business--any business--may produce a variety of products, these products exist in groupings, or "families," which have common characteristics. Even though detailed designs may change for a particular order, the over-all characteristics of the generic "family" still will be present. We all use similar principles in daily life in the words that are used to describe the products we manufacture. The "family" concept is a natural product of human thought processes and language.

For example, if one were to describe an object, one might begin with a

descriptor, say, "animal." This would conjure a general image, eliminating a
wide variety of other possibilities, such as trees, rocks, etc. The addition
of the word "dog" to the description makes the mental image more precise.
Adding the term "Collie" would for many purposes provide all of the
information necessary to complete the picture and to plan for many of the
tasks associated with dog ownership, such as buying food and building a dog
house.

For other purposes, even greater detail may be required through a fourth
descriptor that would provide, say, the dog's name, sex, color, age, height,
length, medical history, etc. Given this final set of descriptors, enough
information can be provided to perform virtually any task associated with
that particular animal.

Steam-Turbine-Generator's Part Recognition Code--and its manufacturing
vocabulary--operates in virtually the same manner with four distinct grouping
of code elements (see Figure 1). Although the Part Recognition Code has been
developed for parts as complex as sculptured surface airfoil shapes, the more
trivial example of a bolt will suffice to show how the code works.

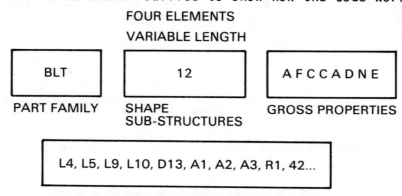

Figure 1. Generative Automated Process Planning System driven by the Part
Recognition Code.

For the first element, the family name "Bolt" is selected. This name
implies the overall geometry of the part and, for Steam Turbine-Generator
manufacturing, particular shops and procedures. For the second element, add
the code for "steel" (as opposed to brass), and the machine tool selection
starts to become specific. For the third element, qualify the description by
saying that the diameter is greater than two inches and the length over 14
inches, and that the bolt has a hex head, and machine tool selection is
defined. Include the thread length in the fourth element along with pitch,
head size, etc., and a complete description has been provided. More
importantly, this description is one that is intelligible to a computer
program in a way that a series of lines, curves, and points on a drawing or
interactive graphics model is not.

Application

Actual application of the Part Recognition Code and the integration of all
systems begins in Steam Turbine-Generator sales offices around the world (see
Figure 2). For the sales representative to get a quotation for a customer, he

is linked to the mainframe computer in Schenectady, NY, via GE's GEISCO communications network (1). The primary elements of the parts to be quoted are identified using either the customer's history, catalog numbers, or descriptive data. Once these elements have been provided (the equivalent of

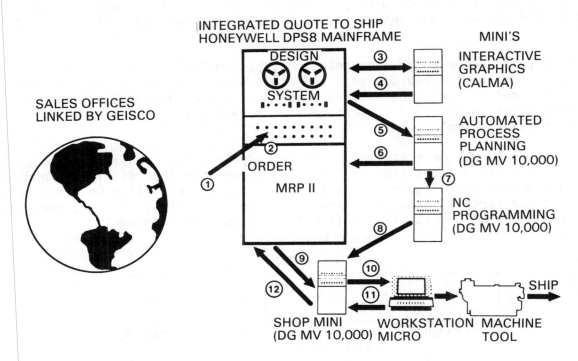

Figure 2. General Electric Steam Turbine--Generator Computer-Integrated Manufacturing.

"animal, dog, Collie" in the example above), Finance's costing programs are able to analyse the manufacturing elements involved, establishing the cost impact and returning price and delivery terms to the sales representative in a few seconds, real time. The obsolete manual methods of delivering a quote could have taken up to a month for some parts. The system also tracks a quotation's status, converting it to an order on a successful closing of a sale, and triggering subsequent production-oriented business systems. (2) While the first three elements of the Part Recognition Code may have been sufficient to provide price and delivery terms, additional, detailed engineering design may be required to establish fully the properties of the final item to be produced. This again is accomplished using the Part Recognition Code and Steam Turbine-Generator's Calma Interactive Graphics (IAG) systems.

In this case, instead of creating the lines and arcs traditionally required to prepare a new drawing manually or on an IAG system, the designer begins with the first elements of the Part Recognition Code. The code informs the design system which part is being called for and draws the appropriate programming into the IAG system's memory (3). Over 1,000 unique design files exist as a resource on the Honeywell mainframe. The designer then provides the detailed information needed to complete the code via a question and answer format. The computer uses this information to "create" the part drawing, which is then checked by the designer and approved. The system not only defines the part electronically but also provides analytical capabilities such as finite element analysis. This digital process enhances design and drafting productivity enormously by simplifying and expediting the design process. Productivity improvements of over 3 to 1 were achieved in this arena.

Once the Part Recognition Code has been approved, its model resides on the mainframe (4) until it is passed down to the Automated Process Planning System (5) residing on a Data General MV10000. This system interrogates the Part Recognition Code and selects the machine tools, available material, and routing required to produce the part. The system also provides the detailed operational instructions for each machine tool, including planned times and a simplified drawing for reference, giving all of the information necessary for an operator to manufacture the part. The system's flexibility enables it to provide on-line alternate planning if a machine tool is down, and the system will modify the planning to accommodate such conditions as over-size raw material, etc.

Machine Control

Based on capturing planning logic in an "expert-type" system, this generative, real-time process planning system was created by combining the technologies of Steam Turbine-Generator's own unique, Part Recognition Code with a powerful, commercially available software "kernal" called LOCAM from Logan Associates of the United Kingdom. Productivity implications are obvious when the three minutes required to produce new planning on the system are compared to typical industry-wide planning cycles.

Once the planning has been created, it is transferred back to the business systems (an MRPII system is being implemented) on the Honeywell mainframe (6), which schedules the work, and also is transferred (7) to the Numerical Control Programming System if NC machine tools are part of the manufacturing process. Residing on a Data General MV10000, the NC programming system takes the Part Recognition Code and routing information and selects the appropriate family-of-parts program which has been previously written for the particular class of parts. Using an APT-IV pre-processor and the GEPOST post-processor for the specific machine tool, the system develops the digital instructions that control the manufacturing equipment. Having used over a dozen NC languages in the past, Steam Turbine-Generator is keying on APT-IV and GEPOST as common languages for the sake of the efficiencies of consistency and to employ the state-of-the-art technologies, especially in complex sculptured surfaces work, that these languages provide. Structured programming techniques also are being implemented to capture and standardize manufacturing processes and to enable programmers to understand one another's coding logic.

Like the Automated Process Planning, the NC system has the flexibility to react in minutes, in real time, to changes on the factory floor and is generatve in providing fresh NC programs each time a part is called for.

When it comes time to manufacture the part, the NC program (8) and the planning data (9) are down-loaded to the particular shop's Factory Management System, resident on Data General MV10000 minicomputers, to control the actual manufacturing operations. The minicomputer is the "host" for a network of hundreds of factory-hardened, Intel 8086-based microprocessors at the various workstations in each shop. Planning and NC instructions are down-loaded to these microprocessors (10) to produce the part and job status information is fed back to the shop mini (11) and the business systems (12) to close the loop on production control.

The Factory Management System was one of Steam Turbine-Generator's first successful forays into Computer-Integrated Manufacturing and consists of three parts:

1. Distributed Numerical Control does away with the traditional cabinets full of mylar tape and links each workstation back to the NC system for on-line, real time changes. The microprocessor at each NC workstation has memory capacity to store several NC tape images so that if the shop's minicomputer goes down, the workstation can continue production.

2. Factory Communications links the machine tool operator with support functions like methods, foremen, movemen, machine repair, QC, etc. Instead of a worker going to seek out help, these functions rush to his aid at the push of a button on his terminal to keep him as productive as possible. Cycle time improvements have been dramatic.

3. Shop Floor Control monitors material from its arrival in the shop and directs the material's movement through the various work stations, automatically requesting the required moves subsequent to each operation. At each work station, the system tracks the work queue and determines the relative priority of the work available for dispatching. As the operator completes work on a given job, the system automatically selects the next highest priority for dispatching.

The major modules of Steam Turbine-Generator's CIM system were installed and debugged in a pilot shop before being rolled out into the other shops. The phased implementation across all shops occurs throughout the original time frame of the master plan with enhancements added as experience develops the new technologies emerge.

LESSONS LEARNED

There have been five basic lessons learned through the CIM implementation process that have been crucial to its success.

First, technologies have to be targetted to business needs, not the other way around. A new technology may appear quite attractive, but it may not be consonant with the goals of the business strategy. Emerging technologies must not only be consonant with the business strategy but with the systems strategy as well. Each piece must integrate with the other, no matter how appealing an "island of excellence" it may be.

Second, the planning process is an essential element, not only for project management purposes but also to anticipate and to drive the development of new technologies. At the outset, it was recognized that certain needed technologies have not yet been developed, but recognizing these gaps provided the impetus to drive vendors to work toward new technologies and capabilities.

Third, integration of the business's systems was gospel, but to enjoy full synergy, the business functions--the people, their roles, and their methods of operation--must integrate as well. Each function must strive for the most effective integration with the other functions with which it must interface.

Fourth, everyone--from the CEO to the hourly worker--must feel ownership for their piece of the CIM system. The more the system is viewed as the exclusive purvey of a particular system group or function, the less cooperation and integration will result.

Lastly and fifth, top management commitment to CIM is necessary. Major programs required to make quantum changes in a business' productivity cannot be expected to start at the bottom and trickle up effectively.

The Evolution of Computer Integrated Manufacturing at AT&T Technology Works, Richmond Virginia

by Larry W. Phillips and Wade L. Ogburn
AT&T Technologies

INTRODUCTION

AT&T's Richmond Works is a high-volume manufacturer of printed wiring boards (PWBs). It has two locations in Richmond, Virginia about one-half mile apart that provide one million square feet for manufacturing and product control. The Main Plant facility was constructed in 1973. The second location was acquired under a lease agreement to provide needed space for expanded operations to meet the needs of the fast-growing interconnection technology. The facility manufactures a complete range of printed wiring boards with sales exceeding $200 million per year. Included in these are: Multilayer, typically with six or eight layers, Rigid, which have plated through holes. Flexible with the characteristic for bending to meet the contour of its housing such as a telephone handset, and finally Connectorized or Backplane boards.

WHY CIM AT RICHMOND?

Like most PWB plants, Richmond Works is operated as a job shop; that is, the product is in lot form and is started in the shop only when an order is received. Since the job shop environment is highly dynamic, it was recognized early in the plant design process that a flexible computer system would be required to efficiently manage the operation. The PWB is usually the last component designed, yet the first one required for a piece of equipment. It is also the first component changed and the one that is changed most frequently. These considerations require a fast reacting and flexible system. This system also must manage a shop with over a thousand active PWB codes at any given time. The markets for these codes are rapidly changing with an average life expectancy of less than two years. The manufacturing technology is very dynamic because techniques are constantly being improved. These improvements must be implemented quickly and with as little disruption to the manufacturing process as possible.

Another consideration was the short delivery intervals that PWB orders often require, with the attendant need to move lots through more than one operation per day. This requirement motivated a real-time instead of batch product tracking system. Furthermore, these intervals are especially demanding for a new design, so the plant needed the CAM software to quickly generate the required numerical control files and Artmasters. Most recently, competition has become a greater factor for needing CIM. Since AT&T's divestiture in January 1984, our old AT&T customers are more likely to go elsewhere if we fail to meet their needs, plus we now are free to compete in the open market.

This competition places a renewed emphasis on CIM at the Richmond Works and makes it a must to be a successful manufacturer of printed wiring boards.

CRITICAL STEPS

Design and Implementation

The first step is putting together a team to develop and implement the system. This should be multidisciplined group with backgrounds in computer science, engineering, business, mathematics, and management. Another point to consider when choosing this team is the size of the team. There is an optimum size. If the team is too small, the system may not be implemented on schedule or may be poorly designed because of insufficient design effort. If a large team is chosen, with the objective of designing and implementing the total system from the beginning, the development could be hindered because of problems associated with managing large groups of people. At AT&T, a team of 16 professionals was used. These professionals developed the basic modules that have evolved into the totally integrated system that now is used to manage the manufacturing facility.

After forming the team, the next step is selecting the hardware, software, and database requirements. Also, decisions need to be made on whether to purchase or develop this software in-house. At AT&T, the basic modules for the Manufacturing Information Control System and Direct Numerical Control System were developed in-house, as was most of the CAM software.

The DNC System started with a centralized, standalone shop computer system. The experience gained from this system along with the requirement for long-term growth and support of off-site facilities resulted in the development of a system with the following characteristics:

1. A low-cost, modular distributed system, with local storage for machine data capable of supporting one or more shifts of work if the host computer was out of service.
2. A high reliability, durable processor capable of withstanding shop area conditions with minimum maintenance.
3. A capability to interface with the bisync communications method on the host computer and to support EIA RS-232 standard interfacing with shop machines and miroprocessors.
4. An ability to support in-plant data communications, as well as off-site communications. Periodic mobility of a processor is required so it can be relocated as shop areas are rearranged, or swapped with a spare processor. This must be done with both minimum effort and interference to shop machines.
5. The elimination of dependency on vendors by developing in-house software and interfacing hardware. Support for new machines added on a modular basis with a minimum of new software or hardware development and maximum standardization.

The Manufacturing Information Control System evolved into the current system by enhancing it with needed modules. These modules include a Storeroom inventory system, chemical control system, tool control system, product yield system, and a management reporting system. These systems are not described in this paper.

All the systems described here are running on an IBM 3083 computer using
the MVS/JES2 operating system CICS for teleprocessing. To see how AT&T

Technologies' Richmond Works' CIM system functions, the processing of a new
PWB design will be described.

COMPUTER-AIDED MANUFACTURING

New designs are teleprocessed in digital form from remote Bell Laboratories
design locations using a corporated wideband transmission network. This data
includes a definition of the board's circuitry, drilled hole locations, and
test points.

On receipt at the Richmond Data Center, the design is automatically
intercepted by a program that checks the characteristics of the PWB (type,
size, etc.). Usually, it is found to fit a predefined "family." For these,
the program generates and submits for execution all the CAM jobs required.
The output of these jobs include: files for drilling, routing, and testing,
which are added to a central database, and plots that show drilled hole
locations, router cutter paths, and points to be tested. The plotted output
is then reviewed by an engineer before the design is released to production.
As little as six hours may elapse between the completion of the design at Bell
Laboratories and the start of manufacturing at the Richmond Works.

The numerical control data is distributed to a network of 130 NC machines
using minicomputers tied into the mainframe. When a machine needs a
particular file, it may already reside on the minicomputer disk. If not, the
minicomputer will request that the file be downloaded from the central
database. This database is very large and contains some 20,000 files,
totaling about 420 million bytes.

PRODUCTION CONTROL SYSTEM

Printed wiring board requirements are received over the same wideband
transmission network as design data. These requirements are edited for
errors and automatically added to the database two times per week. At this
time, they are analyzed to determine if the requested ship date permits time
for our manufacturing interval. If so, a confirmation of the required date is
returned to the customer over the network. If the analysis determines that
the required date is inside our manufacturing interval, Production Control
negotiates a satisfactory required date with the customer. This date is
entered into the database with a CRT and the confirmation is then transmitted
to the customer. For emergency and non-AT&T requirements, a Production
Control Clerk enters the requirement into the database with a CRT and sends
the confirmation to the AT&T customer over the network.

These requirements are used to load the shop, to reschedule work in process,
to determine ahead or behind schedule position at reporting intervals, and to
produce various management reports. When shipments are made against these
requirements, billing data is created and stored to be transmitted once a week

to our AT&T customers and to a corporate billing organization for our non-AT&T customers. When a requirement is satisfied, it is purged from the active database and placed on a history file for use in our forecasting systems.

PRODUCT ENGINEERING SYSTEM

When the new design is received, the responsible engineer will use a CRT to create a routing for that part number. The routing contains the information the shop requires to manufacture the product, including the sequence of operations, machine parameters at each operation, NC file names, etc. As an automatic part of the creation process, the expected hourly output rates for each operation also are computed. These rates are important not only in administering a wage incentive program, but in forecasting machine capacity. After the tooling data and routing are available, a customer order for that part number will trigger the creation of lots to fill the order.

SHOP STATUS SYSTEM

The Shop Status component of the system maintains a queue for each machine, consisting of the lots waiting to be processed by that machine. The queue is ordered into a priority sequence based on the due date of the customer order that each lot is intended to fill. If order due dates or quantities are changed, this will automatically be reflected in the machine queues.

When a machine operator views the queue on the CRT, he or she will indicate which lot is to be worked on next (normally, the first lot on the screen), and the system then prints the engineer's instructions for performing that operation using a small printer beside the CRT. The fact that the latest engineering instructions are printed on-line is a notable feature of the system and makes it much easier to implement manufacturing changes. With a preprinted routing, it would be necessary to physically find all the lots affected by a change so that the instructions could be modified. It is estimated that this task alone would require more than 60 people if performed manually at Richmond.

If the operator's machine is numerically controlled, the selected lot number is used by the system to determine (from the engineer's routing) the name of the appropriate NC file to "drive" the machine. This file then will be downloaded to the machine.

Once the operation has been completed on the lot, the operator reports the completion to the system using a CRT or a bar code reader. The system then removes the lot from the queue and places it at the proper position (as determined by its priority) in the next machine's queue.

A history of each transaction is also recorded so that batch programs can use it for deriving yield data, machine throughputs, operator efficiencies, etc. Since yield and quality are important issues in PWB manufacture, special attention has been given to developing software to help engineers find the causes of problems in these areas. For example, it might be found that a group of lots with drilling defects were all processed by one particular drilling machine.

At the final operation in the routing, a "ship" transaction is entered. This transaction removes the lot from the system and updates the appropriate customer order to reflect the shipment. It also results in a delivery document being printed and in the updating of the shipping statistics for the plant.

WHAT HAVE WE LEARNED

Before undertaking the development of a CIM system, the support of management is necessity. Without it, the system will never succeed, especially if one must retrain employees who are comfortable with an existing system. At AT&T's Richmond Works, the initial modules of this system were implemented when the plant began operating in 1973. No retraining was required; however, training was an important facet of the system in the beginning and has continued to be as the system has evolved. New training methods are currently being developed by the training organization to meet these needs.

We have learned that successful CIM does not allow for complacency. In fact, it is impossible for complacency to creep in. A successful system is one, as the title implies, that evolves and the evolution appears to be a never-ending phenomenon. The basic modules implemented in the beginning have been enhanced over the years. Frequently, these enhancements have been a result of the users, shop operators, production control clerks, engineers, etc., getting involved and making suggestions because they can see the system helping them do their jobs better. These enhancements have caused the basic software to evolve into a truly integrated system.

If there is any one thing that stands out as having been learned from this development experience is that AT&T, Richmond Works could not operate without it. With the high volume of PWBs, short intervals, design changes, and the competition we experience, AT&T, Richmond Works would not be able to meet the service and quality standards that have been our goals even before CIM became a reality.

BENEFITS

The benefits of a successful CIM system are numerous. The Richmond Works has experienced a reduction in both tooling and manufacturing intervals which results in better customer service. Direct labor has been reduced, resulting in lower product cost. These benefits are measurable; however, one important benefit is the intangible human factor. A successful CIM system frees the user from mundane tasks and allows them to be a more versatile employee. Because of increased job satisfaction and self-esteem, the user has become an integral part of the total system instead of just a button pusher. All this results in higher quality and productivity. These are reasons why there are more outstanding development requests before the CIM development group than any time since the plant opened.

Other benefits derived from this system include manufacturing flexibility and simplified rate calculation, cost estimation and capacity planning; all made possible by having all the data stored on a common database.

In summary, here are some system statistics to help judge the support offered by this system:

1. 100,000 MICS transaction per day.
2. 80% are from the shop floor.
3. 40 transmissions per employee per day.
4. 1,100 designs received per month.
5. 130 DNC facilities.
6. 600 CRT terminals.
7. 115 printers.
8. 55 bar code readers.
9. 10,000 control files distributed each month.

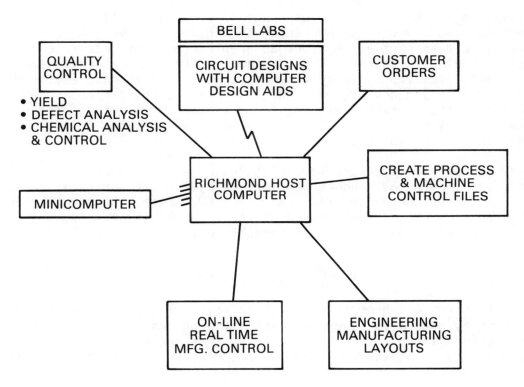

Figure 1. The Richmond Host Computer.

The Importance of Standards

by H. Lee Hales
SysteCon,
A Coopers & Lybrand
Division

THE NEED

To achieve CIM, we need to pass information freely and reliably between different makes of computers, machinery and equipment. We also need the flexibility to make partial upgrades and replacements of integrated systems when new technologies appear. Until recently, these have been technically difficult and often expensive requirements. Our task is made easier with standards--vendor and device-independent specifications for capturing and sending information between systems; for physically connecting different types and makes of equipment; and for a variety of issues related to system configuration, operation and support.

Standards can be viewed at two levels--industry and corporate. Industry standards are adopted by vendors and implemented in the design of their products--software, hardware, machinery, and equipment. Corporate standards are adopted by users and implemented in their purchases of vendor equipment and in the specification of their internally developed systems.

INDUSTRY CIM STANDARDS

Industry standards are beneficial in three ways. First, when widely adopted by vendors they generally lower the cost of doing business. Secondly, they increase options for users when sourcing systems and equipment. Lastly, they tend to simplify the tasks of system development and integration, making it easier for the user to assume a larger role.

Enlightened users can help their own cause by supporting appropriate industry standards. This can be done by participating in standards-setting activities and by including compliance with standards as a criterion in purchase decisions. The specific standards that we each choose to support will be determined in part by the nature of our manufacturing activities. Our first look should be at the dozens of standards already in use. What role do they play in our present manufacturing systems? As we look to the future, we can see a number of emerging standards that are worthy of a deliberately chosen corporate position. The following six are perhaps the most important:

1. MAP (Manufacturing Automation Protocol).
2. TOP (Technical and Office Protocol).
3. IGES (Initial Graphics Exchange Standard).
4. EDIF (Electronic Design Interchange Format).
5. UNIX operating system.
6. EDI (Electronic Data Interchange).

NETWORKS

MAP is a specification that was initially published by General Motors, to promote multivendor data communications or networks in the factory environment. MAP is a collection of existing and emerging communications protocols, each of which has been developed by a standard-setting body. MAP is built upon the work of the Institute of Electrical and Electronic Engineers (IEEE) Standards Committee 802, the National Bureau of Standards, and the International Standards Organization (ISO). A users group has been formed to build support outside of General Motors. This group is now a division of the Society of Manufacturing Engineers.

The goal of MAP is low-cost, multivendor data communications. This will be achieved when the protocols are implemented as integrated circuits. The result will be a MAP circuit board for use in machine tools, robots, programmable controllers, computers and terminals. This board will make it possible to plug equipment directly into the MAP network and communicate transparently with other devices. Such capabilities are several years away. But in the meantime, early versions of MAP can be implemented with special interface equipment and some initial benefits can be gained.

TOP and MAP at a glance

Layer	TOP implementation	MAP implementation
Layer 7 Application	ISO FTAM {DP} 8571 — File Transfer Protocol	ISO FTAM {DP} 8571 — File Transfer Protocol Manufacturing Messaging Format Standard (MMFS)
Layer 6 Presentation	NULL	
Layer 5 Session	ISO Session {IS} 8327 — Basic Combined Subset & Session Kernel, Full Duplex	
Layer 4 Transport	ISO Transport {IS} 8073 — Class 4	
Layer 3 Network	ISO Internet {DIS} 8473 — Connectionless, SubNetwork Dependent Convergence Protocol	
Layer 2 Data Link	ISO Logical Link Control {DIS} 8802/2 (IEEE 802.2) — Type 1, Class 1	
Layer 1 Physical	ISO CSMA/CD {DIS} 8802/3 (IEEE 802.3) — CSMA/CD Medium Access Control 10Base5	ISO Token Passing Bus {DIS} 8802/4 (IEEE 802.4) — Token Passing Bus Medium Access Control

Figure 1. The International Standards Organizations (ISO) 7-layer model for Open Systems Interconnection (OSI) is the basis for both MAP and TOP.

The size of General Motors and its base of 40,000 shop floor devices have gained a good deal of attention for MAP. But it is not the only such effort to provide multivendor communications. In the semiconductor industry, this need is addressed by SECS--SEMI Equipment Communications Standard, a transaction protocol published by the Semiconductor Equipment Manufacturers Institute. In the petrochemical and continuous process industries, the PROWAY standard (ISA SP-72) has been proposed by the Instrument Society of America. It too, governs networks and communications between different vendors' devices. Machine tool builders, through the Electronics Industries Association, also are working on communications between computers and different makes of machine tools.

TOP is a companion specification to MAP, initially published by the Boeing Company and the National Bureau of Standards. The purpose of TOP is to promote multivendor data communications in office and technical design operations. Building on proven means of physically connecting terminals, computers and peripherals, TOP will prescribe rules for representing and exchanging spreadsheets, business graphics, drawings, documents, and electronic mail. The TOP standard, like MAP, will be a set of existing and emerging protocols that implement the International Standards Organization's seven-layer model for open systems interconnection. See Figure 1.

COMPUTER-AIDED DESIGN

In the field of computer-aided design (CAD), transfer of information between different makes of CAD systems is complicated by the fact that vendors format their data in different ways. IGES is an evolving standard that seeks to overcome this problem. Published by ANSI (Y14.26M) in 1981, IGES had its origins in Air Force and NASA projects of the late 1970s. Its use is currently promoted by the National Bureau of Standards. IGES provides a neutral data file that is passed between systems and translated upon receipt. But because of the great differences between CAD systems, IGES does not always do a complete job. Various measures have been taken in response. General Motors, for example, has its own "GM IGES" specification. It contains part of translators also have been developed by Intergraph and Vought Corp. In each case, certain capabilities are provided to address the perceived weaknesses of IGES.

Some large companies have solved their problems internally by standardizing on two or three CAD vendors and writing their own translators. This approach breaks down, however, as we attempt to communicate with our suppliers', subcontractors' and customers' CAD systems. As of 1987, more than 30 CAD vendors offer some degree of IGES compatibility. Fortunately, the graphics community is working on its own internal standards for systems development. As a result, future generations of CAD systems will prove much easier to integrate into multivendor networks of distributed design activity. IGES has been an important step in this direction.

In recent years, the attention of the CAD user community has shifted to a new standards effort called PDES, the Product Design Exchange Specification. PDES will eventually take the place of IGES and will standardize the way in which all product data is represented for digital communications. IGES has focused almost exclusively on graphics and drafting-related information. PDES will address additional key issues such as:

1. Features--standardizing the ways that holes, slots, bosses, webs, etc., are defined. This will improve the integration of design and process planning.

2. Non-shape notes--covering processing or other special instructions for treating, inspecting, assembling, etc.

3. First-level assembly--defining the way that parts mate or fit together. This will aid the application of manufacturability rules during the design process.

4. Administration--addressing the issues of versions, releases and change control.

Such standards are extremely useful when integrating the manufacturing activities of customers and suppliers, subcontractors, feeder and assembly plants.

When it comes to graphics and design information, the microelectronics industry has needs that are quite different from those of the automotive, machinery, and other mechanical producers. Since IGES does not address these needs, leading vendors are promoting EDIF (Electronic Design Interchange Format) as a means of communicating design information between systems, test and production equipment.

OTHER DATA PROCESSING APPLICATIONS

The growing popularity of the UNIX operating system and its lack of standarization is another issue worthy of attention. Originally developed at Bell Laboratories in the late 1960s, UNIX has recently emerged as the favored operating system for high-performance microcomputers and engineering workstations. It clearly has a place in CIM. But unfortunately, the dozens of vendors that offer UNIX do so in a variety of nonstandard ways--over 30 in late 1984. In response, the IEEE has formed a working group on UNIX standards that will eventually reduce this number to a manageable few.

EDI is another emerging standard of potential interest to all industry groups, EDI stands for Electronic Data Interchange. It was published by ANSI's X12 Committee in late 1984. The goal of EDI is to facilitate order processing shipping and receiving, invoicing, and payments between separate firms. With increasing emphasis on close supplier links, just-in-time scheduling, and more frequent order cycles, the importance of EDI will grow.

Many other standards are being defined for data communications, graphics, robotics programming, and the like, some of which will make a difference in our longer-range CIM plans. But as important as they are, these industry standards are often limited to the lowest levels of CIM, i.e. the innerworkings of equipment, physical connections, data capture and transfer. Of equal importance, are corporate standards addressing higher-level issues of system design and sourcing.

CORPORATE CIM STANDARDS

Corporate standards are helpful in several ways:

1. They speed the transfer and diffusion of CIM technologies within the firm.
2. They make it easier to train staff and support the systems in place.
3. They shorten procurement cycles by reducing the technical issues involved.
4. When properly applied and widely used, they lower the cost of CIM.

These benefits are especially important for those with aggressive CIM plans in multiplant and divisional firms. When it comes to setting corporate standards, there are five possible sources:

1. Internally developed.
2. Vendor-specific.
3. Defacto/product/psuedo.
4. Industry-specific.
5. Industry-universal.

Internally developed standards

Internally developed standards are akin to company policies and procedures. A chart of accounts, for example, gives a standard for cost accounting systems. Some firms find it useful to standardize part numbering across plants and products. At Chrysler, the internally developed Cyberman computer model is standard for certain design studies. Specified practices such as these simplify the task of designing CIM systems.

Vendor-specific standards

Standardizing on specific vendors for certain tasks and systems has been a traditional approach. Typical examples include the use of DECNET to link engineering and production; or MacNeal Schwendler's NASTRAN for engineering studies; or Cullinet's Golden Gate for micro-to-mainframe links. This vendor-specific approach risks a poor fit now and then, and it may limit our options.

Defacto/product/psuedo

Defacto standards emerge by popular acclaim--the result of a vendor's or product's market share and related bandwagon effects. The PC-DOS operating system, for example, is a defacto standard in microcomputing. Motorola's VMEbus is both a product and a standard (IEEE PII04). UNIX is another example. With its many variations, it has become something of a psuedo standard for certain applications and systems. As a practical matter, these types of standards are implemented through the purchase of specific vendor's products. When such commitments are made, the buyer should be confident that the underlying "standard" will last.

Industry-specific standards

Industry-specific standards are the easiest to adopt. There may be no choice. In the grocery business it's UPC (Universal Product Code) or else, when bar-coding products. But in the automotive industry it's AIAG (Automotive Industry Action Group). As noted earlier, many suppliers of semiconductor production equipment adhere to SECS for transmitting data between machines and computers in the wafer fab process. In the mechanical industries this same function will probably be covered by MAP.

Industry-universal standards

While they may originate in a single industry or trade group, universal standards are those with wide appeal and use across industry lines. As such, they are often published by ANSI or one of the international standards-setting bodies. EIA (Electronics Industries Association) 1393 is an emerging national standard to govern all types of numerically controlled machines. ANSI MH10.8M is an American standard for bar coding in any industry or application. It differs from the industry-specific AIAG and UPC codes. RS-232 C is a typical universal standard. Governing low-speed, short-distance connections between equipment (the lowest level in CIM) it comes embedded in purchased equipment. In general, such universal standards are of primary use to vendors. Corporate standards will contain them when set at higher levels.

The integrated nature of factory automation makes it hard to set a standard for one activity without considering those related to it. Cross checks are required. And, we need to be sure that the newer emerging standards are workable "as is" before putting them into effect. The general process of setting a corporate CIM standard is outlined in Figure 2.

COMMITTEES AND QUESTIONS

If you have not yet done so, it would be wise to create a standards committee for CIM, or to add this issue to the agenda of your present CIM committee. The first task, of course, is to list the activities and functions that are candidates for standardization. Once defined, the following 10 questions should be answered for each item on your list:

1. Do we really need a standard? Is the lack of a standard hurting us in some demonstrable way? With suppliers? With subcontractors? With customers?
2. Would adherence to a standard improve or hinder our competitive position? How? Will it reduce our cost of automation? How much?
3. Are national or international standards in place (or proposed) that cover the activity or function in question? Do we understand their benefits and limitations?
4. What about industry-specific standards? Are we participating in in their development?
5. If we adopt an external standard, is there some way we can be sure that our suppliers and their products are in compliance? Are there standard tests? Who administers them?
6. How are we performing the activity or function now? Is this consistent with applicable standards? Does our current approach

form the basis of a corporate-wide standard for these activities and functions?

7. Do we have some other home-grown, internal standard that would cover the activity or function in question?
8. Will the adoption of a corporate standard unduly inhibit or delay our adoption of needed new technologies?
9. Will the adoption of a corporate standard hinder or confuse decisions at the division or plant level?
10. Will the adoption of a standard add costs that are not offset by tangible savings or clear intangible benefits?

If standards are the "constitution of CIM," then the last three questions above can be thought of as line management's "Bill of Rights." They are designed to protect us from unreasonable bureaucracy and heavy-handed corporate staffers. Remember, standards are helpful, but they are not prerequisites for action and results.

There are a wider variety of standards efforts underway which ought to be considered in developing a company-specific CIM program. For more information on MAP and TOP, contact the MAP/TOP Users Group at the Society of Manufacturing Engineers in Dearborn, Michigan. For information on IGES and PDES, contact the Center for Manufacturing Engineering at the National Bureau of Standard in Gaithersburg, Maryland.

The International Standards Organization has established Technical Committee 184 to work on Industrial Automation Standards. Figure 3 shows the various subcommittees involved with TC184 and Figure 4 provides key contacts. For additional information on the ISO work, contact the American National Standards Institute (ANSI) in New York City. ANSI's Industrial Automation Planning Panel is currently developing a national registry of standards projects and recommendations for accelerated effort.

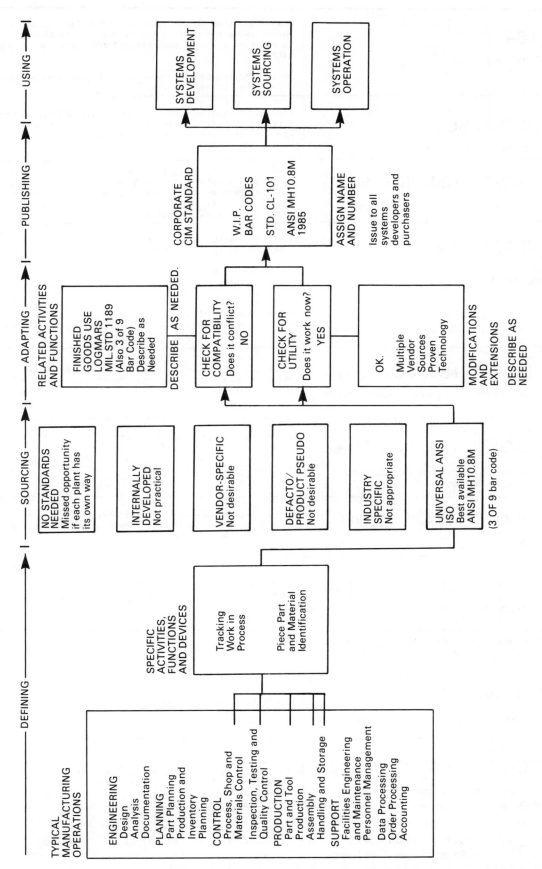

Figure 2. Example of Standards-setting process. This company has decided that ANSI MH10.8M (3 of 9 bar code) is the best way to identify work-in-process.

ISO/TC 184 INDUSTRIAL AUTOMATION SYSTEMS	Standardization in the field of industrial automation systems encompassing the application of multiple technologies, i.e., information systems, machines and equipment, and telecommunications. Note : The programme of work shall be coordinated with that of the IEC and the ITU.
ISO/TC 184/SC1 NUMERICAL CONTROL OF MACHINES	Standardization of codes, formats, axis and motion nomenclature, data structures, command languages and related systems aspects for the numerical control of machines.
ISO/TC 184/SC1/WG1 EXTENDED FORMATS AND DATA STRUCTURE	Revision of TR 6132 to incorporate DP 6983/4. The task covers the needs of real-time interactive applications which allows for modifications of data and process parameters. This should be implemented by means of extended formats and data structures. It covers also the application layer for information exchange.
ISO/TC 184/SC2 INDUSTRIAL ROBOTS	Standardization of : - Définition - characterization - Terminology - Graphic representation - Performances and performance testing methods - Safety - Mechanical interfaces - Programming methods - Requirements for information exchange
ISO/TC 184/SC2/WG1 TERMINOLOGY AND GRAPHIC REPRESENTATION	To consider the preparation of standards for definitions, characterisation, terminology and graphic representation of robots under programme of work of SC 2.
ISO/TC 184/SC2/WG2 PERFORMANCE CRITERIA AND RELATED TESTING METHODS	To consider the preparation of standards for performance criteria and related testing methods for robots to serve users with understandable specifications on robots and to verify specified performances by standardized testing methods.
ISO/TC 184/SC2/WG3 SAFETY	To consider the preparation of standards for safety in the design, construction, installation, use and maintenance of robots under the programme of work of SC 2.
ISO/TC 184/SC2/WG4 REQUIREMENTS FOR PROGRAMMING METHODS AND DATA COMMUNICATION	To consider the preparation of standards for interconnections, data communications, communication, control languages and high level languages.
In the near future, possible creation of WG for cover : MECHANICAL INTERFACES	
ISO/TC 184/SC3 NON DEVICE-SPECIFIC APPLICATION LANGUAGES	Standardization of non device-specific languages
ISO/TC 184/SC4 EXTERNAL REPRESENTATION OF PRODUCT DEFINITION DATA	The creation of a standard which enables the capture of information comprising a computerized product model in a neutral form without loss of completeness and integrity, throughout the lifecycle of the product.

Figure 3. International Standards Organization Technical Committee 184 "Industrial Automation Systems." (Source: American National Standards Institute.)

ISO/TC 184/SC4/WG1 TECHNICAL COORDINATION AND SUPPORT	- To provide technical support and recommendations for SC 4 - To coordinate national technical developments - To resolve technical differences - To collate national technical contributions for inclusion in the draft ISO document.
ISO/TC 184/SC5 REQUIREMENTS FOR STANDARDS TO ENABLE SYSTEMS INTEGRATION	To identify requirements for new standards and to develop and define reference models for system integration in the area of industrial automation.in the manufacturing environment, from product conception through distribution.
ISO/TC 184/SC5/WG1 REFERENCE MODELS	- To study existing work and to create a multidimensional, opened reference model which will provide a basis for long-range planning for standardization through the identification of interfaces and their characteristics (e.g., electrical, mechanical, man-machine, informational, procedural, language, etc.) between system automation elements. - To consider at least the following types of models : a) a functional model, possibly data-oriented, illustrating factory (or company) functions, defined as a group of tasks, and their relationships. b) Other models, illustrating such aspects as : . Data structure . Data base organization . Communications . Electrical/physical interfaces
In the near future, possible creation of WG to cover : - guidelines for implementation - procedures for validation - data for specific applications - developments due to new technology	
ISO/TC 184 WG1 COMMUNICATION AND INTERCONNECTIONS	Standardization of interfaces, protocols, data format and message structure to interconnect computers, equipment and systems in automated factories. The quipment includes e.g. NC machines, industial robots, programmable controllers, measuring equipment and other devices for automation purposes.

Figure 3. continued.

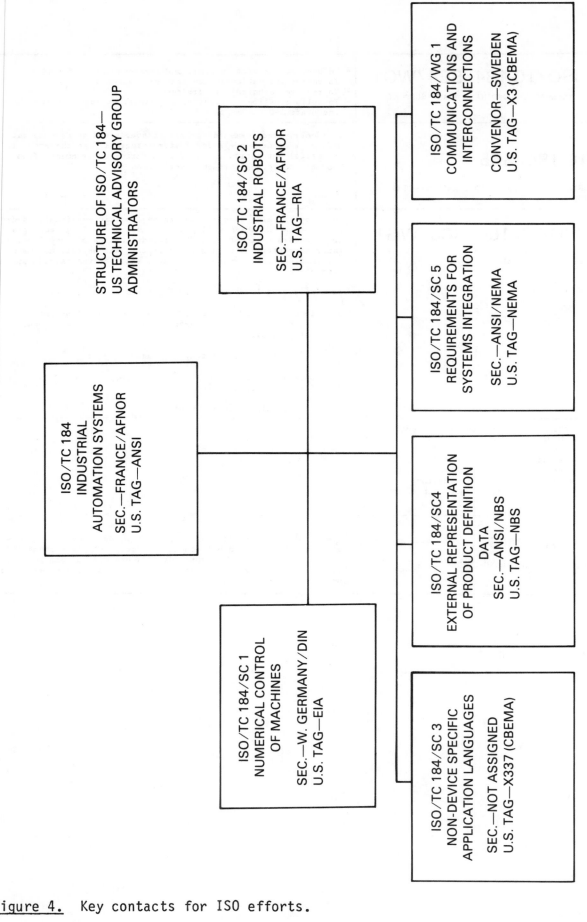

Figure 4. Key contacts for ISO efforts.

Justification of CIM

by George W. Sibbald
Genovation, Inc.

INTRODUCTION

The evidence is overwhelming--CIM can be cost justified in the short term. Many smaller manufacturing companies are getting more results faster than the big firms. Recent technological breakthroughs and business reculturing successes have pushed us down the CIM cost/learning curve (Chart 1). Every day the trade media documents the CIM successes and failures, and as we emulate success or learn from failures, we pave the way for those who follow to achieve a cost-justified, pay-as-you-go CIM development and implementation program.

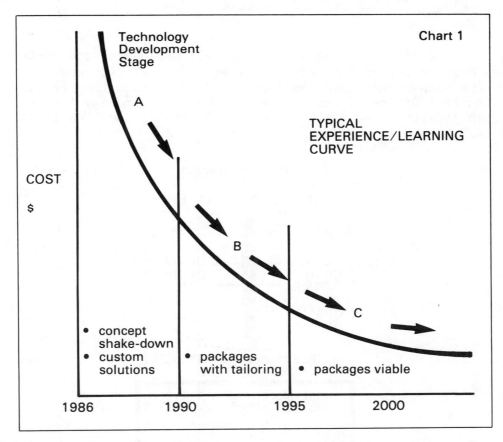

Figure 1. The CIM cost/learning curve. (Source: Genovation, Inc.)

Fifteen years ago when Joe Harrington, the "Father of CIM", began to push the CIM concept, CIM was an idea before it's time and only the largest firms could afford to take up the gauntlet. As Joe put it, "CIM is a policy decision not an investment decision." But now, CIM is an investment necessity, and is easily justified on a simple Return On Investment (ROI) or Discounted Cash Flow (DCF). The issue now is merely in the perspective taken when defining CIM.

Through SME/CASA(1) executive meetings and our CIM client meetings we have reached a concurrence on the definition of CIM (Chart 2).

DEFINITION OF CIM

Computer Integrated Manufacturing and Management, "CIM",
is the computer assisted integration
of production processes and operations control functions
needed for optimal deployment and productive use
of the minimum manufacturing and management resources
required to meet specific strategic business objectives

Figure 2. CIM defined. (Source: Genovation, Inc.)

The significance of the definition is that all management and control processes must be included to achieve integration, whether computers are used or not. And with recent technological advances in both the "Factory of the Future" and the "Office of the Future," computer technology (Chart 3) is creating an industrial economic impact which heralds the "New Industrial Revolution."

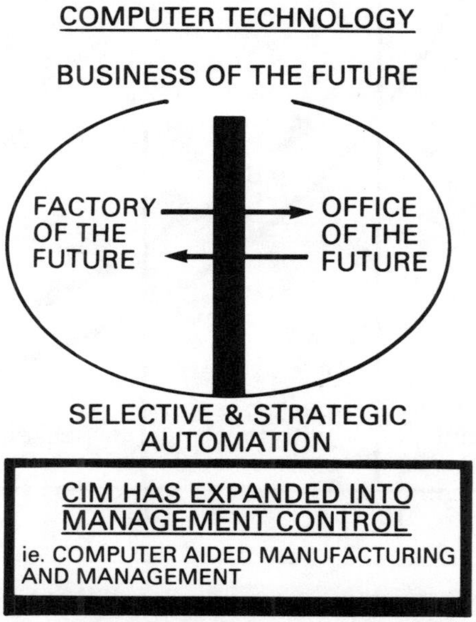

Figure 3. Computer technology. (Source: Genovation, Inc.)

CIM is the keystone of the "New Industrial Revolution" and through CIM the revitalization of our industrial base gives us the opportunity to regain our global industrial strength. But to achieve this, we must design CIM as the simplest, least expensive means to gain cost, quality and delivery advantages over Japan, Germany and other foreign or domestic competitors. There is no room for the NIH (Not Invented Here) syndrome of hidden agendas.

CIM has been costing larger corporations several times what it should with poor returns on their investment; whereas smaller manufacturing companies are reaping high returns in early stages of their CIM program.

Why? The smaller firm cannot afford to make "strategic decisions" that are not financially justified. Also, they look for simpler alternatives first.

Therefore, they view CIM as a road traveled with many small steps, one step at at time.

The remainder of this paper borrows a perspective from smaller manufacturing firms (2), and develops a pay-as-you-go financial justification of CIM under the following sections:

- Management's Job,
- CIM Strategy,
- CIM Risks,
- CIM Justification Roadmap,
- Summary.

MANAGEMENT'S JOB

Management's primary function is to be the guardians of profit. "PROFITS" are the first order of business in our industrial economy (3).

Industrial profits pay for everything else; someone has to generate the income to pay for services of the service sector of the economy. Profits cause businesses to grow, creates new jobs, and pays corporate taxes. Profits give us higher standards of living and income so as individuals we can pay taxes and make charitable donations. Profit is what makes the industrial system work.

But there are people who feel that _profit_ is a dirty word or that profit is a theft from employees and customers. This attitude has been shown as the eventual destruction of a motivated workforce in the Communist industrial system; but we still allow creeping socialism to erode the profit incentive in our system.

Those that seek to buy votes through attacking the profit motive in industry are destroying the most successful economic system ever created. Profit is the economic foundation of the U.S. system, and _political termites_ are at work.

The issue is not profit making, it is the business culture. Decades of excess and entrenched success have made U.S. business fat and lazy. Our ego's have blinded us, and then the Japanese and Germans blind-sided us. We have our government to thank for arming our enemies in this economic war. We destroyed Japan and Germany's pride (a cultural revolution), then we gave them a sense of purpose (i.e. reindustrialization), we recapitalized their industrial base (better than our own), we gave them our best technology and then we gave them access to our markets. Now, after 30 years of single-minded industrial improvement they are passing us. Only our mass and momentum allows us to retain some clout.

The awakening of U.S. industry has come from loss of market to foreign companies. Japan has virtual ownership over much of the worldwide electronics industry and has sizable share and momentum in many other industries (e.g., steel, metals, shipbuilding, and automobile). We need to wake up to the fact we are being beaten at our own game...with our own rules.

U.S. management believes if they beat us they must have a magic new way of doing business, a more disciplined and productive culture, and the support of government. The reality is we are being beaten by their attention to basics; basics learned from U.S. business.

"Job #1" is "PROFIT!"

The road to profit is a return to business basics. These basics also include: sound ethics, employee motivation, corporate good citizenship, cost reduction, market penetration, and strategic focus of all corporate resources.

CIM STRATEGY

There is none! CIM is _tactics_, not strategy.

There is only one strategy, the corporate strategic plan. CIM, manufacturing, and information systems strategies are (or should be) a focused set of tactics to achieve success in specific market segments or strategic business units (SBU).

Basic strategy planning will define the "Success Factors" needed to achieve the strategic goals. "Strategic Opportunity Analysis Methodology" (4) identifies alternative techniques and technologies available to achieve these strategic goals. The selection among alternatives or tactics, is based on resource availability, and SBU strategic direction. Profit is always a key factor, although some SBUs may be looking at long-term paybacks of 10 or more years to the breakeven point. We can only afford to look at the long term if the profits are generated in other SBU's.

This top down strategy must be complimented by a bottom up opportunity identification, where ideas for improvement percolate up and implementation detail must percolate up from the lower and middle ranks of the corporation (5).

Cost justification of CIM is mandatory. But strategic factors may influence the "how to" of justifying CIM.

- •Declining Base: The survival scenario may show that the "do nothing" strategy may see erosion of market share or profits. CIM impact starts from this base.

- Alternative Technologies : (6) Just-In-Time, focused factory layout, human engineered cells and other alternatives may be low-tech/low-cost alternatives to automation. CIM includes all management processes not just automation, integration, and emulation through artificial intelligence. Alternatives must be considered.
- Hurdle Rates: Discounted cash flow (DCF) or return on investment (ROI) often have one hurdle rate for acceptance. This, a sign of poor communications of corporate strategies and grossly misdirects resource allocation. Different SBUs must achieve different strategic goals, therefore, multiple hurdle rates should be set based on strategic needs.
- Technology "Must Do's": Market or strategic dictates makes some CIM technologies mandatory (e.g. Boeing subcontractors often require CAD links to Boeing CAD systems). Note, this could also be cost-justified.
- Approval Cycle: Big ticket expenditures must go up the chain-of-command for approval. CIM, as a "lump", often needs board level approval. CIM a step at a time with pay-as-you-go can often be approved by the factory manager.
- Intangibles: "Although intangible benefits may be difficult to quantify, there is no reason to value them at zero in a capital expenditure analysis. Zero is, after all, no less arbitrary than any other number. Conservative accountants who assign zero value to many intangible benefits prefer being precisely wrong to being vaguely right (7)".

THE RISKS OF CIM

The major risks (8) are: over-design, inflated expectations, false base for justification, and poor implementation.

Over-design is often a result of technical zeal, poor communications, hidden agendas, and a Not-Invented-Here (NIH) syndrome. The Japanese approach is to simplify the problem and then look for the simplest solution. In the U.S., we expand the problem so that our solution covers a broad scope of potential problems. The cumulative effect is obvious.

A consultant's rule of thumb (almost a truism) is "80/20", that means 80% of the results are achieved by the first 20% of the effort, and conversely the last 20% of the results are achieved with the last 80% of the effort. What does that do if the problem is expanded to 120% of the need?

The solution to over-design is the "prototyping" approach which targets at achieving the 80% results level. Emerging computer technologies can give 80% of the results with less than 20% of the cost, time or effort compared to traditional approaches (9).

Inflated expectations have been created by the false impressions of success. "Success stories," according to Dataquest, Inc., San Jose, CA., are G.E. Erie Locomotive, and Yamazaki Machinery Company (10). But G.E. Erie Locomotive is only partly implemented because their market fell from 1,300 units to 270 units over six years (11). What does this say for their communication with the strategic planning function, if there is one?

Yamazaki spent 18 million on FMS but over 20 years the project's rate of return is less the 10% per year (12). What does this say for their capital appropriations? Or are there strategic market leverage considerations (not quantified) by the Japanese company?

False base for justification occurs in the majority of CIM programs. GM justified over $60 billion in automation as a means to compete with Japanese automakers (13). Not only could they have probably bought both Toyota and Nissan for less, but they also backed off their automation program in favor of business basics and good leadership techniques (note, Japanese techniques of business and human engineering were learned from us).

The point is, attention to business basics will often achieve 60 to 80% of the potential benefits that often justifies CIM.

Two excellent examples are Roper Pump Company, and AMOT Controls (14). Both companies did significant house cleaning, method simplification, and human engineering as Phase 0 of their CIM programs. Rates of return on Phase 0 efforts are in the hundreds of percent rather than tens. Further CIM justifications are simpler and less risky because the base is solid.

Poor implementation is most often an excuse for failure. Successful implementation of any change, whether computerized, technical or not, cannot be rushed. Even when done quickly, there are some basic prerequisites to successful implementation. These include, first, a recognition of a need for change, second, an understanding of the proposed changes, third, a concurrence that proposed changes satisfy the need, and last, a willingness to make the change work.

Note, top down commitment, user participation, and education are not the prerequisites. Although they may help achieve the prerequisites, there are many other ways to get results.

Implementation cannot begin without the above prerequisites even if the CIM system is ready to go. The change culture must be created (15).

CIM JUSTIFICATION ROADMAP

This CIM justification roadmap is designed for the company that moves forward one step at a time, and needs to generate results as they go. CIM is not treated as a "lump." CIM is not perceived as as a one-time, top-down strategy. CIM is a new set of technical tactical alternatives which may be used to achieve strategic objectives (nothing more and nothing less).

To establish a frame of reference, we first look at the Five Levels of Industrial Revitalization (Chart 4) and regroup them into the Four Phases of CIM Development (Chart 5). The most critical phase being Phase Zero (0). Phase 0 is the foundation for CIM. Here, we house clean by attention to business basics, we motivate by restructuring to get that 110% effort from employees, and we develop the processes of innovation at every level in the company. That is, we reculture our corporation.

```
Levels of
Industrial Revitalization

1. Motivation
2. Innovation
3. Automation
4. Integration
5. Emulation
```

Figure 4. The levels of industrial revitilization. (Source: Genovation, Inc.)

```
                                    Phases of CIM Development

     Phase 0: Preparation for Change
          Restructure for motivation
          Reculture for innovation & creativity
          Operations house cleaning
     Phase 1: Islands-of-automation
     Phase 2: Bridging the Islands
          Integration
     Phase 3: Automation of the Management Process
          Emulation
```

Figure 5. Phases of CIM development. (Source: Genovation, Inc.)

Internal rates of return from this reculturing process (CIM Phase 0) are often over 100% per year. Although some of the results are from the Hawthorne Effect, most of the results come from a competitive drive and team spirit that is self-directed at perpetual productivity and quality improvement.

Phase I is automation, but automation should not be treated as a lump. Each automation cell should be justified on its own merits. Flexible manufacturing systems (FMS) or equipment groupings should look at low technology alternatives such as Just-In-Time layouts to unveil the true return on FMS alternatives. This leads to automation as islands-of-automation, and so it should. Automation technologies are quickly moving down their cost/learning curves and islands-of-automation are now more easily cost justified. But integrated automation is still early in the learning curve and pioneers are still paying the price for those who follow. Expect integrated automation to become cost-effective in the early 1990s.

Phase II is integration, but not universal integration. We recommend that you treat integration as bridging of systems, where such bridges can be cost justified. Although universal factory networks, standardized protocols and standardized data storage may be philosophically more appealing, these are technologies in a high state of flux and are too complex and costly. By simplifying our integration needs and justifying each piece as we go, we are assured clearer, and likely quicker paybacks. If costs and high-level application development tools come down the learning curve as expected, you can expect your CIM systems to be obsoleted every 2-3 years. Then justify each piece as you go, scale down where possible, and plan to replace them in the next five years.

Phase III is emulation, which focuses on rule based or expert systems. Although we hear a lot about expert systems, they are for the most part small domains or small isolated applications. The broad scope open domain expert systems development capabilities are just now emerging on the market. This emerging technology will be the basis of future CIM problems, primarily because the application shell is passed to the user who prototypes his/her need and develops his/her own simple knowledge-base (shallow expert system). Emulation in this sense will emulate management more than labor. Yet current expert systems should be treated as islands-of-automation and justified as stand-alone cells.

Phase I, II and III tasks will overlap as projects in each phase take higher priority over some projects in other phases.

Justification of CIM is relatively straightforward if we follow some simple steps.

STEP 1: ESTABLISH THE STRATEGIC DIRECTION

In smaller companies, strategy may be implied in the action of the top executives; this is not enough. A clear (well-communicated) set of goals and objectives for the corporation and its business units is needed.

A strategic and resource planning process (16) is a simplified strategic planning model integrated with project justification and resource allocation. This process is designed for integration into a closed loop system including the corporate planning, control and operations from the CEO to blue-collar labor and back (i.e., CIM planning).

STEP 2: TACTICAL PLANNING

As well as market tactics, this step includes both acquisition of pivotal CIM technologies for strategic positioning and the use of CIM technologies to achieve specific results measured by business unit strategic "success factors." Both can and should be justified on an ROI or DCF, but the long-range strategic positioning on strategic "success factors" of SBU may cause the hurdle rate (acceptance decision criteria) to change. Additionally, the intangibles impacts should be quantified. Perfect accuracy in quantifying intangibles is not needed, because tactical selection methods are only rough tools.

Tactics need to look at the alternatives including productivity improvement ideas generated from factory workers. Low technology and low-cost alternatives must be included. Note, one client budgeted $5 million for FMS with the objective of reducing lot size to one. One-half million dollars did the same with redundant, old equipment having permanent setups across part families.

Risk, uncertainty, and interdependence of tactics, as well as cost/benefit are key project selection criteria.

STEP 3: CIM PROJECT IMPLEMENTATION

This is where most formal strategic planning processes fall apart and fail to integrate well with capital budgeting procedures. Informal communications usually drives capital budgeting or "manufacturing strategy."

The typical drive is: "Here's the product lines and expected dollar volumes for the next five years; now tell us what manufacturing needs to make it happen. Give us a three-year capital spending program." And so, we create a communication gap and hand off an "empire building" opportunity.

Simplified resource allocation techniques should be used to justify each project in your CIM program.

First, we develop one-page project overviews which describe the elements of the project, estimate potential costs and benefits, identifies critical resource needs, timing, potential risks and project interdependancies. Mutually exclusive projects may be used both for downscale or upscale projects and for alternative approaches. This task is the explicite tie or bridge of strategic and tactical planning to operations. It provides the opportunity to implement the strategic plan while assuring the capability to feedback results for periodic review and corrective action.

<u>Any project which improves manufacturing or management capabilities or processes is a CIM project.</u> This includes most information systems projects. Other market or growth (non-CIM) projects also would go through a similar project formulation.

Second, we select first-pass candidate projects by ranking all candidates on a predetermined selection criteria, such as:

- Maximize DCF or ROI,
- Maximize returns on the utilization of scarce resources,
- Minimize "downside" risks,
- Generate cash for internal funding, and
- Achieve specific corporate goals or timing.

The portfolio of selected projects then begins refinement.

Third, we develop project pro formas by time phasing the interdependant projects, by defining project resource needs, by interpreting strategic success factors into project measurements, and by securing commitments to benefits achievement.

Fourth, we iterate the first pass selection until we have a portfolio of project pro formas that meet first pass selection criteria.

Fifth, we pass the portfolio of pro formas through a resource loading, to assure that the project time phasing adequately utilizes available resources, or we have additional projects identified to acquire needed resources. This again is an iterative step.

Sixth, we roll-up pro formas of the time phased portfolio of projects to produce the operations budget. Note, if we include status quo operations as a project, then we have a "zero base" resource allocation of all manufacturing resources.

Seventh, we drag forward the project measurements, and project benefit commitments by budget center to produce departmental strategic success criteria or "pulse point" measurements. This creates a "hierarchically distributed performance measurement" system that dynamically communicates the corporate focus performance expectations, and that establishes strategic planning feedback loop.

Eighth, we measure and feedback both operations and CIM project performance. through this feedback the CIM program is modified to limit risk of failure and to maximize return on investment.

STEP 4: CIM PROGRAM MANAGEMENT

CIM justification is the operations budgeting process, where strategic and tactical planning is integrated through a zero base resource allocation or operations budgeting process. This type of operations budget is the sum of the time-phased projects and carries with it the organizational department performance measures, as well as financial information. Routine project control then allows actual cost and schedule tracking to provide performance visibility on your CIM program.

This CIM Justification Roadmap provides a simple integration technique to focus your CIM program on corporate objectives and on the eventual integration of computer-assisted strategic and tactical planning into the operations control process.

SUMMARY

CIM can only be justified through the justification of its elements.

CIM is a moving target. Emerging technologies are radically improving our options. Pioneers, other CIM implementation sites, are driving CIM down the COST/LEARNING CURVE. CIM results are getting better and costs are coming down.

Pay-as-you-go or internally funded CIM programs start with a return to business basics, including communications (formal) of hierarchically distributed performance measures and job expectations, realignment of responsibility and control to the lowest levels possible, capturing American motivation potential, securing a sense of "common cause" or purpose and stimulating creative and innovative processes that focus on a combination of corporate, community, family and personal goals. This is Phase 0 of a CIM program and though house cleaning and morale bolstering Phase 0 is likely to produce 60-80% of the CIM benefits (17).

Up-front costs of a CIM program are minimal, only required for refocusing management on the processes of communications, motivation building, work simplification and change. These processes will generate the cash flow necessary to continue your CIM program. This is a cultural process and does take time. Although a consultant may facilitate the process; YOU must take on both the responsibility and accountability for your own CIM destiny.

REFERENCES

1. Society of Manufacturing Engineer, Computer and Automated Systems Association, Santa Clara, CA. Chapter.

2. Roper Pump Company, Commerce, GA. Derrick Key, President, and AMOT Controls, Richmond, CA., Bob Miner, Director of Production.

3. Extracts from CIM Review, October, 1987, "Roadblocks to CIM Success", George W. Sibbald.

4. Autofact '86 Paper. "CIM Today and In The Future", George W. Sibbald, Figure 14: Integration of Planning, Guide book available from author.

5. Production, March 1987, "Planning for Manufacturing in Large Organizations", Sandra Brooks Dornan.

6. Production, February, 1987, "Cells and Systems: Justifying the Investment", Sandra Brooks Dornan.

7. Harvard Business Review March-April, 1986, "Must CIM Be Justified On Faith Alone?", Robert S. Kaplan.

8. Extracts from CIM Review, October, 1987, "Roadblocks to CIM Success", George W. Sibbald.

9. SME/CASA, Fall, 1987, "CIM Implementation Guide", "Prototyping", Leonard Bertain and George W. Sibbald, Guide book available from authors.

10. Production, February, 1987, "Cells and Systems: Justifying the Investment", Sandra Brooks Dornan.

11. Industry Week, March 9, 1987, "Justifying your CIM Investment", Thomas M. Rohan.

12. Harvard Business Review March-April, 1986," Must CIM be Justifies On Faith Alone?", Robert S. Kaplan.

13. Business Week, June 8, 1987.

14. Roper Pump Company, Commerce, GA. Derrick Key, President, and AMOT Controls, Richmond, CA., Bob Miner, Director of Production.

15. SME/CASA, Fall, 1987 "CIM Implementation Guide", 2nd Edition, "Reculturing for CIM", Leonard Bertain.

16. SME/CASA Autofact '86, "CIM Today and In The Future", Figure 14, Page 1-34, George W. Sibbald, Guide book available from author.

17. Northrop, Hawthorne, CA: "Aerospace Manufacturing in the Information Age", Bill Willoughby.

Nuts and Bolts
Dollars and Sense

by Gary K. Conkol
Picker International Incorporated

THE EFFICIENCY OF IMPLEMENTATION--MEASURING RESULTS

The expression "throwing money at a problem" is often used to describe a situation where something has been made to happen by paying more than what was required.

This applies to CIM more than any other program.

The statement that integration must be built and not purchased echoes this lesson. It is very easy to believe that the purchase of particular equipment will ensure success and that it is worth up to the amount that integration will save over the lifetime of the equipment. The high cost of the systems, software, and hardware gives a false sense of credibility to the claims of performance and benefit. The combination of high cost/benefit ratios and the uncertainty can prevent management from taking even the smallest step. By efficiency, we mean the amount of benefit derived from a given amount of capital or hours spent on the effort of integration.

While it would be easy to review an integration effort after the fact, it is very difficult to tell when the costs are exceeding the minimum. One of the best ways to keep a watchful eye on the implementation effort is by the use of ratios rather than absolute figures. The use of characteristic ratios is commonly used to tell the health of a business or the benefit of a particular installation. A few ratios will be introduced here to guide the reader in the evaluation of their particular integration effort. The absolute value of the ratios is not as important as the trends that routine evaluation will provide.

Integration efforts are concerned with the business needs and production impact rather than the health of a particular computer system or processor. For that reason, the classical ratios and numbers such as CPU utilization and fault rates are not the pertinent values to watch and are really quite worthless in evaluating the efficiency of implementation. The ratios of interest are those with the standard measures of productivity in them such as labor hours, units produced, jobs completed, or rework percentages. The first requirement is that this data is routinely collected and validated.

Take a CAD/CAM system as an example. The units that should be tracked are often the same ones used to justify the system originally. Hours spent at the terminal and the number of jobs completed along with an estimate of the manual time required for the same result need to be tracked. Most systems provide utilities to record the amount of time spent on a terminal but lack a very important piece of information--that is "what" is being done for that time. The "what" refers to activity related to detail, design, analysis, NC work, or programming. The following ratios and trends are defined;

$$PRODUCTIVITY \ RATIO = manual \ hours/system \ hours$$

$$SAVINGS = (manual \ hours-system \ hours)*standard \ hour \ rate$$

$$SPECIFIC \ PRODUCTIVITY = SAVINGS/SYSTEM \ HOURS$$

Benefits can be defined in dollars or in hours.

A typical monthly machining report is shown in Figure 1.

FOR THE MONTH OF _____

category/department	manual hrs	CAD/CAM hrs	ratio	rate $/hr	savings
1) DESIGN	120	80	1.5	30	$1200
2) DETAIL	160	160	1.0	28	-0-
3) ANALYSIS	160	40	4.0	40	$4800
4) NC PROGRAMMING	80	40	2.0	30	$1200
5) NC PROOFING	80	40	2.0	30	$1200
6) OTHER	20	15	1.33	40	$ 200
TOTALS THIS MONTH	620	375	1.65		$8600

RATIOS   AVERAGE PRODUCTIVITY = 1.65

SPECIFIC PRODUCTIVITY = $22.9 DOLLAR/HOUR SPENT

COST OF SYSTEM = $15/HOUR

PERCENTAGE OF TIME SPENT VERSUS PERCENT OF SAVINGS

1) DESIGN	21.3%	13.9%
2) DETAIL	42.6%	0%
3) ANALYSIS	10.6%	55.8%
4) NC PROGRAMMING	10.6%	14.0%
5) NC PROOFING	10.6%	14.0%
6) OTHER	10.6%	2.3%

Figure 1. Example of the way productivity improvements may be tracked.

While its thrust is primarily dollars saved, it must be noted that the hours of production time saved is in direct proportion to this. The detailing application should be reconsidered especially if the analysis function needs more time on the system. What is not shown is the other tangible benefits of integrating these applications on that particular system.

The real benefit of this type of tracking is two-fold. First, it will be much easier to satisfy the financial types who will be asking if the projected savings were realized. The records will be available and the whole job of an internal audit will take a few hours instead of a couple of weeks. Secondly, it allows trends to be quantified. Many executives are surprised when they see that a particular department is out pacing all others while that function was never considered to be a serious application. Establishing this tracking during the implementation phase will make future directions much easier to chart and people will already be used to reporting their figures on a routine basis. The figures that are tracked for an organization will depend on how the organization does business. The important point is that you must keep track of what the efforts of integration are returning. That efficiency of implementation must be watched to keep the integration effort from becoming a "golden fleece."

In addition to having a method of capturing the actual results of implementation, it is also necessary to set realistic expectations in introducing CAD/CAM systems.

SETTING REALISTIC EXPECTATIONS

Expectations from the initial installation of CAD/CAM systems fall into two major categories: financial return and operator proficiency. Overall results are determined by the company's ability to integrate engineering and manufacturing. The two operations are related, but are usually treated separately due to the different organizations involved. Most importantly, when these expectations are not realized, the organization is split in a long-lasting battle which makes integration difficult, if not impossible, as well as affecting capital availability, operator attitude, and management perspective. This is a battle many companies are still fighting.

Justification of the technology is traditionally centered around classical return on investment, although some "survival return on investment" strategies have proved successful. Risk is quantified through calculation of time saved. Additional benefits of increased quality and other related items have only been quantified in a few companies that have the capability to easily track statistics, such as the number of engineering changes required as a product matures. While this financial return fascination should not be allowed to get out of hand it is a good indicator of the productivity increase possible due to the decision to get into CAD/CAM.

There is much literature available to predict the ratios of manual labor improvements. Each organization must decide for itself which ratios are realistic based on actual case studies and others who have been successful. The ratios are a function of the particular job involved and the type of equipment available. Figure 2 shows a matrix whose numbers represent the ratio of improvement over manual methods. The numbers shown are for illustration only and each organization should include its own. The impact of the matrix is the relationship between expected result and the equipment required, assuming an adequate level of performance from both man and machine.

CAD APPLICATIONS

	PLOTTING	BASIC DRAWING	DETAILING	ENG'R CHANGE	AUX VIEWS	SURFACE DSPLY	SURFACE MODIF	SECTIONS	NC VERIFY	NC PATH GEN	WTS & VOL	FEM PRE-PROC	FEM POST-PROC	SOLIDS	ROBOTICS	PACKAGE	INQUIRY	VIEW ONLY	SCHEMATICS	PICTORIALS	PLANT LAYOUT	KINEMATICS	ANALYSIS PROG
2-D	2	2	1	2	◇	◇	◇	NA	1	1	NA	1	1	NA	NA	NA	1	1	1	1	◇	◇	1
2½-D	3	2	1	2	1	◇	◇	◇	1	1	1	1	NA	NA	NA	1	2	1	2	3	◇	◇	NA
3-D	3	3	1	5	5	4	4	3	2	3	3	4	4	4	5	5	2	2	4	4	◇	◇	5

NUMBER REPRESENTS A PRODUCTIVITY RATIO FROM 1 TO 2 TIMES THE NUMBER SHOWN.

Figure 2. Typical increases in productivity based on a survey of CAD.

Figure 2 is based on a survey taken of 51 Canadian and American companies by the Canadian Institute of Metal Working. While the maximum improvement is a function both of the company's philosophy and of the definition of the task, the time required to reach these expectations is relatively common. As can be seen in Figures 3 and 4, the productivity increases for engineering-related jobs is quicker than that of the manufacturing, owing mostly to the definition of the task. The time required to reach a 3:1 improvement ranges from 12 to 24 months. This number does not represent some of the newer opportunities available.

The maximum value of productivity increases will grow with time. These values can only be obtained if both the equipment and people deliver near 100% capability. While it would be hard, if not impossible, to determine 100% capability, 75-80% capability is usually an apparent point. Hardware capability is clinically determined, but operator proficiency is much harder to measure.

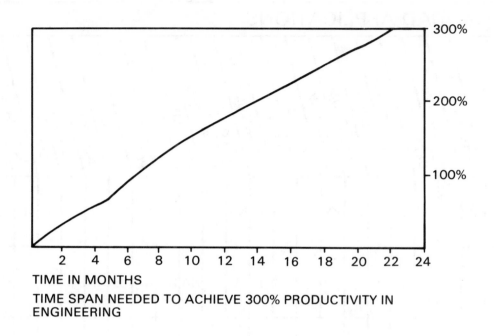

TIME IN MONTHS

TIME SPAN NEEDED TO ACHIEVE 300% PRODUCTIVITY IN
ENGINEERING

<u>Figure 3.</u> Time span to achieve 300% productivity in manufacturing. (1)

ENGINEERING

TIME SPAN NEEDED TO ACHIEVE

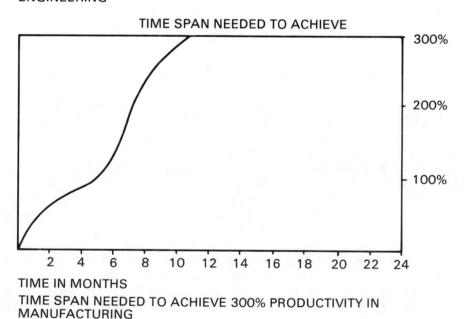

TIME IN MONTHS

TIME SPAN NEEDED TO ACHIEVE 300% PRODUCTIVITY IN
MANUFACTURING

<u>Figure 4.</u> Increases in productivity based on a survey of CAD users. (1)

92

Figure 5 shows a plot of proficiency versus time. While this is largely subjective, it is the result of a professionally done survey. The time of 18 months of dedicated operation to reach a level of 80% proficiency is a good estimate. Contrast this with claims of turn-key vendors of three months time

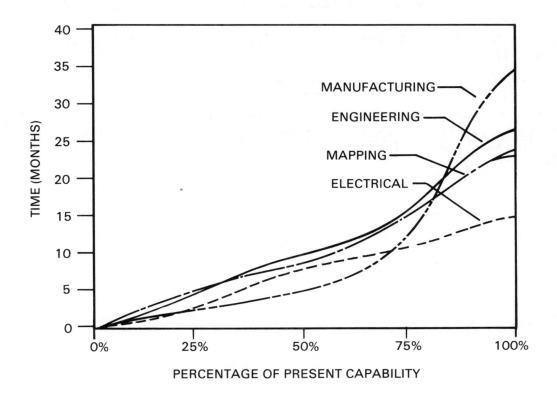

Figure 5. Proficiency increases over time. (1)

to learn their system. The problem lies in the definition of proficiency. After three months, an operator should be able to exercise all of the capability of a particular system. Thus, the vendor's claim of three months is reasonable. What industry needs, though, is an operator who can apply the system's capability to the job at hand. This takes an additional 12-15 months. The difference often results in employee turnover when management expects three months and hard working employees return a 12-month result. This can be seen in Figure 5, which shows that 44% of the companies surveyed had less than 50% of their original staff left after initial implementation. Again, reasonable expectations of both return and operator skills will not only ease the implementation, but speed the integration aspects.

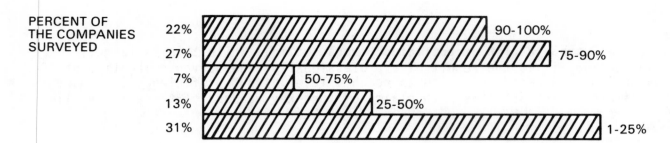

Figure 6. Percentage of present staff after the implementation of the system. (1)

REFERENCES

1. Kyles, Shannon. A Study To Identify The Manpower Requirements For The Effective Utilization Of An Interactive Graphics Design, Drafting, and Manufacturing Systems. Ancaster, Ontario: Canadian Institute of Metalworking, 1982.

Editorial Overview of Part Three

This part of the *Program Guide* is about the needed tools and techniques to acquire and build integrated systems. Dr. Ralph Bravoco provides an excellent overview of the IDEF methods for modeling information systems and structures. The second paper, by Dr. Leonard Bertain and George Sibbald, covers the area of rapid prototyping as an alternative to traditional methodologies involving the sequential approaches of written specification and refinement. Finally, Mr. Oscar Rhudy outlines the numerous issues to be considered and managed when sourcing systems from integrators, software houses, and equipment suppliers.

STRATEGIC THINKING

CONCEPTUAL PLANNING

SYSTEMS DESIGN

INSTALLATION

Part 3

Systems Design

Planning a CIM System Using System Engineering Methods

by Dr. Ralph R. Bravoco
Texas Tech University

INTRODUCTION

One of the primary objectives of manufacturing industries is to increase productivity. There are other objectives--technical, economic, social, and legal--but the desire for productivity seems universal.

A major factor in increasing manufacturing productivity involves enhancing the managerial skills brought to bear upon the day-to-day problems. For two centuries, management of manufacturing has been an art, based upon hereditary rules and precepts, or upon intuitive wisdom. Certain basics could be taught in schools, but experience on the job was indispensable. Regretably it was not easily transferable.

More recently, electronic data processing technology has assisted the manager in day-to-day tasks of information gathering, planning, decision making, and order dissemination. By relegating many of the tasks to the computer, two benefits have been accomplished:

- The information in use is more accurate, more timely, and better recorded.
- The manager can devote more time to key decisions which cannot be delegated to the computer.

As a result, the art of manufacturing management is becoming a science. A science implies a rigorous discipline, understanding of governing principles, and an ability to measure events.

Specifically, the planning and application of the computer to manufacturing management requires a precise understanding of manufacturing as a science.

One must understand the inherent structure of the activity; one must observe the rigorous data handling requirements of the computer. Given these abilities, we stand today at the beginning of an era of very rapid change in the techniques of manufacturing management.

The computer is simultaneously being profitably applied to the control of individual manufacturing operations, such as the numerically controlled machine tools, the analogous-controlled processing operations (heat treating, for example), and automated materials handling operations. It also is being used for logistic control--purchasing, scheduling, and production control. It is important to note, that the data moving in these latter channels are the same data that moves in the managerial information and command channels.

It is obvious, therefore, that to utilize the powerful assistance of the computer, it is essential that the infrastructure of manufacturing be clearly understood. Manufacturing is corectly seen as a complex structure. The network of interrelationships in production sequencing, time scheduling, and spatial relations is so complex as to defy any simple planning approach. The application of a computer to assist in the control of any of detailed activity can be a long and difficult task; the application of computers to all the detailed activities, and to their integration is a monumental task.

The solution to these problems is embodied in the concept of computer-integrated manufacturing (CIM) systems. Any CIM program must address both the definition and design of the integrated manufacturing system and application of computers to provide the information link and to replace planning and control functions where economically feasible.

THE ARCHITECTURE APPROACH

To implement such an integrated system, one must recognize the need to establish a definition of manufacturing (8). The "Architecture" is that set of blueprints, drawings and specifications that captures a formal definition, not of a product, but of a system to produce a product (i.e. manufacturing).

There are different versions of manufacturing which include how each individual plant within a company does manufacturing within the plant. These versions of the Architecture of manufacturing have been called "Factory Views." A simplified version of Factory View is presented in Figure 1. In this figure, each plant is considered by management as a single, individual entity.

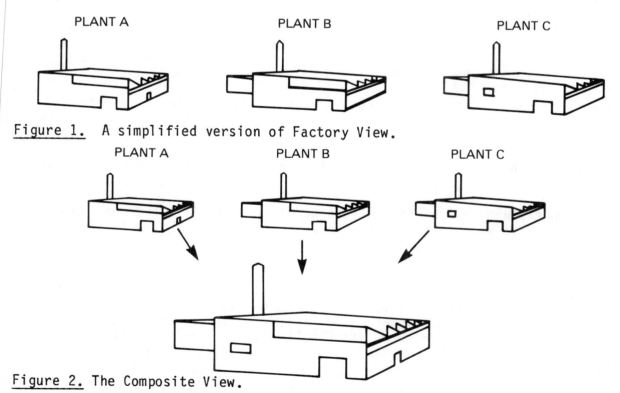

Figure 1. A simplified version of Factory View.

Figure 2. The Composite View.

These different Factory Views (as indicated in Figure 1) are synthesized in their commonality to produce a "Composite View" or total view of the three plants. The Composite View is one step removed from company specific practice, organization, structure, technique and format--yet it is representative of each of the Factory Views. It is the total view of the company considering the individuality of each part (plant) (Figure 2).

Using the Composite View as a baseline, "subsystems" within manufacturing (such as material handling or manufacturing control) are extracted for further definition. In the example in Figure 3, these subsystems are materials handling and manufacturing control. These subsystems may be found in one, two, or all three of the plants.

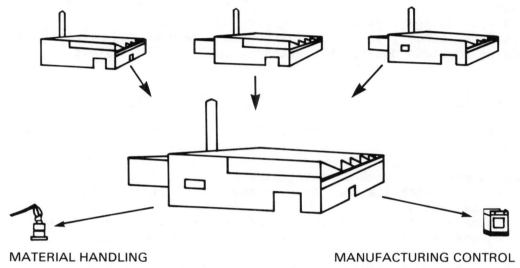

MATERIAL HANDLING   MANUFACTURING CONTROL

Figure 3. Subsystems within manufacturing.

These individual views of some aspect of manufacturing are called "Subsystem Views." Once extracted and completely modeled, Subsystem Views are integrated back into the Composite View to identify and define interfaces between each subsystem and the rest of manufacturing as well as between individual subsystems.

As previously mentioned, the Architecture is that set of blue prints, drawings and specifications that captures a formal definition of a system that manufactures a product.

The "AS IS" Architecture of manufacturing is the Architecture of current or existing manufacturing. Some examples of activities in AS IS manufacturing are:

- Plan Manufacturing.
- Provide material resources.
- Perform the manufacturing.

The previous steps all related to an Architecture of existing manufacturing or AS IS Architecture and are necessary to better understand, communicate, and analyze current operations.

To improve productivity, a new method of operation needs to be understood, communicated, and analyzed. Through analysis of the AS IS Architecture, major manufacturing problems and needs are identified. Based upon these findings, the "TO BE" Architecture begins to take shape. The TO BE Architecture may be a completely new Architecture or a modification of the AS IS Architecture.

It is at this point in the manufacturing process, that simulations, economic studies, and other similar techniques are conducted to determine the optimum improvements and to pave the way for the eventual "business as usual" design and implementation of an integrated manufacturing system.

A system development methodology that establishes a formal definition of the current manufacturing system, prior to the specification of the future integrated system, and uses System Engineering models rather than a specification to accomplish the definition is a recommended planning tool. The following sections detail this planning tool for CIM systems.

INFORMATION SYSTEMS ENGINEERING METHOD TO CIM SYSTEM PLANNING

A unified Systems Engineering Method (SEM) approach consists of four major components:

- A management approach to integrated systems development.
- A standard mechanism for the development and documentation of the technical analysis.
- A common approach to developing and validating system models.
- An integration approach to utilize the data developed.

A Management Approach to Integrated Systems Development

The management approach to integrated systems development utilizes a System Development Life Cycle as illustrated in Figure 4.

Understand the Problem	Needs Analysis
	Requirements Definition
Formulate the Solution	Preliminary Design
	Detailed Design
Build the Solution	Construction and Verification Testing
	Integration and Validation Testing
Implement the Solution	Implementation and User Acceptance
	Maintenance and Support

Figure 4. The Development Life Cycle.

This life cycle provides a framework for technical development and provides management visibility and control standards. Each phase of the Life Cycle is controlled by communication analysis and is implemented through systematic application of definition and engineering methods.

The following paragraphs provide a brief description of each of the eight phases of development listed on the right in Figure 4.

The first phase is titled "Needs Analysis." The primary objective of this phase is to establish the goals and directions of the system to be developed.

This phase is the initial stage in the structuring of the problem environment and determination of the scope of the effort. The activities associated with preliminary organizational planning and technical approach also are determined. It is critical that during this phase that management has an understanding of, and commitment to, the SEM techniques and approach.

The activities associated with the needs analysis phase of system or subsystem development can be characterized as follows:

- Area of impact assessment.
- Capability assessment.
- Problem conceptualization.
- Cost identification.
- High-level cost/benefit assessment.
- High-level return on investment (ROI) assessment.

"Requirements definition" is a description of the existing environment which captures both the consistencies and anomalies. This description is show using models. These models are tools to describe:

- the functions performed,
- the data flow,
- the relations between pieces of information,
- the major events, and
- the system's performance in time.

The philosophy of "observe before you analyze" involves the following.

- Establishing the scope and plan for the requirements effort.
- Constructing the function, information and user-mode interface models according to the standard modeling procedure.
- Integrating of the three models among themselves.
- Integrating the three models back into reference models.
- Evaluating, on a preliminary basis, the need analysis results against the current system definition to prioritize the area for further evaluation.
- Prepare a strategic plan for design activities.
- Reassess the project development costs by prioritized areas.

The primary objective of the preliminary design phase is the identification and allocation of sets of functions to various subsystems to meet the prioritized needs initially identified during the needs analysis phase.

Developed during the preliminary design phase are:

- initial definition of the future system,
- processes, information, and dynamics of the system, and
- strategic plans for transitioning the current system into the future system.

The principle activities of the preliminary design phase include:

- Decision of prioritization of needs and tactical planning of the design activities.
- Formulation of alternative technical approaches.
- Evaluation of alternate approaches based on technical feasibility, cost/benefit trade-offs, projected development time, compatibility with existing facilities, and capability to meet the desired needs.
- Decision on the scope of the build.
- Detailing of the specification of the selected priority areas.
- Configuration control plans.

The utilization of a formal modeling method to describe the alternate designs offers a convenient communication vehicle for the evaluation of the new system by the users. The structure inherent in the functions models should be the reflection of the alternate designs. This allows for the development of version release schedules and a finer detailing of the expected costs by elementary pieces rather than by complete systems. Evaluation of the future system architecture against the current system's architecture allows for projecting and analyzing costs associated with each of the systems.

The objective of the detailed design phase is to refine the results of the preliminary design. The scope of alternatives is reduced but the level of detail is increased. Thus, a designer is no longer strictly concerned with the existence of an interface because, supposedly, all of the interfaces have been identified. Rather, a designer is concerned with how the interfaces which do exist should be designed.

It is only during the detailed design phase that sufficient information exists to identify if existing capabilities can be used again, bought or modified. This decision is made from a cost-effective or performance evaluation viewpoint. From the management point of view, the detailed design phase is the point at which tactical plans--including scheduling, resource allocation and facilities planning--can be established for the construction and verification testing activities. The activities of this phase center around the functions which follow.

- Algorithm development and specification.
- Detail module specification.
- Interface definition.
- Preliminary test plan definition.
- Preliminary implementation planning.
- Physical schema development.
- Tactical planning of the construction phase.
- Design validation via review, or simulation.
- Reevaluation via review, or simulation.
- Reevaluation of costs and planning criteria and assessment of priorities.

In conjunction with the National Bureau of Standards, a set of software documentation has been developed including specifications as:

- system/subsystem,
- program,
- data,

- detailed design, and the
- verification and validation plans.

These documents and appropriate modifications to the preliminary design documents reflect the tactical decisions which are made as the detail of the various modules is established. Configuration control of the documents and the models is coordinated with the configuration control and the system/software documentation system established at the program level.

Within SEM, the objective of the "construction and verification testing" phase is to build the modules identified in the detail design phase. The modules are tested for internal consistency, performance characteristics, and their ability to meet the specifications of the design. Techniques for structured development of software programming can be applied to construction and documentation of the other subsystem being developed. This "constructive" approach emphasizes the concept of physical system quality assurance as opposed to post-production quality control.

There is one disappointing aspect of this phase. Due to the vigorous application of analysis and design techniques, one would expect that this development would proceed smoothly--almost automatically.

However, consistent with the correct application of these methods, many decisions will invariably cause problems. Preliminary testing, modeling of existing systems, and extra schedule slack can alleviate some of the problems.

The primary objective of the "integration and validation tests" is to build the interfaces between the various subsystems and modules and to test these modules against the total system design specification. It is during this phase that simulation can be utilized to predict the performance characteristics of the system under a variety of system loads. Tactical plans implement or phase in the new system including preparation of teaching materials.

Major activities during this phase include:

- subsystem level testing;
- interface testing;
- detailed environment support specification;
- analysis of performance against the original needs and design specifications, and
- development of a logical implementations strategy utilizing the current system definition.

Through the modeling techniques and review process, there should exist a core of users who were continually involved in the development effort. This group is most familiar with the attitudes and organizational structure within which the system is to be implemented. This group also generally provides the best approaches for an implementation strategy.

During "implementation and user acceptance," the developed system is implemented into the user environment. Users are trained and the initial goals established during the needs analysis are evaluated against the operating system. It has been repeatedly demonstrated that systems have both a technological and a psychological measure of acceptability.

It is the transition, particularly of the human element, (i.e., the learning curve), that is often the most difficult factor. The recognition of this problem forms the strongest argument for prototype development and implementation prior to full-scale development.

During this phase, the inadequacies of the system must be identified and documented. Cost/Benefit and ROI analysis data can be gathered and essentially the cycle starts again, i. e., the needs analysis phase is officially reinitiated and tactical plans can be established for embellishments and revisions. Requirements for system tuning also are established.

This leads to the phase which is titled "Maintenance and Support."

At this time, inadequacies in the system which do not meet the stated goals, are corrected. Plans may be established to enter into another development cycle depending upon the seriousness of the inadequacy and the resource available. It is also during this phase that performance tuning and implementation problems are addressed.

THE MODELING TECHNIQUES AND METHODOLOGIES

The previously described phases of development are the management structure around which the technical activity is coordinated. This structure was developed to accommodate the philosophy of defining the current system prior to future design and the approach to integration.

The second component addresses the technical problems of system definition and design. This component is important because it provides a standard mechanism for the development and documentation of the technical analysis of the current system. It also provides a medium for documentation of the trade-off decisions which must be made when going from the current system to the specification for a future system and working mechanism for integration.

What is needed is a set of tools and methodologies which will allow the manufacturing system planner to establish a frame of reference. This frame of reference will provide a structure of characteristics into which data from observation can be organized. The manufacturing system planner should also establish standard interpretations of the relationship between these structures.

A formal modeling definition can provide a structure around which the tools and methodologies with the previously mention capabilities can be constructed.

The choice of modeling tool(s) and methodology(ies) had to satisify characterisitics, criteria, and interpretation constraints:

- Provide a common basis for communication.

- Provide for establishment of a composite definition from many individual company specific definitions.
- Provide a descriptive and representative documentation of the objects of the component systems utilizing a common set of characteristics.
- Serve as the integration mechanism for application and support subsystems.
- Serve as the basis for system design, construction, test, and implementation.
- Be utilized by manufacturing personnel in an effective manner.
- Provide a formal basis so that automated analyzers and construction aids could be built.
- Be validated by both expert review and simulation techniques.

The decision to go with multiple models was based on a judgement which took into consideration the following factors.

First, independently developed models which are validated against one another as an approach to integration prove a great assurance that the important characteristics will be isolated and documented by at least one of the multiple inquiries.

Secondly, since the primary mechanism for validation is expert review, multiple models allow for simplification of the concepts and syntax for each review and thereby enhance communication.

Lastly, multiple models allow the definition process to be segmented into manageable pieces.

The choice of the three model types was a result of three things. First, the analysis of the characteristics generated from the evaluation of existing techniques. Second, the model types are the result of decomposition of the component set of manufacturing subsystems. Lastly, there should be consideration of the criteria for use imposed by the SDM development cycle, the SDM modeling approach to the development process, and the need for control of the "integration" error.

THE DEFINITION METHOD

The ICAM Definition Method (IDEF) is often referred to as a method, language, or a technique. IDEF is a modeling methodology whose purpose is to graphically capture characteristics of manufacturing (2,3,8). IDEF is intended as a means of discovering what actually does happen within the entire manufacturing enterprise and communicating this understanding. It also provides an effective base line understanding (AS IS model) from which improvements are suggested (TO BE model).

The Function Model--IDEF$_0$

The function model, IDEF$_0$, (3,7,11) provides a description of manufacturing in terms of a hierarchy of functions. These functions are collectively referred to as decisions, actions, and activities. To distinguish between functions, the modeler is required to identify what objects are input to the function, output from the function, and what objects control the functions and mechanisms (people, tools, etc.).

Objects in this model refer to data, facilities, equipment resources, material, people, or organizations, information, etc. The idea is to capture a description of manufacturing from a completely functional viewpoint irrespective of organizational lines and system interfaces.

Figure 5 represents a manufacturing function and the arrows in the figure represent manufacturing constraints which define the function. An input arrow shows the data necessary to perform the function, while an output arrow shows the end product generated by the function. A control arrow shows the constraints under which the function must be performed. A mechanism arrow shows the person or device which performs the function.

The IDEF methodology is typical of other modeling methodologies in that it is intended to answer specific questions about the subject. The questions include the issues which follow.

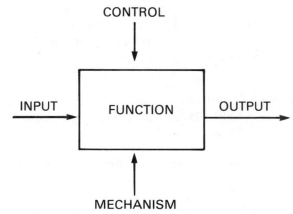

Figure 5. IDEF Function Model.

In Figure 6, what is basic functional breakdown or decomposition of manufacturing? There are three facets: to plan manufacturing, to provide material/resources and to perform manufacturing. See Figure 6.

Figure 6. Basic manufacturing functions.

What is being transformed and what is the result? The product design is transformed into the manufacturing plan and eventually into a product (output). See Figure 7.

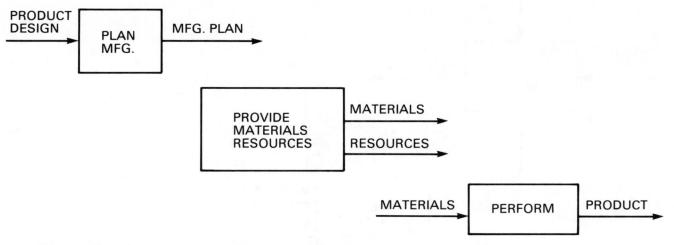

Figure 7. Basic manufacturing functions--inputs and outputs.

What influences these functions that are in the previous two figures? See Figure 8.

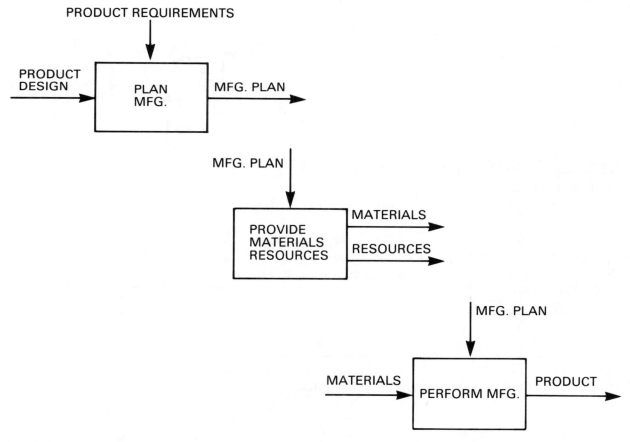

Figure 8. Identifying the controls in the process.

What is necessary to carry out these functions? To manufacture requires resources such as equipment, tools, or staffing. These influences are added in Figure 9.

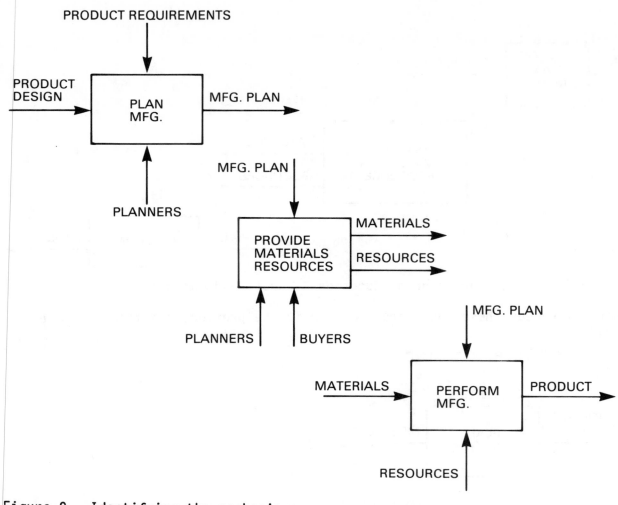

Figure 9. Identifying the mechanisms.

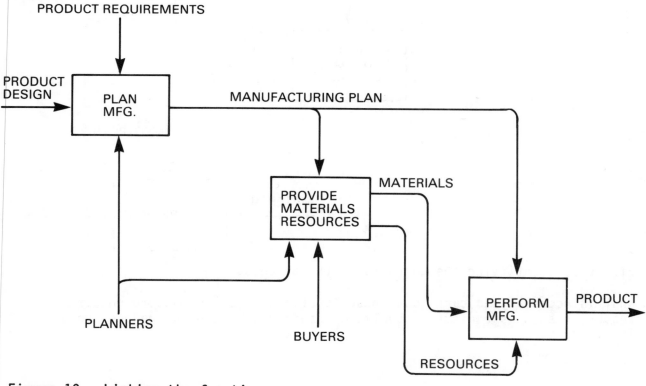

Figure 10. Linking the functions.

Finally, how do these functions, objects, and data relate to eachother? This is related in Figure 10.

Using the IDEF$_0$ methodology, the decomposed function model can show any level of detail. It can act as a "blueprint" description of what is being performed. The diagram is supported by test and glossary.

This structure provides organization, clarity and standardization to a description which otherwise would have taken thousands of words. The hierarchical structure of the description allows it to be developed in a controlled piece-meal fashion. The need for these descriptions to be consistent with each other is controlled by the rules of decomposition. The breakout of a higher level function into subfunctions may only include functions which provide product outputs included in the higher level.

THE INFORMATION MODEL--IDEF$_1$

The Information Model (1,4,6,10) provides a more in-depth description of information by focusing on the structure of information in support of what is being performed.

For example, in the previous model (Figure 10), data arrows represent classes of information or "entity classes." By using IDEF$_1$, the structure of these entity classes can be described as is shown in Figure 11.

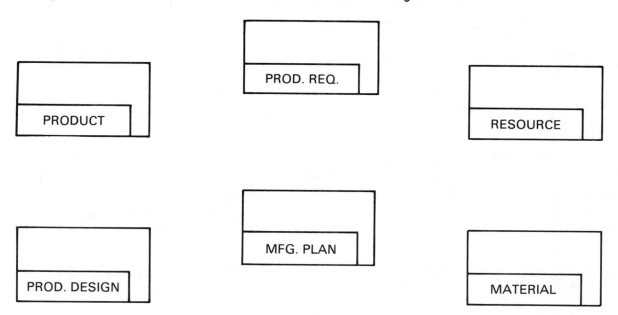

Figure 11. Identification of data entity classes.

The objective of the functional model as represented in Figure 10, is to present pictorially the information structure of an organization. IDEF$_1$ diagrams are comprised of entity classes which are connected by lines and symbols to represent the relationships between the entities (Figure 12).

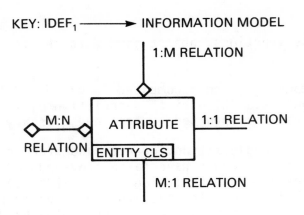

KEY: IDEF₁ ——→ INFORMATION MODEL

Figure 12. Relationships key between the entities.

As in the case of the function model, the information model can answer specific questions, such as: What are the relations between the manufacturing plan entity class and all others? In Figure 13, each manufacturing plan is based on a specific product design, developed for a specific product, satisfies many product requirements, requires many resources and many materials.

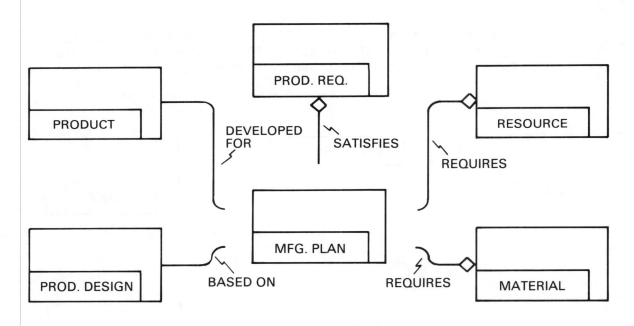

Figure 13. The relationships between the manufacturing plan entity class and all others.

What about the relation of all other entity classes to the manufacturing plan entity class? In Figure 14, each product design has a specific manufacturing plan; each product has a specific manufacturing plan; each product requirement is satisfied by a specific manufacturing plan; each resource is required by many manufacturing plans, and each material is required by many manufacturing plans.

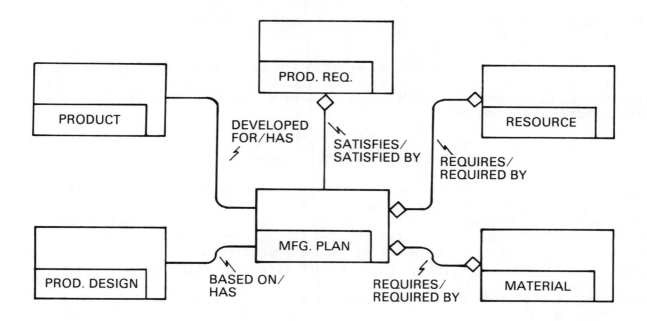

Figure 14. Relationship of all other entity classes to the manufacturing plan entity class.

What unique characteristic of the entity classes reflected in Figure 14 is necessary to identify one entity class element from another within the same class? As is seen in Figure 15, the plan number, design number, product number, requirement number, resource name, and material name provide the answers for each of the entities.

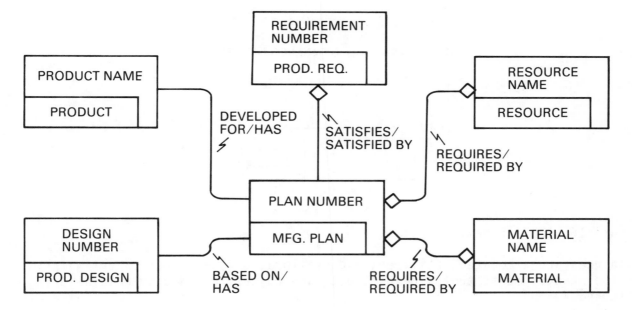

Figure 15. Top level IDEF₁ diagam.

The Information Model is a dictionary or a structured description supported by a glossary which defines, cross-references, relates, and characterizes information at a desired level of detail necessary to support the manufacturing environment.

The advantage of the information model approach to describing manufacturing is that it provides an essentially invariant structure around which databases and application subsystems can be designed to handle the changing requirements of manufacturing information.

THE DYNAMICS MODEL--IDEF₂

The Dynamics Model (5,9) represents the time-dependent characteristics of manufacturing to describe and analyze the behavior of functions and information interacting over time. It answers specific questions about any object or information as it passes through the manufacturing environment. For example: What activities consume time in the processing of a manufacturing plan? The answer is providing resources and acquiring materials.

What time is consumed in waiting to be processed by the activities? The manufacturing plan waits in the Request Queue (REQUESTQ) for processing by the activity listed as "Provide Resources," (Figure 16) and in the Purchase Order Queue (P.O.Q.) for processing by the activity which is called "Acquire Materials."

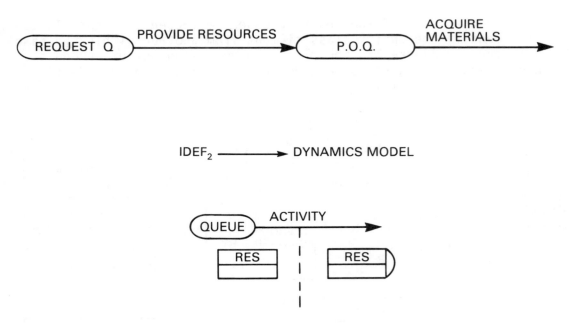

Figure 16. IDEF₂ Dynamic Model.

Resources are allocated, utilized, and deallocated by a number of activities including equipment, tools, people, etc, and buyers requisition materials (Figure 17).

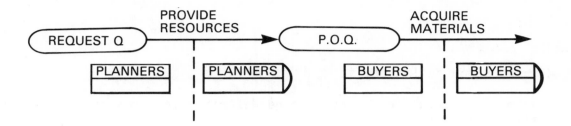

Figure 17. Dynamic Model with resources indicated.

Once questions have been answered, and because of the time-relative information associated with each question, further questions may be answered regarding the performance of flow. These questions include:

- What is the total processing time for a manufacturing plan?
- What is the total time a manufacturing plan is waiting to be processed?
- What is the utilization of the resources?
- What statistics are associated with these items?

These questions are reflected in Figure 18.

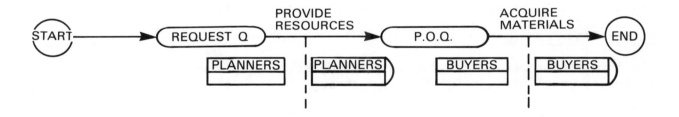

Figure 18. Overview of the Total Dynamic Model.

IDEF2 is used to produce a dynamics model, a "Scenario"--a structured description of the time-oriented behavior of functions and information, and provides quantitative information as to their sequence, duration, and frequency at a desired level of detail necessary to analyze the manufacturing process.

The Dynamics Model Entity Flow Diagram is supported by definition forms which quantify the times associated with the diagram. The Dynamics Model is compressed of four submodels:

- Resource Disposition,
- System Control,
- and Facility Submodels which support the
- Entity Flow Submodel.

IDEF Model Integration

The final component of the SDM is the integration techniques which organize, control, and carry out the actual integration within the system development process.

Integration Philosophy

The ICAM integration philosophy is:

- Complex manufacturing systems can be described in terms of families of common functions.
- Information requirements should be invariant under computerization.
- With a definition of the current environment, future systems can be developed which take advantage of the commonalities in the manufacturing environment.
- Bases of data can be constructed more intelligently by identifying the commonalities in the semantic models of each user class.
- Integration should be a process which: starts during the needs analysis phase; uses system level reference models in the requirements definition phase, and is a modeling process which allows for, but maintains control of, errors.

The utility of this philosophy is being demonstrated in the ICAM Program in the development of an integrated computer-aided manufacturing system for sheet metal fabrication. Through industry coalition participation in planning, development and demonstration activities, an experience base as well as usable products are being established for technology transition.

Integration Management

The integration management technique involves the implementation of the life cycle and modeling techniques of SDM through the use of:

- Standard techniques for the structuring of subsystem development.
- Contractual requirements for integration of needs, requirements definitions and designs as well as (and prior to) the end systems.
- The IDEF techniques for modeling both current system and future system designs.
- Requirements for simulation analysis of both system requirements and designs.
- Standard reporting (including documentation) and cost accounting.
- Standard configuration management techniques.

The standardization of management practices and procedures is probably the most difficult to implement. It is also the key to successful integration. If one key subsystem is allowed to determine its own requirements in its own way, this will certainly cause havoc in future subsystem development and eliminate (or greatly increase the cost of) integration. By implementing the standard development cycles and modeling techniques, the individual managers are given greater visibility into their own project and into the total system development. The techniques and visibility helps to insulate the manager from producing locally optimum solutions. Similarly, the manager is provided with a forum of explaining his or her own development problems especially if the problem is one of an interface nature.

Integration Technology

Integration technology encompasses the following aspects:

- Techniques for extracting preliminary function, information and user interface models from the reference models.
- Technique, for syntax and semantics audit.
- Techniques for integrating subsystem requirements back into the reference level models.
- Techniques for control of error in the integrated system/subsystem.

A similar set of activities are carried out for the information and user interface models. The procedure is again repeated during the design and construction phases of the system development.

REFERENCES

1. Bachman, C.W. "Data Structure Diagrams," Database. New York: Association for Computing Machinery, 1969.

2. Bravoco, Ralph R. and Surya B. Yadav, "Requirements Definition Architecture--An Overview" Computers in Industry. Amsterdam, The Netherlands: North Holland, 1985.

3. Bravoco, Ralph R. and Surya B. Yadav, "A Methodology to Model the Functional Structure of an Organization," Computers Industry. Amsterdam, The Netherlands: North Holland, 1985.

4. Bravoco, Ralph R. and Surya B. Yadav, "A Methodology to Model the Information Structure of an Organization," The Journal of Systems and Software. Amsterdam, The Netherlands: North Holland, 1985.

5. Bravoco, Ralph R. and Surya B. Yadav, "A Methodology to Model the Dynamic Structure of an Organization," The Journal of Information Systems. Oxford: Pergamon Press, 1985.

6. Chen, Peter P., "The Entity-Relationship Model-Toward a Unified View of Data," ACM Transactions on Database Systems. New York: Association for Computing Machinery, 1976.

7. Ross, E.T. et. al. "Structured Analysis for Requirements Definition," IEEE Transactions on Software Engineering. Silver Spring, Maryland: IEEE Computer Society, 1977.

8. U.S. Air Force (no author) Integrated Computer-Aided Manufacturing (ICAM) Architecture Part II, Volume II--Architecture-A Structural Approach to Manufacturing, AFWAL-TR-81-4023, Wright-Patterson Air Force Base, Ohio 45433, June 1981.

9. U.S. Air Force (no author), "Integrated Computer-Aided Manufacturing (ICAM) Architecture Part II, Volume VI - Dynamics Modeling Manual (IDEF$_2$)," AFWAL-TR-81-4023, Wright-Patterson Air Force Base, Ohio 45433, June 1981.

10. U.S. Air Force (no author), "Integrated Computer-Aided Manufacturing (ICAM) Architecture Part II, Volume V - Information Modeling Manual (IDEF$_1$)," AFWAL-TR-81-4023, Wright-Patterson Air Force Base, Ohio 45433, June 1981.

11. U.S. Air Force (no author), "Integrated Computer-Aided Manufacturing (ICAM) Architecture Part II, Volume IV-Function Modeling Manual (IDEF$_0$)," Air Force materials Laboratory, Wright-Patterson AFB, Ohio 45433, AFWAL-TR-81-4023, June, 1981.

Prototyping: A Way of Improving the Delivery of a CIM System

by Dr. Leonard Bertain
Business Spectrum Associates

George W. Sibbald
Genovation, Inc.

INTRODUCTION

A prototyping approach to the development of CIM systems is discussed which enables the rapid delivery of a preliminary conceptual system. As the users understanding of the problem changes during the system development an evolutionary understanding of the ultimate deliverable is acquired. The development of CIM systems is a moving target and the prototyping approach minimizes the risk for all parties involved as well as drastically reducing costs.

Prototyping is not a new concept but it does provide a fresh approach in discussing the development of CIM systems. As was noted by Bertain, "Reculturing for CIM", this Edition, (1) the initial phases of CIM involve a teamwork approach from the factory floor personnel and the engineering staff. Anything that can improve the communications between the people who will use the system and the design engineers insures higher quality deliverables.

What is prototyping? Basically, it is a methodology of systems development that delivers a model of a systems design to management and to users of which they have had a significant input. It is a user-designed system. It is preliminary overview of the system design which contains most, if not all, of the key functional features of the system.

It is not a panacea that was recently discovered. It is a technique, long recognized in the data processing community as a valuable development methodology. There are several new development tools in the market which encourage this technology and are worth investigating.

The users of CIM systems are on the factory floor. The beneficiaries are everywhere in overhead, from the President on down. Prototyping is a major development technique which allows the designers of the CIM system to be effective in their interaction with the shop floor personnel and other users of the system. A "strawman" of the proposed design can be quickly delivered to the factory personnel who can see their ideas materializing as the iterative design evolves. The ultimate deliverable is not a surprise. The users of the system have contributed to the design. The developer takes a tremendous risk in trying to work with users who are growing in their understanding of the problem as the system is being specified. The user takes a tremendous risk in developing any new software regardless of the competence of the developer. It is almost impossible to succeed as a systems developer or an in-house system planner with such risks of failure facing every project.

There are numerous advantages of prototyping (see Figure 1). To name a few:

- Phase 0 User Involvement - The Phase 0 part of CIM systems is the initial step of the process creating the change environment. As part of the process of implementation, the user at the shop floor should be involved in the development. Prototyping allows this to occur. The 60% application shell is prototyped by a small group then as the prototype is evolving, the user modifies the application to meet specific needs, and has a chance to review the progress. The user causes the system design to meet his or her basic requirements and support of the system follows naturally. The user becomes a user-owner (2) of the application.
- Speedy Development - The user has a good notion of what he or she wants the system to do and the screens to look like. With prototyping, a rapid feedback is encouraged to give a visible sign of progress to the user. The prototyping software allows the users to freely consider many different concepts of the design before committing to the final design. This saves much time in the overall system development.
- Risk Minimization - Risk or anxiety? Who cares? They both create uncomfortable situations with the users. CIM systems are new. New is different and different is risky. The user is gradually brought to understand the system. The risks of failure are controlled. By starting with an immediate feedback of a proposed subset of the CIM system, the user has a view of the ultimate deliverable that is not fixed in concrete. The view can change and so can the users perception of the system. This minimizes the risk that the system delivered will be unacceptable to the user. The user changes the system until it is right for him or her. In fact, in actual use, the system flexibility remains strong.
- Reduced Cost - The prototype system gives users a quick fix on the view of the system as they perceives it. They can sit at the terminal with the systems programmer and develop a very quick view of the system. There is an attendant reduction in the amount of paperwork and missed communication. CIM development may easily be self-funding (see CIM Justification Chapter).

Prototyping software will be discussed and an example of a successful project using this technology will be reviewed. It is leading edge prototyping technology, using the latest in event driven expert-system architecture, and is a software model of the capabilities of fifth generation hardware products.

GENERATIONS

First of all, the development methodology to be used consists of fourth and fifth generation development tools. The boundary between the various language generations is not clearcut but a brief overview of the demarcation should suffice.

The first and second generations consisted of machine and assembly languages, respectively. They were the antecedent tools available to the programming profession before the advent of traditional third generation programming languages was that the level of programming was improved to the point that a programmer could rapidly generate programs. However, the corollary to this was that a bad programmer could now generate "bad" programs more quickly. The net result of these third generation tools was volume of program instructions with minimal control of the system generated.

For that reason, systems were developed which forced control onto the programmer. The proper way to program became driven by the proper way to design systems. However, the control of these systems added additional overhead to program development. Programs and projects were late. People lost their jobs for poor quality and costly overruns on system delivery. The requirements of more powerful program development tools emerged in the evolution of a new form of program development tools known as fourth and fifth generation products.

The referenced document (3), available from ADAPSO, is a good source of information on evolving standards of the various fourth and fifth generation development tools. But there are additional concepts of fifth generation technology which need to be reviewed.

PROTOTYPING WITH A E-CIM (TM)

An expansion of the fifth generation software concepts is that of the Event Driven Distributed Expert CIM System (E-CIM) (TM). It provides a new approach to the development of CIM systems (4). It learns as it evolves. A distributed shallow domain approach tailored for the uniqueness inherent in factory control is preferable to the typical application of expert systems used in clinical work. In a typical clinical application, a series of questions is invoked in a sequential manner to narrow the options available for the treatment of a disease. The expert system, in this case, uses the symptoms of the disease to guide the doctor through the options of treatments available.

For the complex situation of major aerospace manufacturer or an electronics board repair facility, an expert system would advise the factory operation as to the best path for a manufactured part to follow or for the board to follow in repair. In any factory, the flow of product through the plant is modelled in the software by breaking every movement and every operation on a product into "tasks."

In either of the above factory examples, the same definition applies. The invocation of such an operation can trigger the execution of subtasks. New tasks and subtasks will be added at any time. The sequence of tasks is controlled by tasks which route the product to the next task based upon the current condition of the product, the current state of available work stations, and the priority of the customer and availability of materials. The ability and facility of the system to accommodate these new "tasks" or directions for operation of the system make up a rule-based expert system. As new tasks are added, the system becomes smarter or becomes more "expert." And all of this can be generated as a prototype model of the factory during development.

The design objective of this architecture, then, is to present an environment to the users which will grow as new rules and new tasks are uncovered for the control of the destiny of each product through the facility. It is expected that this "knowledge base" will never stop growing. Hence, the system will not be able to distinquish development from maintenance. The system will continue to evolve as the knowledge base grows.

The traditional application development methodologies are diagrammed in Figure 1. Many will recognize the layout. We also recognize the costly expense and risk of failure of this development methodology. It has already been reviewed. However, when this is compared to the prototyping approach of the alternative presented, it is clear that the claim of 10 to 1 productivity gain is believable and the cost reduction of 90% is obtainable. The example referenced shows comparable results.

EXPERT-CIM (E-CIM) (TM) DESIGN

The architecture being proposed is like a self-correcting missile targeted to a moving airplane. As the target is initially viewed, one course is set for the missile. As the target moves position, a new course is established until the target is hit. Any predetermined course is guaranteed to fail because we know the target will move.

So it is with prototyping systems. The "software guidance" system is directed to hit a specific "application." As the user progresses in this understanding of the application, the final deliverable will change. The deliverable continues to change until the customer take delivery of the system.

The differences in these analoges is precisely this: the missile hits and destroys its target. A "fait accompli". The prototyped software system is never finished. It will continually change.

The previous discussions were focused around the E-CIM (TM) prototyping architecture. The system consists of a factory control computer and several remote cells running the individual functional parts of the factory. The difference between this design and alternatives is that the hardware is a totally distributed, fault tolerant design, with a distributed database, shared by all components of the network. The uniqueness of the concept is that the Application Development Software allows for a very flexible environment for the development of new applications.

Advantages of E-CIM (TM)

- Ease of Implementation - The main advantage of E-CIM (TM) is the ease of implementation. This allows the user, designer, and programmer a great deal of latitude in the interpretation of the users needs. If the user doesn't convey the precise definition of the meaning to the programmer, it really isn't a problem, because change is make with such ease. The user is encouraged to collect his/her thoughts and present them to the designer/programmer in an ongoing fashion. The objective being that the ultimate goal will be reached more quickly.
- Pay-as-you-Go - The probability of success of most systems is controlled by whether or not the user expectations of the system deliverable have been properly monitored. In any such system, there is a great deal of anxiety on the part of the user, before the system is ordered. As the development evolves, many of the system deliverables

are written out of the contract as too expensive. So the vendor has a careful path to follow in making commitments to he customer. With the proposed methodology, superimposed on the architecture, the best of both worlds is met, the user pays for as much as can be afforded from the developer and takes on the burden of adding the additional enhancements over time.

- Ease of Use - Ease of use is most critical. The facility with which programs can be created, changed, expanded, etc. without massive dependence on a single individual is crucial. The linkage of these two concepts, ease of use and dependence on individuals, is significant. If the programs are easy to use and to an extent, self-documenting, then it is very easy for a new player to spend some time with the system and rapidly understand the design.

- Improved System Control - As any programmer knows, there is no perfect system developed yet for the implementation of systems. The complexity of designing system which extend over multiple processors is phenomenal. The control of the system is unmanageable by a single person or persons. The consistency checking of data element names across multiple developers is difficult without help from the computer. The design aids in recent years for the developer have helped improve the design of systems. However, the conversion of design to application has been anything less than spectacular. So the proposed architecture addresses this problem by proposing a distributed fault-tolerent database system with considerable control aiding the developer in the area of consistency checking of data, records, files, applications, etc., by using the computer to do so.

- Network Data Reduced - The architecture minimizes movement of data on the network by using the concept of "event-driven" systems. Data only finds its way to he network in an exception situation. A schedule of operations for the day is provided to each cell by the central system. The central system assumes that the scheduled work is being done unless it "hears" otherwise. It "hears" of the situation through an "event." The "event" starts a sequence of exception process and consequently directs the cell for the proper follow-up action The significance of this feature is only understood when the number of lines of code are compared or this system and an alternative. In this architecture, one line of code is required. An "If...then...else..execute event" command would effectively cause one of the cells to alert the main system when the "event" of concern occurred. A single line of code would be required to direct the reply to the "event." The mathematical logic of the actual program might not be much different in any other architecture, however, the sequence of programming instructions to the network and the various operation systems can be significant with alternative architectures. For example, a sequence of instructions are required to access the network, and another few might be required to access the master computer, and a few more to access the database and application. The reverse process, when an action is required at the cell, requires few more instructions. The net result is more than 10 times more instructions to handle the process.

- Reduced Data Storage - The E-CIM (TM) architecture only has data elements stored once. There is enough intelligence in the network for the system to know where all data elements are located. this is critical in an automated factory where products move from cell to cell and the location of products is critical to the management of the factory.

● <u>System Expandable</u> - The system is linearly expandable so when additional processing power is required the transaction power of the system goes up proportionately. This is critical in determining the future of the system. You want to be able to add processing power without reprogramming the system and also be able to see a proportionate increase in performance for each dollar invested in the increased power.

CASE STUDY

A rather interesting example of a system which was implemented using this philosophy, is referenced. A rather large aerospace manufacturer required a WIP management and control system and a time and attendance system delivered to the factory floor within two months of project funding. The system was to run in three separate factories, in three separate locations for 24 hours a day. The system was basically a parts repair and maintenance management and control system.

The user had defined a series of screens that needed to be integrated into the system. During the prototyping discussion, that series of 80 screens was reduced to 46. The users had to be involved in the system from the beginning to make sure that the deliverable met their expectations.

The system was delivered one week ahead of schedule by one project manager and five programmer analysts. The system will probable only require one man one-half time to support it in a maintenance mode.

The system was projected to take over 20,000 hours of programming time using conventional techniques. An alternative bid, using one of the many program generators and database management systems, was submitted and was estimated to take over 5,000 hours. The winning bid came in at 2600 hours and billed at 2698 hours to complete the task, less that 4% cost overrun. Spectacular in this day of mammoth project overruns.

The major advantage of this system is that it will pay for itself 20 times over during the first year alone. The system provides all the other benefits of: no lost orders, no sending work out without paperwork (the proper paperwork), and a totally monitored work environment.

For an aerospace supplier, this project is significant. It sets the stage. Large system projects can be delivered cost-effectively and on time.

CONCLUSIONS

The CIM systems of the future will have to justify themselves with more aggressive payback schedules. Prototyping is one way to meet that objective as a pay-as-you-go program is possible. The example reviewed showed phenomenal returns on the investment but with an interesting added benefit. The system was delivered quickly and on time. The user has been able to use the system effectively and the on-going improvements to the system will be handled by a single person.

The prototyping concept is not new. It has been demonstrated to be an effective tool in the development of CIM systems. The users get involved. They have a clearer picture of the deliverable earlier in the project. They can try ideas before the system is ever finalized, (if ever). The final engineering changes are minimized because of the early involvement of the user.

Prototyping provides the methodology which allows the systems analyst and the user to develop a positive working relationship. The resulting system will be a cooperative effort. The resulting CIM implementation will be a success and will effectively contribute to the goal of increasing productivity and reducing the cost of manufacturing.

1. Bertain, Leonard <u>CIM Implementation Guide</u>, second edition.
2. <u>User-owner is a Concept of CIM Applications Development</u>, developed by Roper Pump Company, Commerce, GA.

3. Landry, John <u>ADAPSO Report - 1986</u>.

4. Sibbald, George W., <u>CIM Today and in the Future</u>, Autofact '86.

E-CIM (TM) is a Trademark of George Sibbald.

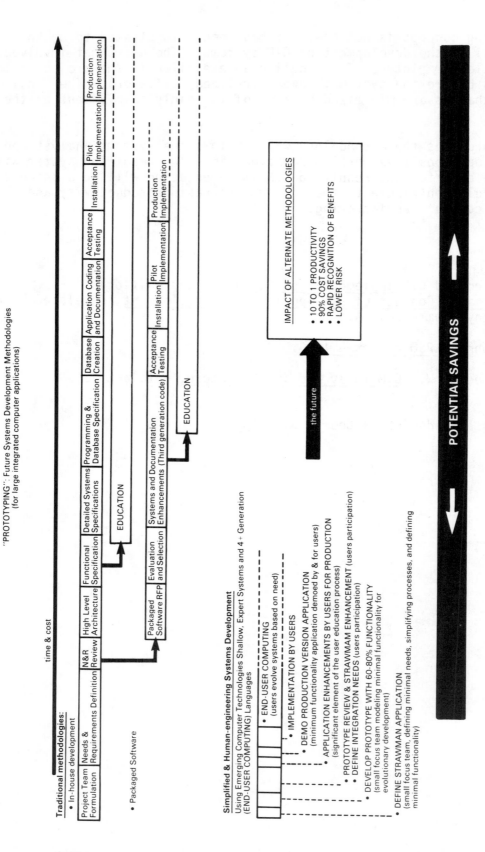

Figure 1. "Prototyping:" Future Systems Development Methodologies (for large integrated computer applications). (Developed by: George W. Sibbald © Copright 1986: Genovation Inc. All rights reserved.)

Software Package
Selection and Integration

by Oscar G. Rhudy
Rust International Corporation

INTRODUCTION

The computer engineering activities for a production facility can be performed effectively for a client by an expert team within a construction engineering business.

The objectives for keeping the process automation within the construction engineering project are to achieve Computer Integrated Manufacturing and to maximize the startup efficiency of each new production facility. The automation project can be grouped into seven successive project activities. These being, in order:

1. project definition,
2. requirements specification,
3. conceptual systems design,
4. detail design,
5. construction,
6. system startup, and
7. continuing support.

Use of this framework for the computer applications project, which is a portion of a total project, is very important for effective project management within the automation team and by total project management. Within the framework, there can be explicit recognition of the requirements of the project. Planning can be consistent. Communication within the total project team will become more fluent. Planners can use the project activities as guidelines for presenting estimates and schedules to the client. The automation team leader can use the project activities for directing assignments and for controlling overall project direction. Communication within the team becomes more effective when everyone understands the project needs and goals.

The three most common problems in software projects are late deliveries, cost overruns, and failure to meet customer needs. The ways to minimize these problems are to begin to explore the customer needs very early in the project and to strive for visibility, traceability, and product integrity throughout the project. Visibility can be attained in automation just as it is achieved with other engineering teams. Visibility is achieved by use of consistent scheduling, consistent activity names, and consistent document names. Traceability is essential for all engineering. Traceability is achieved by standardizing methods and by cross referencing successive documents. Product integrity must be the shared objective of every team member. The focus on product integrity spans the entire software life cycle-not just the final production stages of this life cycle. A Computer Integrated Manufacturing facility will result from the methodical development of automation and control systems during the engineering and construction project.

PROJECT DEFINITION

Project definition involves determining the overall view of the project and producing summary documentation. The design of a complex system proceeds, from the general to the specific through numerous steps. Initially in a factory automation project, one can maintain intellectual control over the project. Early in the design the human cognitive limit is exceeded. The cognitive limit is the number of independent ideas with which the human intellect can deal at a given time. The typical cognitive limit is eight items. At each definition refinement, visibility and traceability can be maintained by summarizing the results in eight or fewer categories. An overall view of the project should include: automation objectives, control objectives, process technology constraints, market place requirements on the product, and an analysis of the process functional requirements. This overall perspective must be understood by the client and all other engineering disciplines involved, not just the automation team.

To understand the scope of the project necessitates a thorough exploration of the steps "upstream" and "downstream" of the process to be automated. The conceptual development focuses on the process flow as depicted by the process flow diagram. The raw materials flow into a process, undergo a transformation, and a finished product emerges. The names and attributes of raw materials and finished products give the general description of the intended facility, e.g., metal door manufacturing plant. In a cursory overview, one may accept that raw materials are perfectly uniform, and infinitely available. As more specific descriptions are developed, a more complicated picture evolves. Raw materials, actually the products of prior processing, come in a variety of sizes, shapes, and weights. The cost and availability of raw materials are functions of quality control tolerance range. Generally, cost increases and availability decreases as the quality control tolerance range narrows.

Similarly, the finished products are not uniform. The variations in raw material, tool wear, process technique, and inspection yield many good products and some defective products. A thorough investigation of the cost of quality raw materials and of the value of quality products establishes the proper perspective for ensuing design optimization.

The expectation of the client's management for their newly automated facility must be fully explored so the best design choices can be made.

Achieving effective communication among the members of a newly organized multidisciplinary team of engineers can be a challenge. Each individual tends to work with a different "world view" of the production facility. That is, an automation engineer often thinks in terms of a computer hardware configuration, and software packages to serve the needs of the facility. Such views are not conducive to effective interpersonal communication in the project definition phase. When the overall view of the project is explored and documented in terms of the succession of material process functions, from acquiring raw materials through dispensing finished products, the individual "world views" can come together to form a total "world view."

A preliminary functional analysis needs to be written. It can be used to estimate the total count of independent functions to be accomplished by software. This count is the basis for early make/buy decisions and an estimate of software cost. The preliminary study is very challenging. Unique needs of the production facility should be investigated and documented. Unique requirements necessitate special-purpose computer hardware and custom software. The most cost-effective way to fulfill normal business and technical needs is to use existing software solutions. The challenge of software estimation for the project scope is to refine the vague functional needs into an estimation model. A preliminary plan calls for making custom programs and buying existing software packages. The software modules fulfilling unique requirements are considered for custom, high-priced, programming. The software modules, available on the market in software packages, are considered for purchase. This is indeed a crude approach but it serves the purpose of making a visible automation system model with a cost estimate. Additionally, the model is traceable back to the preliminary functional requirements.

The written functional analysis clarifies and defines the diverse perspectives and goals for the proposed production facility. Now, list prices for software packages can be checked; software development cost estimates determined and a software cost estimate issued. The majority of the effort is investigating and writing the functional analysis. This documents the requirements on the entire facility. All functions, manual and automated, are included. For writing convenience, the perspective may be in terms of a manual operation. The decisions of manual versus automated will be made later, in the conceptual system design phase. The foundation for all future design is established by the functional analysis. The goals and requirements have to be considered carefully across production areas. This document presents the unity of the facility. Any synergistic effect of multiple processed, materials or operations have to be defined here or else they probably will not be retained through the ensuing refinements.

A hardware cost estimate can be made based on list prices for typical hardware components. With a detailed concept of the requirements, a project schedule can be proposed and written.

Accountability for each requirement is achieved by reference to the person or department, or standard from which information is obtained. The integrity of the functional requirements specification is verified through review and approval by client's project management.

REQUIREMENTS SPECIFICATION

The requirements specification phase involves intensive concentration on the production facility functions selected for automation. New project team members can orient themselves by reading and discussing project definition documents. The preliminary functional hierarchy is reconsidered. Higher levels are organized to achieve consistency with the material handling engineers' conclusions of process flow, and work-in-process storage. Just as the process flow diagram is the focus of discussion for control strategy design, the process flow is the unifying theme for all the automation investigations. Each material transformation is documented from eight perspectives. These are process operation, bill of materials, inventory control, production scheduling, equipment maintenance, personnel administration, material cost accounting, and quality assurance.

During the development of each process function, automation parameters are identified, (e.g., run status of a particular hydraulic pump, total pump run time since overhaul, pump average lifetime, pump lifespan variance, etc.) Each automation parameter is recorded in the data dictionary. As many relevant attributes as can be identified are recorded. Major attributes for data dictionary entries are: data name and synonyms, subject area of data, range of values, definition, functions using this datum, related data structures of higher and lower levels, and frequency of usage. When frequency of usage of all data names become known, the real-time communications network requirements can be inferred.

Visibility of the automation engineering activities is achieved by explicit documents: the hierarchical chart, the Process Function Descriptions and the Data Dictionary. This set of documents is called the Functional Requirements Specification. As the automation team is enlarged, the work assignments can be delegated most coveniently along process functional areas.

Product integrity is a concern during this activity. The engineers must be persistent in exploring each successive refinement of the process functions. They must also be vigilant in understanding and documenting the diverse perspectives from process control through quality assurance.

Conceptual System Design

The project phase, Conceptual System Design, is performed as a sequence of five activities: System Requirements Specification, Vendor Selection, Vendor Specific System Recommendation, Software Quality Assurance Plan, and Scheduling. A computer system oriented specification is produced from the user-oriented Functional Requirements Specification. The system design is represented as a system of modules.

This is the time to formalize an agreement on system design philosophy. An example of an automation architecture follows:

The Disc Brake Components Plant is a fully integrated facility. This may lead to the conclusion that the control system needs to be a fully integrated system. However, in order to increase the integrity of any control scheme, it is desirable to distribute the control system "intelligence" as far as is feasible. This enables areas of the plant to run independently of other areas which may be shutdown due to routine maintenance or breakdown, thus increasing overall plant integrity. To split the process, it is necessary to identify the buffer areas of the plant. A buffer or work-in-process store separates parts of the plant so that operation of one can continue without synchronized operation of other parts.

A System Architecture Diagram depicts the logical relationship of the modules. A visual table of content diagram organizes the modules for descriptive purposes. Availability of required software and hardware components in the marketplace is checked. Alternatives are evaluated in consideration of data flow, data-timing, constrained budget, constrained time, make/buy guidelines, and vendor bid evaluations. The module requirements are documented in terms of functional requirements and organized by module. Modules are clearly described and multivendor relationships are delineated.

For each module, the functional requirements are combined with project requirements to produce the Inquiry Specification. The emphasis is on the set of functions accomplished by the software. The brand of computer will be selected for compatibility with the software package. The selection of software before the selection of hardware strengthens the bargaining position with software suppliers. The vendors are considered on the merit of their offering of software functions rather than equipment.

This phase must include the client in tradeoff decisions. The resulting understanding by the client of system configuration and function gives more chance of a happy acceptance test team.

The traceability of the Conceptual System Design phase is based on a large set of documents: the Conceptual Design, and Approved Vendor List, Inquiry Specifications, a Technical Evaluation Summary, a List or Risk Items with Risk Ratings, the Purchase Recommendation, Technical Points and Schedule for inclusion into Purchase Specification, Project plan, Schedule, and Estimate of Cost.

The organization of the System Requirements Specification is by automation system functions. Topics are man/machine interface, batch language functions, training, system diagnostics, hardware, system performance and coordination communication. Each of these topics is developed to require state-of-the-art software engineering practices. All the process functional requirements are synthesized into qualifications for these topics.

Let's explore the coordination communication topic in more detail. One of the application program systems is material resources planning, MRP II. The functional specification of the MRP II system includes the description of manual and automated functions. The vendors are invited to propose the division between manual and automated functions. The paragraphs for the MRP II functional specification are: the Logic of MRP, Master Production Scheduling, Bill of Materials, Inventory Transaction Subsystem, Scheduled Receipt Subsystem, Shop Floor Control, Capacity Requirements Planning, Input/Output Control, Purchasing, Distribution Resource Planning, Tooling, Financial Planning Interfaces, Simulation, and Performance Measurement.

The experience of engineering and operating personnel in a company might suggest other necessary functions that could be part of the software. For example, Production Planning Logic might be implemented as a knowledge-based expert system. The tables of rules would be available for validation and reuse throughout a multifacility corporation.

Software quality assurance is planned and systematic pattern of all actions necessary to provide adequate confidence that the software product conforms to established technical requirements. In the conceptual system design, software efforts are initiated for embedding controllers in individual pieces of process equipment, process equipment, process area control, and process coordination. There may be dozens of software projects for a production department or hundreds of software projects for an entire facility. The success of the entire project clearly depends on the reliability of software. Fortunately, the discipline of software engineering has matured sufficiently so that there is a consensus of opinion on how to obtain a reasonable degree of confidence that each software product is in the process of acquiring the required attributes during software development. The IEEE Standard for Software Quality Assurance Plans standardizes the topics which a quality assurance program should address. Compliance with a software quality assurance plan must be one of the general statements of each inquiry specification. After the vendor-specific system recommendation is presented, a software quality assurance plan can be tailored to the special software to be developed. Among the topics addressed are documentation, standards, practices, conventions, reviews, and audits. Section six of the Standard for Software Quality Assurance Plans clarifies methods for reviewing software design documentation. It calls for a series of reviews to control compliance with good software engineering principles. Four reviews address required documentation. Three audits verify function and consistency. A managerial review is held periodically to access the execution of the plan.

The final activity for the Conceptual System Design phase is scheduling the detail design and construction phases. The software tasks identified in the Software Quality Assurance Plan are copied onto a schedule form. The milestones for the tasks include the reviews, audits, and planned documentation delivery. The minimum amount of schedule detail would be to schedule a Software Requirements Review, a Preliminary Design Review, a Critical Design Review, a Software Verification Review, a Functional Audit, a Physical Audit, an In-Process Audit, and monthly managerial reviews. The minimum amount of schedule detail is essential to establish visibility of the software effort. Depending upon the project manager's perception of the criticality of software, additional software subsystems can be placed on the schedule. Additional software configuration management reviews and audits can be used as milestones.

Detail Design

The Detail Design phase of the project is characterized by intensive activity in multiple areas. Teamwork and careful project management are essential to modularizing tasks and maintaining a unity of design.

Vendor-specific specification is the activity of writing the Computer Process Control System Purchase Specification. This includes both hardware and system software modules. This activity is made visible by retaining the document outline previously used for the Computer Process Control System Inquiry Specification. Traceability of the specification activity is completed by checking off the issues list as items are reconciled and changes are incorporated into the draft of the purchase specification. For example, an issues list item may be the need for additional batch language statements. Further discussion with the client reaffirms the need so the requirement is clarified and written into the purchase specification.

The integrity of the purchase specification depends upon the thoroughness with which each issue is explored. The vendor representatives are important contributors to the technical understanding of product capability and adaptability. The automation engineer achieves specification integrity by understanding the project need, comprehending the adaptability of the vendor's standard module, and drafting a purchase specification paragraph to explain the requirement.

A System Acceptance Test Plan is in preparation for formal testing conducted to determine whether or not a system satisfies its acceptance criteria and to enable the customer to determine whether or not to accept the system. This Test Plan is made visible to project management by reference to the IEEE Standard for Software Test Documentation, ANSI/IEEE Std 829-1983. The activity sequence for the Software Test Planning is: identify features, synthesizes a plan approach, design test cases, and implement procedures.

The form and content of specific software requirements specifications are defined. This activity is helped by IEEE standard 830-1984, IEEE Guide to Software Requirements Specification. This guide describes the necessary content and qualifies a good Software Requirements Specification. It presents a prototype Software Requirements outline. This guide does not specify industry-wide Software Requirements Specifications standards nor state mandatory document requirements. The guide is written under the premise that the current state of the art does not yet warrant a formal standard. The goal of this work is to establish the basis for agreement with the supplier on what the software program is to do. The description of the software lends insight necessary for estimation project costs and obtaining approval for bids or price estimates.

The detail design phase involves other control systems work which must be coordinated. The piping and instrumentation diagrams, (P&IDs), must be reviewed for compatability with automation objectives. Any hardwired relay networks or special purpose logic designs are reviewed. The operator interface is approved. The Control System Databases is configured. The site preparation and installation for automation equipment is designed and reviewed. Major equipment specifications are reviewed for consistency and compatibility with other automation systems.

Construction

The Construction phase is often called programming or software implementation. Visibility is enhanced by stressing the analogy to the brick and mortar activities termed construction.

The traceability of the construction phase is straightforward: purchase packaged software, implement custom modules, integrate automation systems, and conduct factory acceptance tests.

The complexity is increased by the sheer number of software modules and the software configuration changes.

The implementation of custom modules is accomplished by developing a software design description, performing software verification, and producing a preliminary software verification report. The software design description undergoes at least two refinements; the first version is the subject of the preliminary design review. The second refinement incorporates needed revisions and additional detail. After the critical design review, necessary revisions are incorporated and the software is coded. A software verification plan is developed to trace the software verification activities. Software verification involves establishing conformance of the software modules with requirements and documenting the process. Establishing conformance is a complex job of reviewing, inspecting, testing, checking, and auditing. The job is concluded with a software verification review. The results of the software verification are written in the software verification report. This includes the results of all reviews, audits, and tests required by the software quality assurance plan.

The audits to be performed at implementation time are the functional audit and the physical audit. The functional audit is performed to verify that all requirements specified in the software requirements specification have been met. The physical audit verifies that the software and its documentation are internally consistent and are ready for delivery.

Startup

System startup phase begins with integration testing of automation and control systems. When sufficient capability is achieved, production is started. With limited production, we can commence collecting performance data and tuning control loops. Operations and maintenance crews are trained and brought to proficieny on the new equipment. When all the integration and tuning has been accomplished, the formal acceptance testing is conducted. Results are acquired, analyzed, and additional system tuning is performed. In this period of full scale operation, there is close observation of system operation. Production performance is monitored. Critical and long runtime software is optimized. The final acceptance test encompasses a review of all specifications and a review of performance results. Products of this phase are test results, change orders, a system evaluation report, and the inevitable system improvement proposal. The startup phase is concluded with a summary report of the acceptance test.

CONTINUING SUPPORT

Continuing support is the ongoing day to day attention needed to keep automation systems, software and hardware, at optimum performance. There is ongoing performance evaluation. This information serves to locate malfunctions and to identify potential improvements. The maintenance activity focuses on correcting hardware trouble, tuning and improving software performance, and devising new ways to do performance evaluation. The visibility of the continuing support improvement proposal.

In addition to this formal activity is a large amount of informal communication. The people responsible for continuing support of an automated facility have to review and expand their knowledge of their software systems. The impetus for the review of software packages in light of current problems yields solutions. Further discussions or tutorial sessions on the flexibility of a software package resolve most problems. This ongoing process permits the operations people to respond to changes in the business climate.

BIBLIOGRAPHY

1. "IEEE Standard Glossary of Software Engineering Terminology," IEEE Standard 729-1983.

2. "IEEE Standard for Software Quality Assurance Plans," IEEE Standard 730-1981.

3. "IEEE Standard for Software Configuration Management Plans," IEEE Standard 828-1983.

4. "IEEE Standard for Software Test Documentation," IEEE Standard 829-1983.

5. "IEEE Guide to Software Requirements Specifications," IEEE Standard 830-1984.

Editorial Overview of Part Four

Virtually every company today has had some experience with the installation of computer and automated systems. The issues and potential problems are not new, and the actions required are generally understood. Still, the integrating technologies of CIM do add some extra dimensions, and require extra emphasis on coordination among various specialists, suppliers, and operating departments.

The challenges of installation come alive in Mr. David Scott's paper on a MAP network pilot at Deere and Company's Harvester Works.

We close this section, and the Guide, with the *CIM Checklist* by Dr. Charles Savage. Published in the first edition of this book, it serves us well here as a summary of the attitudes and actions required for successful implementation.

STRATEGIC THINKING

CONCEPTUAL PLANNING

SYSTEMS DESIGN

INSTALLATION

Part 4

Installation

Making MAP a Reality
a User's View

by David C. Scott
Deere & Company

THE MOVE TO CIM

Since the advent of Computer Integrated Manufacturing (CIM), most
organizations have reached only a few concrete conclusions. The first is that
achieving true CIM will be an evolutionary process. The second is that the
computing environment on the shop floor will include a multitude of different
vendors. They will include those selling computers of varying types, Computer
Numerical Control (CNC) machinery, process controllers, reliability and
quality inspection and computing equipment, robots, and automatic material
handling and storage systems.

Having reached these conclusions, the need for a flexible yet powerful
communications infrastructure for the factory floor becomes obvious. In fact,
putting such a system in place should occur relatively early in the move to
CIM, as it will provide the foundation for factory automation.

In General Motors' case, this realization led to the initiation of their
Manufacturing Automation Protocol (MAP) effort, which is aimed at developing a
specification for a set of standards to allow for a multiple vendor computing
environment on the shop floor. The rapid growth of the MAP Users Group over
the past three years proves the wide acceptance of these conclusions.

One of the early supporters of MAP, outside of General Motors, was Deere &
Company, the large manufacturer of agricultural, industrial, forestry, and
consumer equipment. Deere has often been recognized as a leader in the areas
of factory automation and Computer Integrated Manufacturing. In 1981, the
Computer and Automated Systems Association (CASA) awarded Deere's Tractor
Works in Waterloo, Iowa its first LEAD award, presented annually to a company
in recognition of a leading edge implementation of CIM. There are many other
examples of advanced automation and integration of of computer-based systems
throughout the company.

Deere, like many other companies, historically has paid a high price for
integration. As automated processes and systems have been introduced, up to
50% of the final costs have gone to installation and integration of
computerized equipment with existing systems. The bill for ongoing support of
such systems from a communications/integration viewpoint has limited the
advantages gained. And the current CIM direction could potentially amplify
these problems, as it emphasized the use of many new shop floor computing
devices. These include powerful microcomputers and engineering work stations
in a distributed computing environment for functions such as "cell
controllers," Distributed Numerical Control (DNC), adaptive control of

137

processes, and "real time" scheduling to accommodate concepts such as just-in-time manufacturing. These devices will be required to communicate among themselves and with the various computers arriving on virtually every piece of new manufacturing equipment. Thus the rationale behind the MAP effort is very appealing to Deere, as it strives for "plug-in" automation and shop floor communications, basics for the realization of true CIM.

A CIM PILOT PROJECT

To emphasize Deere's commitment to the effort, what turned out to be the first manufacturing production MAP-compliant network was incorporated in a CIM pilot project in 1984. This pilot was initiated in the sheet metal facility of the John Deere Harvester Works, in East Moline, Illinois. The Harvester Works covers over 260 acres (95 under roof), and is located on the Mississippi River. The facility performs complete design and manufacturing from punching and welding of sheet metal, machining of bars and castings, through assembly and inspection for a full line of grain harvesting combines.

As depicted in Figure 1, the intent of the project was to demonstrate CIM in a just-in-time manufacturing environment by developing techniques to transform computerized designs to completed manufacturing instructions which could be transmitted directly to and from the shop floor. The system was to support sheet metal parts which would be manufactured in a cell including a turret punch with laser and a straight shear. The chosen equipment was a Behrens

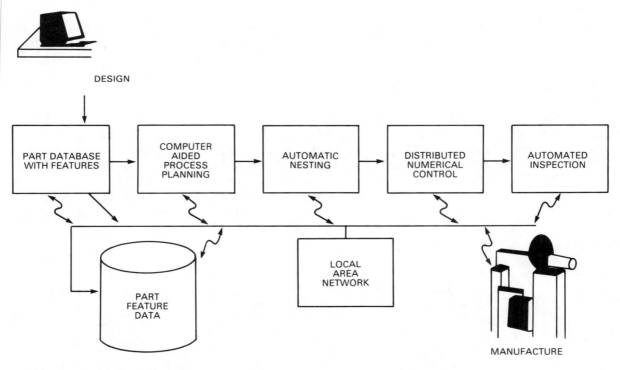

Figure 1. A CIM Pilot

turret punch press with laser and a Fischer CNC straight shear. The punch uses a GE 1050 CNC control and the shear a CNC control from the German firm Heckler & Koch.

A project team with members from the Computer Systems, Plant Engineering, and Production Engineering Systems departments was formed. The members were to design and install a system that would integrate the entire process of sheet metal part design and manufacturing.

Each member of the team had an important reason to make the pilot succeed. Production Engineering designed needed distributed NC, as well as the two new machines, for efficiency. Plant Engineering designed the network for general utility purposes to take full advantage of its benefits, and Computer Systems wanted to gain valuable shop floor and network experience.

The NC programming and design engineering specified a distributed numerical control system. They chose two Numeritronix microcomputer-based DNC systems (one as backup) with 20 Mbyte hard disk drives and communication ports for the ability to communicate with outside devices. The Production Engineer evaluated and procured the DNC system and worked with the vendors to design the screens to be used at the CNC equipment.

MAP SELECTED

A Local Area Network (LAN) work package was added to accommodate the needed communication for the plot, as well as the future growth of Distributed Numerical Control. The use of MAP broadband network was suggested. The timing was right. Not only was DNC a requirement, but new CNC controllers and machines were also on order. Although the cost of the network was higher than point-to-point links, corporate management was encouraging the effort and communications cost was only a small portion of the total project cost. The risk was low for a new installation because the equipment could always be connected using point-to-point links.

In May 1984, the requests for proposals for an 802.4 MAP-compatible LAN were sent to several vendors. At that time, the only supplies of MAP-compatible communications equipment was Concord Data Systems (CDS). Though the installation of a broadband backbone communication utility and associated one-time startup costs would be more expensive than traditional point-to-point twisted pair wiring schemes, the expenditure was approved with the belief that it would save cabling dollars for future additions; accommodate machine rearrangements; and, most importantly, be a major step towards CIM and essential network experience.

The Plant Engineer developed a computer program which allows graphical design of cabling schemes while automatically computing signal levels and other parameters and then inserting required components (amplifiers, couplers, etc.) as needed. This program allowed several alternatives for cabling to be quickly evaluated for feasibility and cost. The 3500 feet of broadband backbone cable was installed by a cable television contractor. MAP-compatible Token/Net Interface Modules (TIMs) and a headend remodulator were purchased from Concord Data Systems and all electrical connections were made by Deere Harvester electricians.

The network was 802.4 compatible because the cable and TIMs implemented the lower layers of the seven-layer model while the terminal server software in the TIM coupled with software in the DNC and CNC systems, implemented the higher layer protocols. Although messaging and file transfer protocols have now been standardized for MAP, in 1984 there were no standard upper-layer protocols to specify. So, the DNC and each of the CNC systems came with a different protocol. To service queries to the operator and requests for downloading data to the shop floor, the same software protocol needed to be used by all systems. For a fee, Numeritronix wrote protocols to match those used by both the GE and H&K controllers.

This protocol problem will be alleviated by fully functional networks in the future. Eventually, simply specifying MAP will provide easy connection. As machine controllers and computers are available with full MAP interfaces and networking equipment has been tested for all seven layers, the pieces will fall together. This is beginning to happen, but will not be widespread for several years.

THE CHALLENGES

The project team realized that the protocols would be a problem and got them in hand before any connections were attempted. Meanwhile, the network was being installed, and by November 1984 all of the equipment was in-house.

The next step was to connect the machines' CNC controllers to the DNC system. The production engineers had specified an RS-232 interface with terminal mode for the CNC controllers. But they had not specified male or female connectors or format for terminal mode. As a result, they received something different with each piece of equipment.

Connectors should have been specified as RS-232 type D female. The H&K controller came with a 15-pin connector. Deere electricians made a special adapter to accommodate the H&K connector at one end of the one-foot cable and an RS-232 type D female on the other.

Once the connectors were standardized, the team realized that the TIM networking boxes require pin 20, data terminal ready, to be used. Neither the distributed NC system nor the two controllers had used pin 20, so all had to be strapped to be usable. The standard cabling was no longer standard. Future service and maintenance could be tougher because of this, even though the team documented all changes made.

If the communications parameters of the systems to be connected are specified in advance, all of these problems can be avoided. In this case, by finding out Numeritronix and CDS specifications, the CNC controllers could have been ordered with compatible cable and connectors. Of course, in this case, the needs for distributed numerical control and for the CNC machines had been evaluated separately, with a melting into one networked project later. Once the physical connection was established, the DNC system and controllers were hooked up and a program download to the CNC was unsuccessfully attempted. Speed, number of bits per character, and parity were all set differently on the two controllers, but were not documented by either control manufacturer. To determine how they were set, the team disconnected the network TIM boxes and connected a terminal, breakout box, and datascope (relatively common test equipment in data communications, but not in most factories) to the CNC to check parameter settings.

The plan was to use a line speed of 9600 bits/second, so all ports were configured to correspond to that speed. Changes to the Numeritronix system required hardware configuring; the CNC controllers needed Exec changes. Speed, parity, and other parameters for each port on the TIM box were software configured via terminal.

Another difference encountered was the format for terminal mode. H&K provided internal screen formating at the controller depending on menu choice and GE allowed one line x 80 character prompts from the DNC host. The menu of operator options from the Numeritronix DNC system originally appeared as 10 lines. Changes had to be made so the options appeared one line at a time.

After these modifications, connection could be made, but problems in getting a full dialogue between the DNC system and H&K controller still existed. One feature, auto line feed, was set wrong on the Numeritronix system. With that DNC system option set of "off," things began to work on the H&K controller-- sometimes.

Using the datascope, documentation of the problem was compiled. It was discovered that downloads were running at 9600 bits/second, a function (undocumented) of the DNC system designed to run at 1200 bits/second. So speed settings at the TIM boxes, DNC computer, and CNC controllers needed to be changed. The team had to order a special EPROM from Germany to make the H&K controller run at 1200 bits/second.

Speed matching is always necessary with point-to-point links using traditional wiring and modems. The original network software from CDS also made it necessary in this case. The new CDS software called SPA, which replaced the PDL protocol used initially for this system, allows different-speed products to communicate across the network. Several other communication parameters that may vary from one piece of equipment to another also are now handled internally by the network. With a full complement of MAP products for both computers and NC controllers, companies with less data communication experience will be able to easily install a full MAP network before long.

LESSONS LEARNED

Finally, in January 1985, the first NC programs were downloaded from the DNC system to the laser punch and the shear. Now, NC programs generated and nested on two Computervision Designer 5X systems can be downloaded to the Numeritronix DNC system for storage. Programs can be uploaded across the network, as well, so if a program does not run properly on the shop floor, it can be modified in the memory of the controller and uploaded to the DNC system in the new usable form.

It took considerable communications expertise and about three months to progress from getting equipment in-house to using the DNC system for production. Most of the problems lay in not specifying all of the communications features needed at the time of equipment acquisition, partly because this pilot project came together as the culmination of three separate evaluations of need within the company at the same time.

In summary, the project helped gain practical experience in networking and MAP, and in developing specifications for equipment for this environment. At a minimum, the communications section of a machine process specification must include consideration for:

* cable type and pin-out,
* connectors,
* number of bits per character,
* parity,
* protocols, and
* speed.

Consistent protocols and speed difference compensation are advantages of broadband networks. New CDS and other full MAP products provide those services now. MAP was in its infancy in 1984; Deere and Concord Data Systems were pioneers.

NETWORK EXPANSION

Other existing equipment was also connected to the network. A TIM was added in a room where a Visual 50 terminal acts as a console device for the DNC system. Several Lear Siegler terminals used by engineers to access the CV CAD/CAM systems for data management and file manipulation also were connected. With these terminals on the network, a user at any terminal can access either system. An Okidata printer also was added when new software which accomodated hardware handshaking became available.

A VAX 11/750 that is used as backup on another system in the plant also was added. As long as the system it backs up is operational, it is used for development and software testing. It is now also being used for network management. A program was written for the VAX that allows statistics on all of the devices on the network to be collected with one command.

Four Wiedematic punch presses with GE 7500 NC controllers have also been added to the DNC network. For this retrofit installation on less intelligent controllers have been added to the DNC downloads menus and NC programs to operators on the 1502 terminals. The 1502 then supplies the machine controller with one block of the program at a time as the NC machine requests it, similar to reading a tape. To add these NC machines, on four-port TIM was needed, as was some coax cable to drop from the main broadband; the initial backbone utility cable topology was designed to permit future additions such as this.

The LAN also has been extended for a separate project being installed in the welding operations. This system links a VAX 11/730 and two cell controllers each controlling up to 16 controls on manual spot welders. The system, designed mainly to improve the quality of spot welding, is being supplied on a turnkey basis by Medar. The total network configuration is shown in Figure 2.

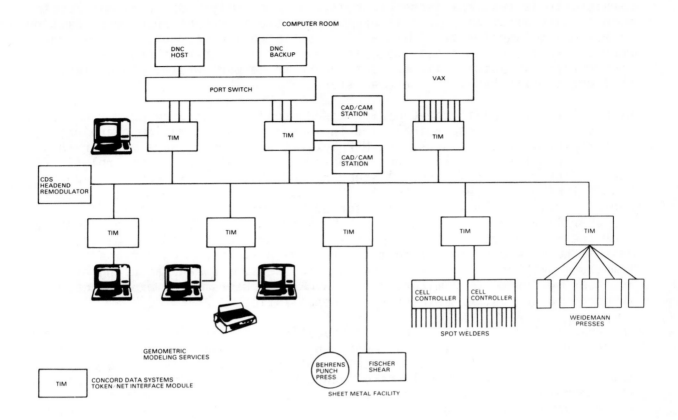

Figure 2. Deere Harverster MAP Network.

THE FUTURE

Since completion of this project, a team was formed to update the strategy to
address CIM for the factory. Most of their proposals will not require large
capital investments, but instead involve finding better ways to use equipment
already in-house. Integrating systems already in use, finding common formats
for related software programs, and optimizing equipment usage are some key
portions of the plan. Based on the success of the MAP pilot, the team
recommended expansion of the network throughout the entire facility to provide
an essential communication utility to support these CIM concepts.

The prices of MAP equipment are dropping, but even now, the LAN would not be
cost-competitive if there were no side benefits. For example, terminals that
were once dedicated to one of two computer systems can now access either
system. The status of the machines and computers connected to the LAN are all
available from one point on the network. Network experience allows
exploration into newer and wider uses of the utility.

Perhaps the largest challenge remaining, on a company-wide basis, is how to plan for and manage the shop floor communications, computing, and automation directions to facilitate CIM in a large decentralized company such as John Deere. Experiences such as those in the pilot need to be shared and incorporated in future efforts if they are to be worthwhile. To address this challenge, Deere has taken several steps.

At the Corporate office, a Computer Aided Manufacturing Services organization was formed. Their responsibilities include factory automation planning, factory local area networks, and MAP activities, among others. Under this group's leadership, a Shop Floor Computer Communications and Control (SFCCC) Users Group has been formed. A steering committee with members from corporate Manufacturing Engineering, Computer Systems, Quality and Reliability Engineering, and CAM Services was formed to coordinate and provide input to the overall group. This general group is composed of factory representatives from the same disciplines as the steering committee. As in the pilot, each unit is being encouraged to form a "core" shop floor communications team with members from Plant Engineering, Computer Systems, and Manufacturing Engineering Systems. Similar to the GM MAP/TOP Users Group experience, the response to the SFCCC has been very enthusiastic.

The role of the SFCCC is three-fold:education, coordination, and direction. At the meetings, educational segments on topics such as MAP are included with unit updates on experiences, current problems, and issues being faced. Members are asked to share lists of vendors, contacts, informational sources, and other such data which may be useful to others. Based on discussion of the issues surfaced by the group, plans for their resolution to provide future direction are formulated.

At the first general meeting, the users decided to form three interim working groups to develop guidelines for the three primary issues identified during the meeting. The first developed "boilerplate" specifications for inclusion in shop floor equipment specifications which will deal with the desired capabilities of the computer control. It covers physical and electrical characteristics, protocols, and general capabilities required to integrate the equipment into an overall CIM system. Basic examples are upload and download commands and terminal mode. The application layer of MAP using the EIA-1393 specification will be the ultimate answer when complete. The second group worked on guidelines for the communication utility and physical cabling schemes, including plans on how to evolve from current systems (e.g. point-to-point) to the "ultimate" broadband for MAP in a cost-effective way. The final group addressed flow and placement of data in the evolving distributed hierarchy on the shop floor.

Another obvious need identified is training at all levels. To address this, outside training vendors are being contracted to provide courses ranging from overviews of LANs, to MAP, to detailed broadband engineering instruction. Extensive contacts are being maintained with vendors of LANs, controllers, and computer equipment to obtain education on their directions and products and encourage their participation on future pilot projects, stressing MAP.

CIM will become a reality on a broad scale within the next few years. However, to be ready, the foundations must be laid now. The communications schemes for the shop floor are essential and the MAP approach offers a very attractive alternative, with an expanding support base from both users and vendors. But rather than just waiting for MAP to "happen," it is important that those companies which hope to realize the CIM potential begin planning and learning now through activities such as pilots and users groups. The benefits are tremendous.

CIM Checklist

by Dr. Charles M. Savage
D. Appleton Company, Incorporated

The following items are designed to stimulate thought and they act as a check list in developing a Strategy and Implementation Program for Computer Integration of the Management of the Manufacturing Enterprise.

A successful Computer Integrated Manufacturing Program (CIM) best begins from the perspective of the management of the entire enterprise. Although every company is different, this list reflects the types of issues more advanced companies are addressing.

- Clear statement of business strategy and goals.
- List of Critical Success Factors (CSF) to support the business strategy. What key things must go right to achieve this strategy?
- Clear statement of CIM strategy which supports business strategy and CSF.
- CEO/GM charter for CIM Strategy and Implementation Program and top support from all functions.
- Identification of the company's starting point:
  Level I--Integration--policy and data architecture,
  Level II--Interfacing--Standards, and
  Level III--Isolated Islands.
- Strong commitment to overall integration, not just excellence in functional islands or convenience in interfacing activities.
- Survey existing systems to determine levels of compatibility. How are many software and hardware systems capable of communicating together?
- Agreement to manage data as a corporate asset.
- Support from the MIS Department and good cooperation with engineering and manufacturing.
- Commitment to move information between all functions in digital form.
- Agreement on standards and protocols.
- Use of integration methodologies like those which have grown out of the USAF's ICAM Program.
- Development of an architecture for a common logical database.
- Development of phased process to support the transition to CIM:
  1. Goals/plans.
  2. Conceptual design.
  3. Detailed design.
  4. Implementation.
  5. Benefits tracking and fine tuning.
- Ability to learn from and receive support from the hardware and software vendors.
- Ability to learn from experiences of other companies.
- Willingness to streamline or simplify existing operations. (Reduce the

complexity index).
- Reviewing use of Just-In-Time and Group Technology.
- Adjust departmental charters and work assignments to support a networked organization.
- Ability to move from an individual application-bound approach to a data-driven approach, where the same data can be used by different functions for their own unique needs.
- Use of outside resources (universities, professional associations, and consultants).
- Identify potential financial benefits.
- Develop new ways of working with and exchanging information with vendors and customers/clients.
- Make use of public domain information from the various federal projects, such as NASA's IPAD, USAF's ICAM, and the Advanced Manufacturing Program of the National Bureau of Standards.

This is not an exhaustive list. Each company will have to develop its own set of items to address. What is critical is that CIM can only be achieved through a blending together of a wide variety of technologies, procedures, policies, and imaginative leadership.

Appendix A

Resources

Resources

For more information on these and other published resources, contact: Publications Sales, Society of Manufacturing Engineers, One SME Drive, P.O. Box 930, Dearborn, MI 48121, (313) 271-1500, extension 418 or 419.

CAPP: Computer Aided Process Planning, 2nd Edition
Editor: J. Tulkoff
250 pages
1987

This newly updated second edition focuses on how the latest CAPP system applications and integration help improve the interface between product design and the manufacture of the product. A special section on artificial intelligence and expert systems applications is also included. Other sections examine the benefits of computerized process planning, system applications, CAD/CAM integration, and new directions in CAPP.

CIM SERIES BOOKLET

This booklet includes four documents on CIM. Computer Integrated Manufacturing by Richard G. Abraham defines computer-integrated manufacturing and provides a common understanding of what is included in such a system. This book develops a scenario for the factory of the future and the benefits if the recommended approach for phased implementation is followed. Achieving Integrated Automation Through Computer Networks by Nathan A. Chiantella describes how plant automation application concepts can be brought together to achieve communication networks in which all computers within the plant are linked. The individual applications described provide for the automation, optimization, communication and control aspects of plant operations.

Preparing for the Factory of the Future by Dr. Charles M. Savage presents a case study focusing on the technology, societal attitudes, and foreign competition that are reshaping the industrial structure. A hypothetical case describes the challenge of transforming a capital-intensive, industrial-age company into a knowledge-intensive, information-era enterprise. Finally, The CIM Database by Daniel S. Appleton, describes the issues associated with the concept of the Computer-Integrated Manufacturing (CIM) database. It portrays the CIM database from both the user and the technical perspectives. Many technical concepts are addressed.

THE CIM GLOSSARY
Editor: Dr. Thomas V. Sobczak
98 pages
1984

This glossary provides clear explanations of over 3,000 terms relating to CAD, CAM, NC, MRP, CAPP, production control, and more. The book is the result of an exhaustive search through computer-related manufacturing publications. Each term is incorporated into the volume to promote standard meanings and usage of important manufacturing terminology. Every effort was made to include those terms that are most relevant to professionals communicating in the mainstream of rapidly advancing technology.

JOURNAL OF MANUFACTURING SYSTEMS
Quarterly Refereed Research Journal

An explosion in systems technology has brought critical issues to the surface. Published quarterly, The Journal of Manufacturing Systems is devoted entirely to the study of the systems-related topics that are changing the face of manufacturing. Selected papers cover research programs worldwide, delivering intricate details on the most advanced manufacturing systems. A 36 member International Editorial Board carefully selects those papers relevant to current industrial situations--on topics such as: CIM, flexible manufacturing systems, robotics, group technology, sensors, adaptive control, and other vital subjects.

CIM TECHNOLOGY MAGAZINE

CIM Technology is the authoritative editorial voice in the field of computer integrated manufacturing. It provides highly sophisticated technical features and up-to-date coverage of the latest automated technology.

CIM Technology serves manufacturing managers, engineering personnel, and technicians in the metalworking industry who make use of CAD/CAM systems, computers, and related equipment such as microprocessors and flexible automation systems. This includes computerized machines in fabricating and processing, inventory controls, and applications in testing, inspection, quality control, and other automated sequencing operations. CIM Technology goes to the end-user and relates to hardware/software and turnkey systems.

CIMTECH '87 CONFERENCE PROCEEDINGS
150 pages
1987

This new book has 14 technical papers offering new CIM implementation strategies and justification techniques. Topics include an enterprise analysis, software diversification platforms, and standards for factory communications and data exchange.

The CIMTECH papers cover a diverse range of topics. Examples include: "The Simplify-Automate-Integrate Approach to CIM and Competitive Advantages", "Factory Control Using MAP", "Case Study-Generative Process Planning in the Smaller Company", "Simulation Analysis of Asynchronous Material Handling in High Volume Manufacturing Environments," "Computer Integration of CAD/CAE/CAM Using TRW's Data Engine", plus case studies and many other CIM topics.

AUTOFACT '87 CONFERENCE PROCEEDINGS
1,000 pages
1987

This comprehensive proceedings examines the implementation and management aspects of CIM. Containing over 90 technical papers, this one book offers a practical perspective on CIM strategies, examples of successful implementations, ways to overcome implementation problems, just-in-time techniques and CIM justification.

Other topics covered in this set of papers include: CALS (Computer-aided acquisition and logistics support); systems architecture; simulation; configuration management; socio-technical engineering; local area networks; solid modeling; artificial intelligence/expert systems; TOP and office automation; designing flexible control systems; MAP graphic application development; and more.

SME BLUE BOOK SERIES
CIM and Fifth Generation Management (1986): A Roundtable Discussion
CASA/SME Technical Council
10 pages
1987

A selected group of CASA/SME members participated in a roundtable discussion to exchange ideas on their visions of Fifth Generation Management. Topics discussed include: the nature of work; comparisons between the Industrial Era and the Information Era; CIM as it encompasses the total enterprise; reward systems and the combination of databases.

Solid Modeling: Roundtable Summary Document
CASA/SME Technical Council
10 pages
1987

This document summarizes the CASA/SME Technical Council discussion of solid modeling and its key role in the process of computer-integrated manufacturing. The early history of solid modeling and CAD/CAM is also explored. Other topics discussed include: upstream applications of solid modeling; the performance of solid modeling systems; kinematics and robotic applications of solid modeling; data management with respect to the geometric database; standards; benchmarks for a company interested in buying a solid modeling system; and more.

Image Processing Applications In Manufacturing: A Roundtable Discussion
CASA/SME Technical Council
10 pages
1987

This booklet summarizes the viewpoints of a panel of CASA/SME members on image processing applications and tools pertinent to improving productivity and quality in the manufacturing process.

Fifth Generation Management For Fifth Generation Technology
CASA/SME Technical Council
10 pages
1987

This document summarizes the roundtable discussion of CASA/SME members which focuses on defining Fifth Generation Management (FGM) and how it can support the overall integration of manufacturing enterprise management to give it a competitive advantage. It covers the need for a new leadership style and more employee interaction in order to achieve success with FGM. It also takes a look at managers, professionals, and employees who use computer-based resources to enhance their decision making capabilities.

CIM WHITE PAPER
Configuration Management and CIM
CASA/SME Technical Council
24 pages
1987

This paper discusses the goals of CIM and the importance of establishing and maintaining a strong configuration control system to achieve success with automated methods. It also provides insight into the techniques for good configuration management, including the development of software to automate configuration control.

CIM: FOCUS ON SMALL AND MEDIUM SIZE COMPANIES VIDEOTAPE
Length: 30 minutes
1987

This videotape examines how smaller firms stand to benefit from implementing CIM. Case studies illustrate the specific structures, applications, and external factors that need to be integrated for a successful system. The videotape goes on to examine the importance of careful advance planning, how to re-evaluate existing structures, and how to restructure them to fit CIM concepts.

You'll also study two successful examples of CIM implementation at smaller companies: Modern Prototype Division of Modern Engineering Service Company (Warren, Michigan) and Cone Drive Division of Textron Corporation (Traverse City, Michigan).

IMPLEMENTING CIM: A STRATEGIC CHALLENGE VIDEOTAPE
Length: 26 minutes
1987

This 26-minute videotape examines the state of the art as it was presented at the AUTOFACT '86 exposition. It begins with a close-up look at computer-integrated manufacturing and the CIM "wheel". Developed by the Computer and Automated Systems Association of SME (CASA/SME), the CIM wheel depicts integration of the entire manufacturing spectrum from design to assembly through finance and management.

Next, innovations in CAD, CAM, CAE, and other areas are featured to illustrate how islands of automation are linked together into a cohesive unit. It also features new personal computer uses for keeping costs low, for simplifying operations, performing design, analysis, simulation, data collection, and work cell monitoring, and for transmitting to and receiving information from other computers, peripherals, or machining equipment, and more. Also discussed are the latest in hardware and software, sensors, machine vision systems, plotters, optical encoders, and much more.

CAD/CAM, 2ND EDITION
Productivity Equipment Series
631 pages
1985

This book is a convenient and time-saving catalog to the available CAD/CAM manufacturing systems and components. Over 800 companies and products are represented, including their names, addresses, and phone numbers.

Each product description is one or two pages in length and highlights the product's outstanding features, benefits, applications, and specifications. Detailed photos and diagrams are also included to illustrate what the product looks like and how it functions.

The book is conveniently organized into nine sections for easy access to specific facts on products including: computer-aided design and drafting systems; CAD/CAM systems; NC tape prep; software packages; CRT's, workstations, and recording systems; plotters and printers; digitizers; computers; and special CAD/CAM systems.

CAD/CAM INTEGRATION AND INNOVATION
Editor: Dr. Khalil Taraman
460 pages
1985

This compendium of over 25 journal articles, technical papers, and reports brings together information on successful and innovative uses of computers throughout the total manufacturing process.

Beginning with design and geometric modeling and proceeding through the industrial production process, this book contains practical advice from experts on the factory of the future, computerized machine controls, interactive graphics, CIM databases, cost benefit analysis, and much more. Examples of the papers included are: "Computer-Aided Manufacturing: An International Comparison", "Interactive Computer-Graphics CAD/CAM Interfaces to Existing Design and Manufacturing Systems", "Geometric Modeling Based Numerical Control Part Program Verification", "Processing Planning--The Vital Link Between Design and Production, "A Conceptual Schema for a CIM Database", and more.

The book concludes by providing case studies of successful CAD/CAM integration at British Aerospace, Westinghouse, Battelle Columbus Laboratories, IBM, and many others.

NEW DIRECTIONS THROUGH CAD/CAM
By: W. Beeby and P. Collier
230 pages
1986

This informative book includes fundamental knowledge for achieving success with CAD/CAM integration. It discusses how American industry uses CAD/CAM to develop design and manufacturing processes for products in a fraction of the time it takes when manual design methods are used. Concise examples of the CAD/CAM tools, technology, and standards are also included.

The book's nine chapters cover: The Phenomenon of CAD/CAM; The CAD/CAM Tools; Group Technology, The Family of Parts; Setting the Standards; The Design Side of the House; The Right-Hand Side of CAD/CAM; CAD meets CAM; Managing a CAD/CAM Project; and Goals and Directions.

CAD/CAM VIDEOTAPE
Length: 25 minutes
1987

This videotape begins with a brief introduction to computer-aided design and manufacturing (CAD/CAM) benefits and a profile of industry growth.

Then, four case studies featuring successful CAD/CAM installations are examined. First, K2 Skis uses CAD/CAM for ski design and production control. Second, product design and instantaneous prototyping are studied at Flow Systems, Inc. Third, Toro Outdoor Products utilizes CAD/CAM for product designing and CNC control for fast prototype development. Fourth, CAD/CAM reduces the amount of prototyping required between design and production at the Oster Division of Sunbeam Corp.

Five CAD/CAM experts present their views on the state of the art and future application possibilities. Featured experts are Dr. Gordon Kirkpatrick (Flow Systems, Inc.); Rich Thau (MICRO-MRP, Inc.); Dana Lonn (Toro Products Div.); Neal Jeffries (Center for Manufacturing Technology); and Bud Runnels (Autodesk, Inc.). Areas examined for future growth include better hardware and software, integration, and three-dimensional holograms.

CAPABILITIES OF GROUP TECHNOLOGY
Editor: N. L. Hyer
400 pages
1987

This book is the perfect introduction to the time-saving and cost-effective benefits of group technology (GT). It includes 35 documents prepared by industry leaders. Each article, report, and technical paper offers guidance on how to organize and classify part designs and experiences when developing new designs.

Topics covered include: how GT increases your productivity; the relationship of GT and CIM; cost-effective parts coding; GT applications in aircraft manufacturing; implementing GT in a machine shop; productivity techniques for job shops; scheduling GT lines for optimum productivity; the new role of GT in factory automation; and more.

ROBOTS 11/17TH ISIR (INTERNATIONAL SYMPOSIUM ON INDUSTRIAL ROBOTS)
CONFERENCE PROCEEDINGS
1,488 PAGES
1987

With 93 papers and over 1,400 pages of new information, this publication covers systems-based approaches, sensors, manipulators, controls, and off-line programming for improving the productivity of robot applications. Included are examples of robots and robot systems handling assembly, grinding, deburring, sealing and painting, welding, and a variety of other tasks.

The book's 21 sections, cover: remote system applications; aerospace applications; automotive applications; kinematics and mobile robots; special purpose software; manipulator tooling; mechanical assembly; multirobot systems and networking; plus several more. The Robots 11 Conference Proceedings also includes presentations from the 17th ISIR--International Symposium on Industrial Robots.

PERSONAL COMPUTERS IN MANUFACTURING VIDEOTAPE
Length: 28 minutes
1986

Personal computers have revolutionized the business and communications fields, and are rapidly becoming valuable time and money-saving manufacturing tools. The flexibility and compatibility of today's PC systems make various applications possible without costly add-ons or upgrades.

Examine five in-depth case studies of personal computers at work. First, personal computers monitor particleboard thickness and production flow of architectural doors at Weyerhaeuser Company. Next, IBM Corporation uses personal computers to control a sorting machine and an automated storage and retrieval system. At Caere Corporation, personal computers run a manufacturing resources planning system. Personal computers reduced NC programming time and increased design flexibility at GSE, Inc. Finally, Pillsbury Company uses personal computers in the computer-aided design of food cartons.

Presenting their views on the state of the art are Richard Schulte (Manager of Marketing Requirements and Development for the Manufacturing Technology); and Rick Thau (President, Micro-MRP, Inc.). Also covered are integration with mini-computers and mainframes and closed-loop integration with other manufacturing systems.

THE EXPANDING ROLE OF PERSONAL COMPUTERS IN MANUFACTURING
Editor: J. Heaton
220 pages
1986

This book has 35 articles and papers containing details on PC-based applications for testing, automatic systems, maintenance, estimating, operations scheduling, and simulation.

This book offers an overview of how microcomputer applications can be integrated into a CIM system, as well as an example for operations scheduling and simulation. Also featured is the potential of microcomputers to replace dedicated function systems and their cost advantages and flexibility.

SMART MANUFACTURING WITH ARTIFICIAL INTELLIGENCE
Editor: J. Krakauer
275 pages
1987

This book focuses on the promising potential of Artificial Intelligence
(AI). Over 20 recent articles and technical papers offers a better
understanding of AI's role in automation. These papers include AI
applications at work in design, scheduling, and process control, and
explains how AI can help reduce lead times and lengthy calculations.

AI's role in CIM and how AI interfaces with the sophisticated control
requirements or robots, vision systems, and flexible manufacturing systems
is also covered. Smart Manufacturing with Artificial Intelligence can be
used in three ways: as a technology and applications overview; as a
detailed review of today's AI applications; and as an analysis of case
studies.

INTIME MANUFACTURING DATA BANK

Electronic computerized searches of the SME INTIME Manufacturing Data Bank
are now offered through the SME Search Service. The INTIME Manufacturing
Data Bank contains computerized abstracts of every technical paper, book,
and magazine article published by SME from 1974 to the present. In all,
there are over 10,000 records.

A user will be able to find information on any aspect of manufacturing with
INTIME, from broad investigations to more specific studies or applications.
Computer printouts are given with the abstract of each article or paper
related to the subject. The information allows the user to secure the
complete text of the article or paper. Each listing includes the author's
name, affiliation, the page count, and reference number to facilitate
ordering the document. To use the service, simply call SME and ask for
"INTIME". A trained information specialist will work with you to develop a
search strategy that will pinpoint the information you need.

CIM-RELATED ACTIVITIES AT CASA/SME

The Computer and Automated Systems Association of the Society of
Manufacturing Engineers (CASA/SME) was founded in 1975 to provide
comprehensive services to advance computer automation and integration of
manufacturing.

CASA/SME is applications-oriented and addresses the integration of all
phases of research, design, installation, operation and maintenance of the
total manufacturing enterprise. As an educational and scientific
association, CASA/SME has helped engineers and manufacturing managers
worldwide focus on new developments in computer integration and automation.

CASA TECHNICAL COUNCIL AND LEADERSHIP

The CASA/SME Technical Council is an industry-driven, proactive project
management group that provides technical direction for the development of
educational tools.

Automation users, consultants, vendors, academics, and representatives from
the government and laboratories compose the Council--bringing varied
perspectives to the group's activities.

CASA/SME activities are designed to:
1) Provide professionals with a single vehicle to bring together the
   many aspects of manufacturing which utilize computer systems and
   automation.

2) Provide liaison among industrial, governmental, and educational
   organizations to identify areas where computer and automation
   technology development is needed.

3) Encourage the development of the totally integrated manufacturing
   plant.

PUBLICATIONS

More than seven current books on CIM, Computer-Aided Design and Computer-
Aided Manufacturing (CAD/CAM) and other systems-related topics have been
written or edited by CASA/SME members.

CASA/SME is a sponsor of the quarterly scholarly refereed research journal,
the Journal of Manufacturing Systems.

EDUCATIONAL EVENTS

AUTOFACT, the ten-year-old, premier conference and exposition on the
automated factory, is annually held in the Fall--attendance 25,000+.

Over 100 major national and international educational conferences, seminars,
workshops, and in-plant programs each year are sponsored or co-sponsored by
CASA/SME.

THE LEAD AWARDS--"LEADERSHIP AND EXCELLENCE IN THE APPLICATIONS AND DEVELOPMENT OF CIM"

The Industry LEAD Award, sponsored by CASA/SME, is presented each year to a team of technical and management professionals responsible for developing and incorporating an "innovative, leading edge" CIM installation that results in significant productivity gains.

For more information on CASA/SME, write to CASA/SME, Society of Manufacturing Engineers, P.O. Box 930, One SME Drive, Dearborn, Michigan 48121, or call (313) 271-1500, extension 521.

Appendix B

Selected Readings in CIM

A Brief History
of CIM

by Warren L. Shrensker
General Electric Company

INTRODUCTION

The challenges of today--the need to improve productivity, product quality and reliability and reduce costs--cannot be met by just better machines and skilled operators. There must be better managerial tools and integration of the various disciplines to define and produce the products that will allow you to take advantage of existing resources--both machines and operators. The one single tool that can meet those challenges in a cost-effective manner is computer technology.

Computers are not a recent innovation. The first computer, as we know them today, was created around 1946, but a commerically available computer did not enter the marketplace until 1951. In 1954, numerical control (NC) was introduced. Then in 1955, development of the first automatically programmed tool (APT) processor marked the premier of computer-aided manufacturing (CAM), although today CAM encompasses many more manufacturing disciplines. Computer-aided design (CAD) appeared publicly early in the 1960s with high-technology design businesses (auto and aerospace) with design augmented by computers.

In the late 1960s and early 1970s, with the advent of microelectronics, came the minicomputer, and more importantly, the microcomputer--the "computer on a chip." Performance of these systems were excellent, costs continually dropped, and the systems found their way into more manufacturing applications and into computer-aided design products such as interactive graphics In 1974, Dr. Joseph Harrington coined the concept "Computer Integrated Manufacturing" (CIM) in a book he published by the same name. However, it was not until 1981 before the term became widely used. Today, computer-aided design and manufacturing systems, in an on-line, real-time environment, are just beginning to touch the surface of their full capabilities. Computer-aided design has grown in the early 1980s into a new discipline called computer-aided engineering (CAE), which utilizes graphics with powerful analysis programs including solid modeling. This has been joined by a wide range of other computer-aided systems for manufacturing process planning, inventory control, and decision support.

Industrial technologists of the world have forecast that the overall future trend in engineering and manufacturing between now and the year 2000 is toward the development and implementation of the computer-integrated manufacturing. Very significant economic and social incentives are at work to provide the motivation for this to happen. The strategy being followed is to develop and implement a sequence of viable economic steps in a shorter range program to bring about the eventual realization of the overall objectives. These objectives include development and implementation of new optimization technology, including integrated engineering manufacturing databases, group technology, cellular systems, and full manufacturing management systems and their applicable, complex software systems, including the latest development in interactive graphics, computer-aided engineering, computer-based business systems, and office automation--including word processing, electronic mail, teleconferencing, etc.

A major boost to the CAM technologies actually came from the Department of Defense, when in 1975 they started the AFCAM program (Air Force Computer Aided Manufacturing) which was intended to erect a scientific approach to better manufacturing technology. Out of this, in 1976, the ICAM (Integrated Computer Aided Manufacturing) program was born under the direction of the U.S. Air Force's Materials Laboratory and under the guidance of the National Academy of Engineering's Committee on Computer Aided Manufacturing (COCAM). The ICAM Program was dissolved in 1985 and replaced by the U.S. Air Force's CIM Program.

The Computer and Automated Systems Association of the Society of Manufacturing Engineers (CASA) has spearheaded the use of the term computer-integrated-manufacturing (CIM) system developed by Dr. Harrington that provides computer assistance to all business functions from marketing to product shipment. It embraces what historically have been classified as "business systems" applications including order entry, bill of material processing, inventory control, and material requirements planning, design automation, including drafting, design, and simulation; manufacturing planning, including process planning, routing, tool design, and numerical control parts programming; and shop floor applications such as numerical control, assembly automation, testing, and process automation.

A fully integrated CIM system involves the design, development, or application of each of the systems in such a manner that the output of one system serves as the input to another. For example, at the business planning and support level, a customer order servicing system receives input from the sales force relating to descriptions of products to be purchased by prospective customers. The product description serves as a input to the engineering design function. If the product contains previously designed components, a computer-aided design system would output the engineering drawing information to the bill of materials processor and process planning system. If the product description contains new components, the description would serve as input to a computer-aided design system where interactive graphics could be used as a design aid to provide engineering and manufacturing information. Complete inplementation of CIM results in the automation of the information flow in a business organization from entry of an order through every step in the process to shipment of the finished product.

Project Selection
within the CIM Program

by Jerry Kaser
Rockwell International Corporation

OBJECTIVES

The object of an "Integrated System" is to have separate programs perform
separate functions with communication and data passing between the separate
programs. Interfacing is the connecting of one system to another system; in
most cases, of another design. To suggest that a large organization might
have a totally integrated manufacturing management system without interfacing
existing systems is probably not feasible.

Most functional groups or departments within an organization have discovered
that their process can be improved and they can adapt to changes easier when
they utilize some type of computing system. Typically the groups have used
the computers to automate their process and generate reports, drawings and
other documents that fell within the group's responsibilities. When this type
of computing system does not allow for communication with other computer
systems, it becomes known as an "island of automation."

In the early planning stages, every island of automation should be considered.
The questions to be answered are:

- What type of data inputs are required for this system and where do
  those inputs come from?
- What kind of outputs do I get from this system and where do those
  outputs go?
- If the answers to both questions are a single point (me, one group
  or one department) then leave that island alone!

Once it is discovered that it will be necessary to have several systems
talking to each other, then the first project will be to provide the data
links and software necessary to make this possible. The physical link is the
network lines (local area network) that tie the systems together. It is the
local area networks that will coordinate the material and the information
between processes.

When the designated systems have been tied together and communication software
put into place, you will be ready to tackle your CIM structure on a project
basis. It is suggested that projects be kept small and one completed before
another is started. You may want to start with the front end of your business
or you may prefer to start with what you feel is a problem area that will show
the greatest advances.

STRATEGIC BUSINESS PLANS

The strategic business plan will set the stage and put the factory processes into motion. The main drivers are the number of units to be produced, the budgets and delivery dates.

First phase programs that will need to share information might be the following:

- Budgeting.
- Material and scheduling.
- Make or buy.
- Process planning and scheduling.
- Cost estimating.
- Inventory.

These types of programs should draw from and contribute to a common database. A Management Report Program should draw from this database and feedback any top management directions. A complete and comprehensive report should be drawn from the database and sent to all management involved to the downstream processes.

The second phase programs would be the various engineering functions that might employ (among others) the following programs:

- Structural analysis.
- Thermal analysis.
- Aero analysis.
- Vibration analysis.
- Mold flow analysis.
- Environmental analysis.
- Structural design.
- Propulsion and power design.
- Hydraulics design.
- Producibility.

Programs for engineering will probably reside on all kinds of computers from personal computers (pc's) to mainframes. This area will be difficult and should encompass several projects. The engineering processes can have an effect on the activities preliminary to engineering and on the post activities.

Therefore, the integration efforts will require the various disciplines to be reporting to each other and to upstream and downstream management that will be affected by their activities. A common database for all engineering disciplines could become very large and cumbersome. For this reason, a structured group of engineering databases would probably be more easily handled.

Third phase programs will involve manufacturing functions. Manufacturing will need access to the engineering database having part and assembly drawings. Their required programs might be:

- Machining systems (CAD/CAM, APT, Compact II).

- Material status.
- Part status.
- Process status.
- Robotic controls.
- Mechanized system.
- Tool Design systems.
- Sheet Metal systems.
- Template layout systems.
- Inspection systems.

Manufacturing will probably employ everything from pc's to mainframes. Like Engineering, their activities will have an effect on the upstream phases of the operation. Their common database would probably not be as complex as Engineering's but would need to be structured for reporting purposes. The common database would probably be a very comprehensive statusing of the total product.

ORGANIZATION

It might be easier to think of the organizational process in the terms of "puts" and "takes" (See Figure 1).

The first phase will take forecasted information, refine this information, and build a database that reflects their refinements. First phase will then put out reports of their plans, schedules and expectations. First phase will also put out purchase orders. It will then be in a mode to expect feedback from downstream that will alter their database and their course of actions.

The second phase will take reports and plans from the first phase and start an interaction to create their databases. They will put out reports; both upstream and downstream, that will call for changes upstream. They will put out common databases that can be used by first phase and by third phase. The second phase will now be in a receiving mode and expecting feedback.

The third phase will take reports and plans from the first and second phases and databases from the second phase. They will use engineering databases and

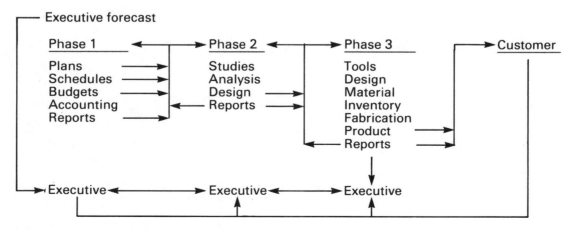

Figure 1. Puts and takes diagram.

create some of their own databases that will be concerned with operating machine tools, robots, and mechanized operations. They will put out reports and product. This group is always in a receiving mode. Third phase activity will call for alterations in first and second phase data.

The key for selection of projects with the greatest paybacks will be to look for programs that perform similar functions (inputs or outputs). You probably will want to keep both (all) programs but may find a shared database or a management report program which will reduce the work effort and make both (all) programs tell the same story. Programs that are mostly into report generating also will be the shortest projects to complete. Programs with analysis or number crunching technologies will be the most difficult to plan and take the longest time for completion.

It is important to remember in the selection of projects that "AS IS" may not be the optimum method. If a better way is in the offing, this will be the time to take advantage of change. An example might be in a shop that is producing NC tapes for machine tools: they should consider distributive numerical control. This will eliminate one step in the process. When all phases are complete, the organizational information system (network) will be of a dynamic nature; thus, supplying direction to all functions as quickly as possible.

All of the functions of a large organization have obviously not been included in this section. The CIM program approach will work for every function within an organization. The intention is to stimulate your thinking about your particular application and how it fits into your organization. Can it be retrofitted to mesh a little better?

What are Companies Spending on CIM and How are They Justifying These Expenditures

by Ralph G. Bennett
Arthur D. Little Incorporated

INTRODUCTION

Industry is spending on CIM at an ever-increasing rate, with current
projections of the overall growth of this market averaging 12% to 15% over the
next five to ten years. (1,2) At individual corporations, CIM investments and
programs are among the largest capital investments and most extensive programs
that they undertake. Companies that are seeking to implement CIM can learn
from the aggregate experiences and trends of those companies already involved
in CIM programs. This overview presents the investments that companies
typically make for CIM, and the accompanying justifications that they develop.
Modifications to the techniques used for justification are then outlined to
make the techniques more effective at evaluating CIM programs.

DISCUSSION

General trends in the amounts that companies are spending on CIM will be
developed from a recent survey of companies involved in CAD/CAM and CAE
implementation, (3) as well as from our experiences with CIM planning. To the
extent possible given the wide variety of companies seeking to implement CIM,
an average profile of relative investments can be developed for the following
categories:

- Planning and System Design.
- Human Resource Development.
- Hardware.
- Software.

Hardware and software are certainly the major share of the CIM investment.
However, planning (and its underlying economic justification) and system
design are a vitally important and a significant portion of the CIM program
cost. In addition, companies are finding that there is a very significant
impact on people and organizations which requires consideration for human
resource development in the CIM program. A current composite profile based on
our experience suggests that companies spend less than 10% of their CIM
investments in planning, system design, and human resource development, about
50% in hardware and installation, and the remaining 40% in software
acquisition and development. The trend is clearly for the software
investments to increase at the expense of hardware investments, as early CIM
implementations have proven software to be more of a consideration than first
anticipated, and as hardware costs come down with improved price/performance.

General trends in the methods used for justification of CIM investments will be similarly developed from the survey. The justifications that support CIM investments are unparalleled in their complexity and numbers of assumptions. They are further complicated by the uncertainty and risks perceived in the programs. Strict adherence to any of the standard financial analysis tools for justification often leads to CIM programs. This may weaken the programs to the point where they fail to produce the strategic benefits that were once within their grasp, or even to where they fail to get underway.

In view of the size and complexity of CIM programs, the underlying economic justification is commonly the most difficult aspect of getting underway with CIM. In performing an economic justification, CIM differs from more traditional capital investments in several important ways:

- CIM benefits are not limited to the initial impact of the equipment. Synergies resulting from the integration of equipment and systems continue to be identified as the program proceeds. These opportunities arise not because of insufficient planning up front, but because of the inherent flexibility of the software which allows a more dynamic response to changing competitive situations.
- CIM costs can decrease with time due to the upward compatibility in the hardware as well as its rapidly improving price/performance reducing the cost of hardware installed at later stages in the program. CIM benefits can increase due to the optimization of system software performance during its life.
- The greatly leveraged flexibility of the manufacturing facility impacts the way that the company does business with its customers and suppliers.
- CIM increases the effectiveness of communications and thereby decreases the time scales with which the company responds to new opportunities and problems.
- CIM affects the people in the organization, and requires new skills, attitudes, and measurements. This requires that management anticipate human resource development, and organizational changes at a very early stage in the program.

Traditional methods for investment analysis include payback period, average rate of return, internal rate of return, and net present value methods, with many variations on this basic set. (4) These can be viewed against a broad historical backdrop of steadily increasing use of Discounted Cash Flow (DCF) methods (e.g., net present value and internal rate of return) and a steadily decreasing use of nondiscounted methods (e.g., payback period and average rate of return). (5) This has happened because of the recognition of the inherent value of discounting cash flows to judge them on a more even basis. Still, the DCF methods are known to suffer from a variety of problems that have been identified over the past few years, with many authors presenting valuable improvements in the way that they should be applied. (6, 7, 8, 9)

Despite this popular trend, CIM program justifications based on these more "correct" DCF methods are too often based on assumptions that neglect the major differences in CIM investments previously outlined. Improvements to the DCF methods can be identified that considerably enhance their application to CIM investment analysis. The major area of improvement is that consideration be given to all of the costs and benefits of the CIM program. This consists of making comprehensive and sufficiently long-term cost estimates, facility investment estimates, and revenue estimates. This may very well mean that a hypothetical value has to be attached to a given qualitative benefit.

An equally important problem is the fact that these methods are often applied to CIM equipment on a case by case basis, which focuses much too narrowly on machine productivity as the basis for justification. A revision is needed in the way that companies approach CIM investments that focuses on the program's relationship to the company's competitive position. (10,11) This requires that the results of the justification be looked at in the broader strategic perspective: CIM programs should not be judged in competition with other less strategically important projects, even though the latter may yield higher returns. When integrated into a broad, consistent and long-term view of the CIM program as a basis to achieve competitive advantage, DCF analyses that are improved in the above ways become a solid foundation for program justification.

REFERENCES

1. The Computer Integrated Manufacturing Market in the United States: 1982-1992, Cambridge, MA, Arthur D. Little, Inc., 1983, p. E-5.

2. "Factory 2000," Iron Age, June, 1984, p. 6.

3. CAD and CAE--The Current and Future Practice, Cambridge, MA, Arthur D. Little, Inc., to be published May, 1985.

4. Granof, M., Accounting for Managers and Investors, Englewood Cliffs, NJ, Prentice Hall, Inc., 1983, Chap. 21.

5. Klammer, T., "Empirical Evidence of the Adoption of Sophisticated Capital Budgeting Techniques," Journal of Business, July, 1972, pp. 387-397.

6. Harrington, D., "Present Value Methods," Colgate Darden Graduate School of Business Administration Note, 1979.

7. Hayes, R., and Garvin, D., "Managing as if Tomorrow Mattered," Harvard Business Review, May-June, 1982, pp. 71-79.

8. Hayes, R., and Wheelwright, S., Restoring our Competitive Edge, New York, John Wiley & Sons, 1984, pp. 142-143.

9. Hodder, J., and Riggs, H., "Pitfalls in Evaluating Risky Investments," Harvard Business Review, January-February, 1985, pp. 128-135.

10. Magaziner, I., and Reich, R., Minding America's Business, New York, John Wiley & Sons, 1984, pp. 142-143.

11. Hayes, R., and Wheelwright, S., Op. cit., pp. 329-330.

Cost Justification and New Technology Addressing Management's "NO!" To the Funding of CIM

by Madden T. Works
Aerojet Electro Systems

INTRODUCTION

However clear the need for Computer-Integrated Manufacturing (CIM), its value is generally not accepted by those in the corporate hierarchy who have the power to say "NO." The equipment is expensive. CIM changes the way people are used to doing things.

Management's seemingly reflexive "no" is understandable. Their expectations usually have been set by direct experience with previous information system failures. Often they are scarred survivors of the rough adolescence of data processing as it evolved from a catalyst for failure into the religion of the database. After all, says management, they're not virgins.

Early attempts at implementing computer-dependent MRP systems were generally not successful. Even today, the failure rate of computerized systems (MRPII, business information systems, CAD/CAM, management analysis systems) has been estimated to be as high as 75% by the American Production & Inventory Control Society (APICS), the Organization for Industrial Research (OIR) and others. According to the Institute of Industrial Engineers (Figure 1) such productivity programs prove ineffective 30% to 45% of the time. With historical failure rates ranging from 30%-75%, most bankers will rate any "new-tech" proposal as "risky" at best.

This no-win record would induce battle fatigue and a strong avoidance reflex in Godzilla. Is it any wonder that a new data system proposal faces significant resistance?

- Formal employee involvement in productivity improvement planning and evaluation; 37% of events judged ineffective.
- Introduction or improvement of quality control/methods; 27% of events judged ineffective.
- Introduction or improvement of inventory control methods; 29% ineffective (others say 70%, above).
- Evaluating performance and establishing specific productivity improvement targets; 33% ineffective.
- More worker training to improve product/service quality; 26.5% events judged ineffective.
- Systems innovations; 29% events ineffective.
- Development of indirect labor standards and control; 46% events ineffective.

Figure 1. Effectiveness of productivity programs. (1)

ACQUIRING CIM

To acquire CIM capability the incremental capital expenditures (costs) must be realistically weighed against the benefits that are expected to result from implementing CIM. Unfortunately these benefits usually are not fully appreciated until they have been delivered. It's like explaining the taste of ice cream or the sound of music to someone who has no experience with either. It is similarly difficult to explain that the payouts are cumulative and that a period of time must pass after installation before the potential of CIM can be achieved.

Calculated cost justifications are a waste of time unless the program includes a solid commitment by everyone involved. In an effective and successful request to purchase CIM technology, both the requestor and management must have empathy for CIM's payoff benefits.

Seriously consider abandoning the project if the request to purchase has to go through traditional justification procedures. New computer systems--unlike straight "business" data processing systems--elicit a narrowly focused cost justification syndrome in those who control the company's purse. They don't want to kill enthusiasm, just inhibit it.

Since justification for the cost of today's new manufacturing technology comes from nontraditional sources, attempts to provide cost justification in terms of ROI/payout will fail. By definition, the benefits of any emerging technology are not yet solidified. The outlaw Jesse James supposedly once said, "Carts didn't even have wheels until somebody thought of it."

Likewise, no standard valuation of CIM benefits has emerged. Implementation tactics are as fresh and young as their simple tally. Because the specific benefits of CIM are still hard to list, (much less to rank or quantify), the reflexive question the company's financial officer will ask is: "How will this CIM save money? All I am shown are capital expenditures...what are the specific costs which will be either reduced or avoided?"

While it may be clear to some in management that a failure to integrate computing into manufacturing will threaten the company's survival, even that warning is ineffective. They've heard the cry of "WOLF!" before. Why should they react this time?

Enlightened management knows that cost justification rests on two key factors: (2)

1. Traditional cost benefits. These are direct (objective) quantitative, financial payoffs to the company.
2. Nontraditional noncost benefits. These are payoffs which are indirect (subjective), qualitative and personal to CIM user groups.

If the value of both direct and indirect CIM benefits justifies the cost of acquiring CIM technology, then it is easier to justify the capital expenditures. Obtaining budget approval is an early roadblock to most CIM proposals. Adequate justification must be provided if approval to proceed is to be received.

So what is the value of the benefits which may accrue from CIM implementation? Since the vague promise of "increased productivity" resulting from successful CIM implementation may not be justification enough for your company, other nontraditional (noncost) benefits need to be clearly presented as well.

CIM BENEFITS

The following figures present benefits of some of the various aspects of CIM. Figure 2 discusses the benefits of computer-aided design (CAD). The benefits of computer-aided process planning (CAPP) are reviewed in Figure 3. The advantages of group technology (GT) are listed in Figure 4.

There are two types of manufacturing planning and control systems: quantitative and qualitative. Benefits of both are outlined in Figure 5. In Figure 6, two aspects of computer-aided manufacturing (CAM) are discussed. They are numerical control (NC) and flexible manufacturing systems (FMS). Finally, Figure 7 lists the high points of industrial robot application.

> Enables productivity gains of 3:1 or 4:1.
> Increased product quality.
> Reduces new product design leadtime.
> Eliminates prototypes.
> Reduces paperwork load.
> Allows examination of dynamics and kinematics.
> Highlight in color complex designs and assemblies.
> Allows myriad views of parts.
> Provides a valid geometric part description for easy access via CRT from database.

Figure 2. Benefits of computer-aided design. (Source: Arthur D. Little, Inc.)

> Reduces new part introduction cost.
> Standardizes routings.
> Utilizes more optimal processes.
> Reduces need for process engineers.

Figure 3. Benefits of CAPP, (Source: Arthur D. Little, Inc.)

> Reduces new product design leadtime.
> Reduces new part introduction cost.
> Increases capacity utilization.
> Reduces setup time.
> Reduces scrap.
> Rationalizes and reduces the number of parts in database.

Figure 4. Benefits of Group Technology (Source: Arthur D. Little, Inc.)

QUANTITATIVE

Reduces inventory levels by up to 33%.
Increases customer service.
Reduces purchased parts cost by up to 6%.
Reduces overtime by up to 50%.
Increases labor productivity by up to 10%.

QUALITATIVE

Improves customer relations due to ability to react quickly to changing market conditions.
Provides a company game plan with no "hidden numbers."
Increases teamwork between company functions.
Increases workforce and management morale.
Allows foremen to be managers, not expediters.
Allows buyers to become purchasing managers, not expediters.
Reduces scrap and rework.
Allows better planning.

Figure 5. Benefits of manufacturing planning and control systems. (Source: Arthur D. Little, Inc.)

NUMERICALLY CONTROLLED MACHINE TOOLS

Enables 3:1 productivity gains.
Increases product quality.
Reduces scrap and rework.
Reduces operator skill requirements.
Reduces overall setup time.
Allows higher machine utilization through off-line programming.

FLEXIBLE MANUFACTURING SYSTEMS

Improves productivity due to unmanned operation capability.
Increases product quality.
Reduces scrap and rework.
Increases production flexibility.
Increases machinery utilization.
Reduces production floor space requirements.

Figure 6. Benefits of computer-aided manufacturing. (Source: Arthur D. Little, Inc.)

Increases productivity.
Increases product quality.
Increases flexibility with respect to hard automation because of reprogrammability.
Increases reliability of "workforce."
Reduces production floor space requirements.
Substitutes for humans in hazardous, monotonous, or drudgery-laden work.

Figure 7. Benefits of robotics. (Source: Arthur D. Little, Inc.)

Both direct and indirect cost benefits must be considered and listed if the total potential of CIM is to be realized. Following is a discussion of some

specific objective (direct) and subjective (indirect) benefits to help justify
CIM in a company (Figure 8).

1. Traditional direct cost benefits.
2. Product quality benefits; less rework.
3. Shorter project span times; fewer hours per unit shipped; on-time delivery.
4. Integrated database; lower paperwork burden; good communication.
5. A risk reduction strategy for the future.
6. Undocumented, unexplainable cost reductions; personal payoffs to users.

Figure 8. Direct and indirect benefits of CIM.

Direct Cost Benefits

The normal approach to justifying capital expenditures includes both pay-out
and return on money invested (ROI). As Daniel S. Appleton has noted in his
discussion of financial considerations in achieving CIM:

"The traditional financing strategy for automation is a
"bootstrapping" concept. Dollars are spent on islands of automation
from departmental budgets. However, there is rarely any significant
money invested in building assets which are to be shared. Capital
is spent on fixed assets, i.e. hardware systems, software and
communications.

"CIM financing strategies make capital investments in shared,
value-added assets such as databases. These assets cannot be
bought; they must be built. Unlike current strategies, CIM
financial strategies do not allow common assets to be bootstrapped.
These assets are "owned" by the enterprise, not an individual user
group. Nonshared resources are locally funded, but much money is
spent on the care and feeding of highly valuable shared enterprise
assets." (3)

Unfortunately, "bootstrapping" traditional cost savings is still the standard
approach in many companies. It is not the best approach, but it is one that
corporate management and finance people understand. Management focuses on
acquiring hard data that unequivocally proves the value of a proposed
expenditure. The fact that such proof is desirable does not mean that the
proof is available.

Accurate data is expensive to acquire. Controlled research proof-tests which
compare conventional techniques to CIM techniques are difficult to set up and
even more difficult to analyze against background "noise." When controlled
tests are conducted, they often cannot meet rigorous verification and strict
application of the scientific method. Thus they are very costly and often
inconclusive.

Adroit number manipulation can become a two-edged sword in supporting or not
supporting a conclusion. Such research is especially unstable in times of
flux and change. Immediate production needs may change the priorities,

conditions, and motivations for the research efforts. Even the measurement of job time is not simple.

Nevertheless, agreement about levels of productivity gain through use of CIM elements has emerged. CAD/CAM, FMS, JIT, MRPII, shared data resources and automated data collection all produce a high-confidence level in the favorable comparison of productivity gains between CIM and non-CIM systems.

For example, Chansen and Dow (4) describe several specific benefits for CAD, and L. Harmon, formerly of Lockheed-CADAM (5), has developed specific benefit/value numbers for CIM. General Electric, IBM, and others have documented impressive gains through CIM, and list CIM benefits. (6)

But even "hard" numbers can be dismissed by corporate sharpshooters with remarks like "...Yeah, but we're different from them... We have unique problems...real problems..."

Product Quality

Using CIM, potential fit and function problems in the actions and interactions of the manufactured part, its tooling and assembly procedures can be successfully investigated sooner and remedial action taken earlier.

The resulting data has significant value for statistical quality control. The end-product is more easily produced and is less costly to make. Customers get a better product. CIM makes it easier to investigate those "special" manufacturing headaches and develop tooling alternatives before production problems actually occur on the shop floor. (7)

The fact that a CIM system improves reliability and producibility contributes to the justification of CIM costs. Can your manufacturing division put an economic evaluation on improved production? To paraphrase Dow: "The loss of a critical flight assembly in manufacturing is a rare event, but the tangible cost of such a failure is enormous and the intangible costs are extensive and immeasurable."

These concepts should be factored into any benefits analysis for CIM. The shop foreman can provide suitably graphic examples.

If the product is manufactured to strict design tolerances, CIM will lessen the probability of a tolerance or "fit" problem. CIM can significantly reduce both defects and rework with resulting cost savings and cost avoidance.

Shorter Project Span Times

Manufacturing time equates to money--big money. Shorter elapsed time for a task is a sound basis for avoiding overhead expense and increasing productivity.

Don't overlook the potential for CIM on "short" projects either. Short project span times and long problem-solution times characterize many CIM applications. In manufacturing engineering there are many one-time applications in which the total span time of a project and the selected solution technique are critical considerations. CIM allows short span times with no attendant loss of solution time. Indeed, CIM broadens the tactical arsenal for providing timely solutions.

Many manufacturing needs or problems cannot be anticipated in advance. These are "Unk-Unk's" (unknown-unknowables) that are recognized when it is already too late to acquire the technology to resolve them. The ability to respond and correct these "special" problems within available time is a strong justification for CIM. Discovering and resolving "Unk-Unk's" before it is too late has obvious value but is difficult to quantify.

Simply put, CIM can help you avoid Murphy's Law: "That which can go wrong, will; at the worst possible moment."

Integrated Database, Reducing Redundancy, Less Paper To Push

For most manufacturing companies, CIM represents a distinctive facet of high-level automation. In an integrated database environment, a great deal of descriptive data and documentation resides within the computer's memory for access, update, change, same-as use and design feedback.

Typically, the engineering drawings require considerable data manipulation. Once the data for an application has been input to the CAD system, they can be retrieved selectively by attributes, by drawing section, by "windows", by overlays or layers (each containing certain classes of information,) or by a host of other options.

The ability of Manufacturing Engineering, Quality, Test, Inspection, and Production to transform design drawings, portions of drawings, notes or parts lists automatically has great value. Redundant data-entry is avoided, accuracy is improved, the as-designed-and-built products conform to space, costs are reduced for similar follow-on work, old problems are solved and not reinvented anew, and subsequent users act as data quality "checkers" so that mistakes are corrected permanently in all user areas.

Even when the drawing has little benefit in itself, use of the descriptive CAD data for that drawing in follow-on manufacturing activity (CAM) can be immense. In the manufacture of hybrid computer chips, for example, a microscopic area can be "zoomed" and enlarged for a better assembly aid than hand-drawn sketches.

Users of the CIM database may extract from the database exactly the data that are relevant--no more, no less. Tedious entry and reentry of the bill of material by successive users, with the possibility of perpetuating errors, is specifically avoided.

In a non-CIM system the same data is output and input many times to satisfy user needs which appear to be distinct but which actually have elements in common--properties that lend themselves to productive interfacing and integration.

The improved communication link between Engineering and Manufacturing means that engineering designs can indeed be manufactured--a rare event in conventional nonintegrated manufacturing.

CIM--Risk Reducing Strategy for the Future

Industry leaders and the Department of Defense agree that integrating computer technology and manufacturing is not optional for a company that intends to remain in business. If your company's objective is to prevail over both foreign and domestic competitors, CIM is the strategy of choice.

There are many critical problems of corporate survival that can only be solved by the implementation of CIM. CIM permits the adoption of improved manufacturing techniques before production starts. Time proven shop methods can be automated, frequently with only slight adaptation during preproduction activity. CIM permits immediate access to the design drawings. Different users can download drawings and change scale to meet a specific need for detail (or lack of detail).

Part definition can be optimized, working off a local workstation to adjust tool or cutter path for numerical control. This is considerably preferable to ruining parts to reach the same end.

Correct fit and mating of parts in assembly is another essential requirement which is assured using CIM. Reducing risk in transitioning from product development to production is likewise assured. (8) The existence and proof of the extent of clearances is clearly established before production ever begins. Henry Ford would be proud of us.

Unexplainable Cost Reductions

Enhancements to the quality of work life fostered by CIM installation and implementation are benefits which are often overlooked.

There are many manufacturing tasks that are boring, repetitive, unrewarding and tedious. These same characteristics identify areas of a job that will benefit from CIM. It is these tasks that are well-suited to computer-integrated assistance.

New federal laws for two-way part traceability and the data requirements of MRPII, serial numbers, lot coding, and just-in-time inventory requirements all conflict with the ideal of a paperless factory. The U.S. Air Force has characterized excessive paperwork as "our biggest problem."

Instead of expediting the production process, paperwork robs workers of time which is better spent on actual "touch" production. CIM provides relief.

An example of an elementary and simple CIM application offering easy rewards is the use of optical scanners for data collection. Many companies are using bar codes on their parts to accomplish this. Even greater benefits will accrue from bar coding the shop paper which accompanies each part on its trek across the factory. Data collected at each workstation along the way provides work-in-process status (WIP) quickly and with near-perfect accuracy. Integrating this information throughout the entire plant, including receiving, inspection and purchasing lowers costs, increases speed, improves accuracy and helps eliminate boredom for people responsible for these tasks.

CONCLUSION

In conclusion, if management understands both the short-term problems and the long-term potential of CIM and agrees that CIM cost justification is both objective (traditional) and subjective (nontraditional), the case for CIM will not fall on deaf ears.

Overcoming the corporate "NO!" is a matter of setting management's expectations so that even if they don't understand your vision, they at least invest in it.--Pat Works

REFERENCES

(1) Institute of Industrial Engineers productivity survey of members, "Keeping Current-Operations," Production Engineering. Cleveland, Ohio: Penton IPC Publishing, March 2, 1985.

(2) "On Communications," Computer World. Farmingham, Massachusetts: CW Communications, Inc., November 1984.

(3) Appleton, D.S., "Building a CIM Program," A Program Guide For CIM Implementation. Dearborn, Michigan: The Computer and Automated Systems Association of SME, 1985.

(4) Chansen, S.H. and Dow, S.W., "Task 140 Preliminary Cost-benefit Analysis," The Guide for the Evaluation and Implementation of CAD/CAM Systems. Atlantic: CAD/CAM Decisions, 1981.

(5) Thompson, H., "Computer Aided Planning," The Aerospace Engineering Conference and Show, Education Session. New York: American Institute of Aeronautics and Astronautics Inc., 1985.

(6) Various papers. CIMCOM-85. Dearborn, Michigan: The Computer and Automated Systems Association of SME, 1985.

(7) Harrington, J. "Can I Justify the Cost?," Computer Integrated Manufacturing. Malabar, Florida: Robert E. Krieger Publishing Company, 1979.

(8) No author, "Transition from Development to Production," Dept. of Defense Directive number 4245.7, Jan. 19, 1984.

Guidelines for Developing a Cost-benefit Analysis for CIM Investments

by William T. Muir
Price Waterhouse

INTRODUCTION

The implementation of advanced computer integrated manufacturing technologies has often been hindered by antiquated cost analysis (capital equipment investment analysis) processes which emphasize only direct labor savings. The reality of advanced manufacturing technologies is that cost-behavior patterns are shifted to a lower percentage of direct labor and a higher percentage of other "value added" costs (i.e. overhead).

Cost-Benefit Analysis is the analytical process which assists in (1) identifying those operational areas where the introduction of enhanced manufacturing technology will have the greatest financial impact, (2) evaluating the project economics of potential improvement projects, (3) preparing an analysis of and plan to manage project risk and (4) identifying cost-benefit tracking requirements so that the planning/control loop can be closed to monitor if benefits are actually realized.

Cost-Benefit Tracking is the continual determination of the actual level of project investment and associated recurring costs and savings. This information is compared to what was planned during the cost-benefit analysis phase and, subsequently, to current estimates based on any changed circumstances.

COST-BENEFIT ANALYSIS

Cost-benefit analysis uses financial expense information, engineering standards and/or production estimates which have been collected on a manufacturing function basis. Based on this information, proposed capital investment projects are then analyzed according to their productivity improvement potential, economics and implementation risks, and on a manufacturing function basis.

The following guidelines have been prepared to aid the execution of the cost-benefit process. The guidelines cover the topics of:

1. defining manufacturing functions (activities),
2. AS IS cost baselines preparation,
3. AS IS performance baseline preparation,
4. improvement project prioritization ("needs matrix"),
5. selecting improvement technologies,

6. TO BE cost baseline preparation,
7. assessing intangible factors and risk,
8. assessing integration ("islands of technology"), and
9. time-phased economics.

Guideline Number One

Structure factory modernization cost-benefit analysis on a manufacturing function (top down) basis.

Most formal manufacturing management improvement programs support the use of a "top-down" manufacturing activity identification approach that uses a Node structure. These approaches are designed to identify both the manufacturing functions currently performed (AS IS) or proposed (TO BE).

Guideline Number Two

Identify and analyze all significant costs incurred by each manufacturing function. (Prepare an AS IS cost baseline.)

Develop a cost classification model, suitable for both the facility and each manufacturing function, which identifies all significant manufacturing value-added costs. This cost model should be structured using costs that can be easily identified with the Critical Success Factors of production. At a minimum, manufacturing technology improvement projects should analyze the following high-level cost groupings:

    Manufacturing function
       (process) cost   = Direct production labor
                                    + Indirect labor
                                    + Material utilization (scrap)
                                    + Material logistics (handling)
                                    + Operations support
                                    + Information systems
                                    + Engineering support
                                    + Equipment amortization
                                      (including tooling)
                                    + Plant and facilities amortization
                                    + G&A support
                                    + Inventory financing

The AS IS cost baselines of improvement projects, based on a cost classification process similar to the above, are used to describe the predicted impact of an improvement technology of the costs of production. It is important that the assumptions and definitions underlying the cost-baseline (both AS IS and TO BE) be explicitly stated and documented.

Guideline Number Three

Measure the efficiency and effectiveness of each manufacturing function. (Prepare an AS IS performance baseline.)

Each synergistically related group of nodes (Function Group) identified in the "top down" model should be analyzed to determine how efficiently/effectively (relative to current company and/or accepted industry standards) it is being executed. The analysis should emphasize the quantification of problems, diagnose their causes and provide benchmarks against which to measure improvements. Some of the measures (Critical Success Factors) which could be used, other than cost, might include:

- Throughput time.
- Machine utilization.
- Labor utilization.
- Schedule adherence.
- Scrap and/or rework.
- Capacity utilization.

Guideline Number Four

Develop a "needs matrix" to prioritize identified improvement projects.

The identification of high-cost and low-performance Function Groups can be facilitated by developing a matrix of the manufacturing functions, their associated Critical Success Factors, the current efficiency/effectiveness of the function relative to its Critical Success Factors, and its cost.

Guideline Number Five

Evaluate the alternatives for improving the productivity of the Function Groups. Select those alternatives which offer the highest probability of attaining their potential with the highest potential payback.

Once the Function Groups having the greatest cost-reduction potential have been identified, all the available alternatives (within reason) for reducing costs within that Function Group should be identified. Those technologies which, on the basis of their implementation history or technological promise, seem to offer the greatest potential are selected for further investigation.

Guideline Number Six

Determine a TO BE cost baseline for each alternative.

Using a cost-model approach such as that suggested by Guideline Number Two, determine the cost-behavior patterns (AS IS and TO BE) for each productivity improvement alternative being investigated. By using an analytical tool, such as the model described, there is greater assurance that all costs will be analyzed and the cost reduction will actually be attained, not just cost relocation.

Guideline Number Seven

Analyze the impact of intangibles (such as implementation risk, inflation, human factors, and legislative trends) to the extent that they can be quantified.

Each improvement project must be assessed to determine the risk of not achieving the anticipated results, whether due to intangibles, economic conditions or fate. The important point is to recognize most of the environmental factors which will come to bear on the project(s) and:

- Identify the most significant risk factors for each which would result in not achieving the anticipated savings. By performing an elementary sensitivity analysis, a "best case/worst case" condition can be identified.
- Calculate the "worst case" project cost savings for the project.
- Assess the technological risk for each.
- Identify a risk-management plan that would increase the probability of success by focusing project management attention on the identified risk factors. (Do not necessarily give up the project if the "worst case" is not acceptable--improve project management first.)

Guideline Number Eight

Determine the impact of the integration of a single improvement project with others being considered.

The cost-benefit analysis process should quantify (to the extent possible) the synergistic impact of all projects to determine their effect on total manufacturing cost. This can best be accomplished through the use of the Function Group approach which has been previously described.

Guideline Number Nine

Determine the time-phased economics of each of the selected improvement projects.

Cost-benefit analysis should provide management with several levels of economic analysis, including:

- annualized savings (over the planning horizon),
- ROI,
- payback,
- cost impact on: fixed cost, variable cost (per unit), and nonrecurring cost,
- Risk-adjusted savings.

COST BENEFIT TRACKING

The goal of benefits tracking is to measure the actual impact of advanced manufacturing technologies on total manufacturing cost and related performance measurements; and compare this data to the TO BE cost as forecasted by the cost-benefit analysis, adjusting for mix and volume differences. Benefits tracking should be developed from the same database used to report financial results, but must go beyond these minimums and address significant indirect costs.

Current benefits-tracking and cost-accounting procedures are based on traditional accounting practices. This tradition states that manufacturing cost data should be collected by product production work order for direct labor and direct materials, and that all other costs should be collected in aggregate and allocated to product on a quantifiable basis (typically direct labor). This approach was developed for a manufacturing environment where direct labor was the dominant portion of "valued added" manufacturing cost and where the direct laborer controlled the pace of the manufacturing process.

In a CIM environment, however, these practices are no longer universally appropriate. The proposed factory of the future will contain less direct labor costs than those being experienced in the factory of today. This future environment dictates a revised approach to measuring the benefits attained from implementing advanced manufacturing technologies.

Guideline Number One

Monitor those costs and performance measures which have been identified as critical by the cost-benefit analysis.

Develop a benefits-tracking plan at the conclusion of the cost-benefit analysis process. The plan should identify the:

- information required to monitor the Critical Success Factors,
- source of the "Actual" production data to be compared to the TO BE cost baseline.

As advanced manufacturing technology is incorporated into a manufacturing process, the type of information available from the process will change. The information required for the cost-benefit tracking of the advanced technology should be evaluated relative to the information that is potentially available from the new process and from the financial reporting system.

Guideline Number Two

Ensure that cost and performance measures are compatible with all internal and external reporting requirements, including generally accepted accounting principles and cost-accounting standards.

The benefits-tracking system should be structured to provide information from the common database that is being used to satisfy other compliance reporting requirements. One method of ensuring this congruence is to develop a matrix of benefits-tracking, operational management and financial-reporting requirements. Any data not currently being reported should be evaluated to determine whether it is in variance with good management objectives.

Guideline Number Three

The data provided by the benefits-tracking process must be verifiable and auditable.

Document all sources of information which were previously identified in the cost-benefit tracking plan, including report number (by date), person or document number. Each assumption should be explained in detail with supporting documentation where appropriate.

Guideline Number Four

Cost-benefit projections should be tracked for a sufficient time to determine whether actual savings have been achieved.

Since most cost-management systems are not structured on the same basis as a company's capital-investment process, an ongoing tracking of savings can best be achieved either by modifying the existing cost-management system, developing a dual system or performing a periodic review of the project results. The decision whether to restructure the cost-management system should be made relative to the perceived use of the information within the management decision-making process and the cost of modifying the system. Even if the decision is made to restructure the cost-management system, the change should be evolutionary and integrated into the corporate strategic factory modernization plan.

If the decision is made to not modify the current cost-management system, periodic industrial engineering studies could be used to validate savings. In this case, the benefits-tracking plan should include the timing and scope of the audits and the procedures used for verification of the results.

Economic Analysis Study and Case Example

by Mark H. Stern
IBM

INTRODUCTION

All manufacturing investments need to be justified on either financial or strategic grounds to obtain the necessary funding. A problem has arisen in recent years, however, in that the tremendous advances in manufacturing technologies and software solutions have not been met with equal advances in the techniques of justification. Return on Investment (ROI) calculations continue to be oriented towards pieces of equipment, not systems, and towards number crunching, not number development. This can result in situations where sound projects are not approved, and where projects which do not offer the highest return are accepted. The reason for this is that many of the benefits of the solutions such as flexible automation and integrated control systems are not made evident by the traditional justification techniques.

BACKGROUND

The IBM Computer Integrated Manufacturing Systems (CIMS) group, located in Boca Raton, Florida, provides manufacturing consulting services to IBM locations throughout the world. CIMS is a part of IBM's Industrial Systems Organization. CIMS is a part of IBM's Industrial Systems Organization headquartered in Milford, Connecticut. A recent project which CIMS undertook was the analysis of the requirements for a line to manufacture a subassembly found in many IBM products. At the time, this part was being sourced from a foreign manufacturer. The analysis of this case project included an investigation of the material handling and production equipment, as well as a simulation of the proposed solution. In addition, CIMS provided a justification analysis for the capital investment, which was projected to cost over $30 million. The economic analysis favorably compared this investment and the ongoing costs of the operation against the costs of obtaining the subassembly from the alternative source.

CIMS applied to that project an economic analysis package which had been developed under the auspices of the IBM Corporate Manufacturing Staff. This package was the result of a study of the internal issues concerning the justification of automation. These issues are quite applicable to CIM teams in the manufacturing community as a whole. The study concluded that whereas a predominant concern is the acquisition and use of justification software programs, tools such as those are only a part of the overall return on investment problem which CIM teams face. What is acutely necessary is increased education as to the sources of value in CIM proposals and better understandings of the economic models which are being created.

The development of good alternative solutions and an understanding of the assumptions inherent in the concepts being proposed is crucial. For example, an alternative which proposes a flexible manufacturing line could consist of a certain configuration of robots and a material handling system which is quite adequate for today's products. That configuration also makes implicit assumption, however, about the size, weight, and number of parts contained in future products. In addition, the line will be set up for a particular approach to handling product features, model mixes, and volumes. Determining the long-term fit of these assumptions to development and marketing strategies is critical.

ANALYSIS

The first part of the analysis of the subassembly project centered around coming up with alternatives and did not go into economic details of the decisions which had to be made. In every CIM analysis, it is first necessary to determine a set of requirements which must be satisfied: how many, how soon, what color, what design, etc. From this, a generalized definition for the process must be formed. As with any flexible manufacturing system, the goal is to separate the process from the product; as new products come along they should be implemented on existing process equipment.

This generalized process definition need only take the form of block diagrams, such as storage, assembly of type X components, assembly of type Y components, test, final assembly, and packaging. This then enables the CIM team to develop assumptions and constraints about the process as a whole. An example of assumptions which are implicitly a part of the process definition stage can be seen in a recent experience of one of the automotive firms.

This firm was operating a warehouse which supplied parts to an assembly plant. The warehouse was a traditional operation in that most of the material movement was very labor-intensive. After some study, it was decided that the warehouse would be replaced by another, more automated facility. The new warehouse did in fact achieve many of the operating cost savings which had been predicted, and promised an acceptable return on the investment. A few years afterwards, however, the firm became quite involved with just in time (JIT) production management, and wanted to apply JIT techniques to the parts operation. They then realized that the warehouse investment was based on the assumption that what was needed was a way to store parts efficiently. That investment, however, could not be used for JIT. If they had posed a different question to begin with, such as how to deliver parts efficiently to the floor, they would have analyzed a different set of alternatives. This could have included not only the automated warehouse alternative, but the JIT solution too. Answering questions based on incorrect questions and assumptions can suboptimize the solutions.

In the subassembly project the main business choices had to do with the sourcing alternatives. Choices between types of equipment were mostly made for engineering and manufacturing reasons rather than on cost alone. In terms of the product requirements, there were a number of subassembly models which were manufactured at the same time. In addition, these models were occasionally replaced, and new models were added every year. This created the necessity for a high degree of flexibility in the potential solutions.

With regard to the process requirements, change in the engineering technology was expected to occur in the next five to 10 years. This change would require the introduction of new types of assembly machines to satisfy the demand for models utilizing this technology. The financial impact of this had to be evaluated. The volumes for the subassembly were not well-known, and it was necessary to ensure that all demand levels could be satisfied. These process assumptions and constraints led to the formation of three alternatives: continue to purchase the subassembly overseas, manufacture the part within IBM, or purchase the item from a U.S. vendor. These alternatives are diagrammed in Figure 1.

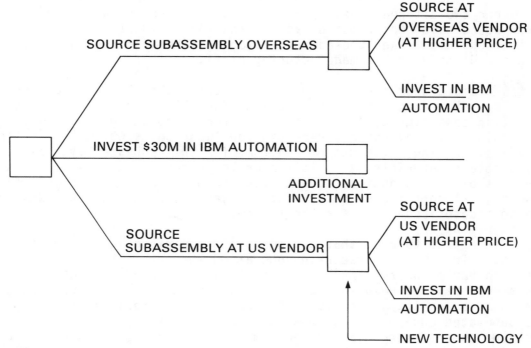

Figure 1. Decision diagram.

OBJECTIVES

It also was necessary to develop a statement of objectives, or rationale, as to how a decision would be made among the alternatives. Typically, the alternative with the highest internal rate of return (IRR) is chosen. Other objectives also could be a short payback period, limiting the amount of capital which can be committed, the reuse of existing hardware, ensuring constant workforce levels, or space constraints. For the subassembly project, it was decided that the IRR would be the primary indicator, with additional emphasis on strategic factors such as being able to stay on the leading edge of technology for this type of subassembly.

ECONOMIC COMPARISON

To determine the IRR, the out-of-pocket cash flows for each of the alternatives had to be determined. These cash flows included the effect of taxes and tax credits, as well as investments in inventories and equipment. Operating costs, such as material and labor line items, also were significant parts of the overall cash flows. Where possible, costs were related to volumes. For example, inventory was specified in terms of inventory days rather than dollar volumes. Changes in inventory were treated as changes in working capital. Carrying costs were used to convey only the out-of-pocket costs of holding inventory, and not allocated interest charges. In addition, inflation was applied to individual line items such as labor, material, and overhead costs.

In doing the costing evaluation, it was seen that the alternative of having a U.S. vendor supply the subassembly was--in all instances--a poorer choice than the other two alternatives. The main reasons were the additional inventory which would have been required versus the IBM build plan, the financing of the capital equipment, and the communications gap between the IBM engineering groups and the vendor's manufacturing staff.

It was decided that for the comparison between the IBM build and the overseas sourcing, that conservative assumptions for all items were to be used. The operating cost figures contained some interesting insights as to the value of automation. The overseas source had low labor costs which were reflected in the final pricing. IBM determined that for this subassembly, however, we could obtain materials at a similar or lower cost than this overseas source. The cost of labor, duties, inventories, shipping delays, and inflation, however, all contributed to driving the yearly out-of-pocket costs in the overseas case above that for the IBM-built part.

It is important to note that the point of comparison in the costs was at the next step in IBM's manufacturing operation where this part was then assembled into another product. Inspection, packaging, storage, and other post-assembly costs were all included in the analysis. In the case of parts costs for the IBM build scenario, the costs of having the raw materials packed for use on the automated equipment also was included. The figures also reflected the costs of establishing quality programs with the raw parts vendor. Only in this fashion was it possible to compare the two alternatives on the same level.

Capital investment was planned so as to allow IBM to take advantage of future changes in production technologies. This was accomplished through the choice of material handling equipment which is compatible with a broad spectrum of production equipment and a layout which could accommodate additional machinery. Most importantly, the capital investments were delayed until absolutely necessary. These steps were important in easing management fears of getting locked into outmoded equipment; by showing the provision for new equipment late in the project life it was possible to ensure that future volumes could be accommodated. The delay of equipment purchases required iterative simulations which showed the manufacturing capacities and manpower levels over time and in comparison to the projected volumes.

The out-of-pocket costs in the overseas purchase alternative necessarily projected the difficulty of establishing good lines of communication over long distances. The effects of this included slower manufacturing learning curves as well as higher scrap and quality costs due to IBM initiated engineering changes. The learning curves were anticipated to be lower overseas due to an inability in that case to implement a program to drive down raw parts costs; such a program would require a good interface with the U.S.-based development and engineering staffs. This interface has been inadequate in similar arrangements with overseas suppliers. For the same reasons, the yearly IBM development expenses were expected to be lower in the overseas alternative.

The base case assumptions are shown in Figure 2. Capital costs include an initial supply of 2.5% spare parts and inflation was applied to equipment purchases after the initial year of investment. Direct labor staffing levels included three months of training and learning. IBM maintenance costs were minimized by having the machine operators trained to take care of minor repairs wherever possible.

			YEAR:	1	2	3	4	5	6
CAPITAL ($M)		BUILD CASE:		0	15	7	0	5	3
	INCLUDES:	2.5%	CAPITALIZED SPARE PARTS						
		1.5M	CAPITALIZED REFITTING						
		6.0%	INFLATION ON EQUIPMENT COSTS						

			1	2	3	4	5	6
LABOR	BUILD CASE:							
	DIRECTS:		4	28	65	70	90	102
	PROFESSIONALS:		19	35	31	31	31	31
	BUY CASE:							
		PROFESSIONALS:	0	8	8	8	8	8

MATERIAL COSTS

BUILD CASE:	(RAW PARTS ONLY):	$40 PER UNIT
BUY CASE:	(COMPLETE UNITS ONLY):	$47 PER UNIT

INFLATION RATES   LABOR: 6.5%
                   SPACE: 3.0%
                   MATERIAL COSTS: OVERSEAS: 4.5%
                                      U.S.   1.0%

INVENTORY	BUILD CASE:	15 DAYS
	BUY CASE:	35 DAYS

LEARNING   BUILD CASE: 5% PER YEAR REDUCTION IN MATERIAL COSTS (PRE-INFLATION)
$650K PER YEAR IN DEVELOPMENT COSTS

            BUY CASE: 2% PER YEAR REDUCTION IN MATERIAL COSTS (PRE-INFLATION)
$250K PER YEAR IN DEVELOPMENT COSTS

Figure 2. Base case assumptions.

Material inflation rates were assumed to be different for raw parts which IBM buys and then assembles itself versus the scenario where the subassembly is delivered complete. The difference in the inflation rates was particular to the type of subassembly being discussed, and extensive investigation supported the difference. In general, a strategic analysis of raw part supplies predicted a price stabilization. Overseas labor costs were projected to rise, on the other hand, and would cause an increase in subassembly costs. This is not to say, however, that management was unconcerned about the inflation differences; on the contrary, a small difference was used in the base case, and the sensitivity to this figure was observed.

RESULTS

The analysis of the base case showed that the IBM manufacturing alternative was favorable and provided a 40% IRR. A sensitivity analysis was then done to assess the impact of changes in certain of the assumptions. The greatest downside risk lies in the area of part costs for the IBM build case and the contract costs with the overseas supplier.

The sensitivity analysis, Figure 3, shows the change in the IRR for a change in the value of the line items. For example, a change of one dollar in the raw parts costs changes the IRR by 3%. The sensitivities as shown were all calculated for small changes in the line items from the conditions of the base case. The sensitivities do change for situations significantly different from the base case. For this reason, it is not possible to add up the sensitivities to equal the base case of 40% IRR.

ITEM	CHANGE	EFFECT ON IRR
MATERIAL COST	$1.00	3%
MATERIAL INFLATION	1%	3%
STARTUP DELAY	1 YEAR	3%
	2 YEARS	10%
ADDITIONAL PRODUCTION	1 YEAR	9%
	2 YEARS	17%
DECREASED PRODUCTION	10% DECREASE	5%
ADDITIONAL CAPITAL	$1 MILLION YEAR 1	2%
	CONTIGENCY (10%)	3%
SPARE PARTS	ADDITIONAL 2%	.5%

Figure 3. Sensitivity analysis (Base Case: IRR=40%).

The projected base case returns, while meeting the decision rationale described earlier, showed limited downside risk as well as upside return potential. For example, one year delay in starting the assembly process would decrease the IRR by only 3%. This limited effect was achieved in part by using conservative first-year volumes in the base case to allow for unexpected, but normal, startup problems. It was determined that volumes which could not be built in the automated facility could be sourced from alternative vendors at prices similar to those of the overseas supplier. This eliminated any cost effect on subassemblies other than those built on the line.

The base case scenario was run for six years out; this was considered conservative in that IBM had firm needs for the subassembly for this period. Needs after this period also were expected, and would increase the IRR by approximately 9% per year for manufacturing in years 7 and 8. Volume decreases had a significant impact on IRR; if the volume decreased by 10% the IRR fell by 5%. This assumed on across-the-board volume decrease, lower volumes in the high-volume years 4, 5 or 6 would have a greater effect on IRR.

The investment also showed very little exposure to slight increase in the capital required. A $1 million capital increase in year 1 caused the IRR to drop by 2%. A contingency which increased the capital needs in every year would have affected the IRR by 1% per million dollars of gross impact. Lastly, the project was fairly insensitive to the need for additional labor, inventory, or spare parts.

CONCLUSION

The recommendations of the CIM team to proceed with the automation effort were accepted by IBM management, although the implementation schedule was later modified to better utilize the production space at the proposed site. It was not necessary to analyze the full effect of the expected technology change on the IRR. This was true because the change would benefit the IBM build scenario and this was the recommended alternative. The IRR is not meant to be a firm prediction of future events and therefore need not be exact. What is crucial however, is that it helps management to make a decision, and that decision would not change if additional information was added to the analysis.

The manufacturing environment of today involves shorter product life cycles, changing process technologies, and quite often, very expensive solutions. Most large-scale manufacturing projects will not provide a quick payback of high ROI when just the first few years or initial product volumes are considered. Only by including many of the nonobvious savings (such as part cost inflation differences) and/or by extending the time frame being considered to encompass follow-on products is it possible to justify many of these proposals.

The primary objective of the justification and review process is to minimize the risk of the company's investment. Extending the time frame being considered can be a risky proposition. However, an analysis of the applicability of the project to future plans and manufacturing strategy are ways to minimize the risk. In addition, the use of sensitivity analyses to explicitly analyze the impact of delays in startup, volumes below projections, or insufficient capital allocations, will aid in the understanding of both the downside and upside exposures of the project.

The use of these techniques by the CIM project team will help in the design of better, less risky projects. Used in conjunction with other tools such as designing for automation and simulation, firms will benefit by the implementation of viable long-term and competitive manufacturing solutions.

Group Technology and Cellular Manufacturing: the Keys to CIM

by William G. Rankin
Deere and Company

INTRODUCTION

Deere & Company is well-known for its innovative use of computer technology in manufacturing. The application of group technology and the formation of focused manufacturing cells have been key elements in achieving computer integrated manufacturing (CIM). Deere's movement toward cellular manufacturing and the use of group technology to improve the information flow from product design to manufacturing are reviewed.

BACKGROUND

Since its historic beginning in 1837 when John Deere invented the self-polishing steel plow, Deere & Company has grown to become the world's largest producer of agricultural equipment. Most of this growth has been steady and deliberate with few opportunities for start-ups of new plants on green field sites. Typically, as volumes increased and new products were introduced, plants grew outward by occupying more space on their periphery. Although each decision made sense at the time, many plants grew to be very large and complex. Material flow patterns were long, often requiring parts to move from building to building and floor to floor in their paths from raw stock to finished product.

This problem became most pronounced in the early 1970s when Deere initiated a major expansion and modernization program for its largest manufacturing facility in downtown Waterloo, Iowa. It was in this facility that farm tractors, our basic product, were built. To simplify and focus manufacturing operations, two new plants were constructed. The first was designed to manufacture a line of diesel engines, thus freeing space at the downtown site for other activities and focusing a portion of manufacturing management and equipment on a very specific product responsibility.

A second plant was built focusing primarily on tractor assembly. The result is the John Deere Tractor Works, a seven-building, 2.1 million square foot complex located in the northeast corner of Waterloo. This factory, which has been in full operation since the Spring of 1981, is probably the most modern and efficient tractor-building facility in the world today. It was for this facility that the Computer and Automated System Association of the Society of Manufacturing Engineers (CASA/SME) awarded Deere the first annual Lead Award for "leadership and excellence in the application and development of CIM."

The remaining operations at the downtown site also were reorganized into what are called factories within a factory. Four major divisions were formed. They included hydraulics, drive trains, special products and the already operating gray iron foundry.

The underlying strategy in this massive reorganization was to simplify and focus manufacturing operations by moving away from large functional, process-based departments and divisions to individual departments and operating units. Emphasis was placed on going from raw stock to finished parts in the most efficient manner with the inefficient cross-flow among departments eliminated wherever possible. The fundamental building blocks of the new organizations were manufacturing cells designed to perform nearly all of the operations on their assigned part families. Group Technology (GT) was recognized early on as the methodology for identifying part families based on similarities in material, geometric features and manufacturing processes.

THE JOHN DEERE GROUP TECHNOLOGY SYSTEM (JD/GTS)

Deere's first experience with GT was gained in 1975 through the purchase of MICLASS, a commercially available GT computer system. After initial applications at the Waterloo complex, MICLASS was subsequently applied at the John Deere Harvester Works located in East Moline, Illinois. Again part families were identified and cells were formed in redeveloping both their casting and bar machining divisions.

These early applications clearly demonstrated the value of group technology, but also identified the potential for a more complete set of part data. Deere began development of its own proprietary GT system in 1978 by interviewing approximately 400 engineers throughout the company to determine the information about parts they required to do their jobs. A state of the art set of software tools was developed to allow the flexible collection, retrieval and analysis of part data.

Heart of the System

The heart of the resulting system is a classification and coding scheme designed to capture the key geometric characteristics of parts. Working from engineering drawings, part coders at factories provide this input on new and revised parts through an interactive, menu-driven computer program. The classification structure records specific information about the parts within the categories of sheet metal, rotational or nonrotational.

The system generates a 35 digit code which acts as a reference to the features on the part. In addition to creating the code, the complete, detailed geometric data about the part is retained and is routinely used for selection and analysis. The system is also designed to access existing production data from other corporate and factory databases. This data includes part standard costs, weights, routings, future requirements, etc.

The resulting GT database is accessible to the engineering user through a variety of flexible retrieval and analysis programs. The software within the system consists of major programs organized into six modules. CODE gets data into the system. EXTRACT isolates a group of parts based on any combination of geometry-based features and/or production data using keywords. MODIFY allows changes to the data to perform "what if" analyses. ANALYZE provides a set of statistical and graphical analysis routines. FILE performs any necessary file handling such as sorting and printing file contents. HELP provides comprehensive on-line instructions and keyword definitions.

As one would expect, this extremely powerful combination of data and software has applications far beyond the formation of manufacturing cells. Currently, there are more than 600 users of the system and more than 145,000 part numbers have been coded.

Daily Access

Users access the system on a daily basis at nearly all Deere factories in both the United States and Europe. The system is used by product engineers for design retrieval to combat part proliferation. It is used to provide reference data for process planning, for part rerouting and methods improvement, for facilities and capacity planning studies, for the procurement of machine tools, to avoid new tooling and to assess new manufacturing technologies.

The John Deere Group Technology System is the key to Deere's movement toward cellular manufacturing and the adoption of just-in-time production concepts. It has increased the productivity of Deere's engineers, allowed analyses to be performed that couldn't even be conceived before its existence and has been credited with providing major savings to the corporation. Perhaps most important, it has provided a foundation for CIM. GT's feature-based representation of parts provides a common, neutral "language" to bridge computer-aided design (CAD) and computer-aided manufacturing (CAM), a fundamental requirement for CIM.

COMPUTER-AIDED PROCESS PLANNING (CAPP)

With GT as an experience base and foundation, Deere is expanding its use of part feature concepts in both design and manufacturing. A major current effort is in process planning. Just as GT is the communications link between design and manufacturing, process planning is the functional link. It entails converting design data into manufacturing plans and costs. It is where CAD meets CAM.

Process planning is a major opportunity area for computerization and integration. It typically consumes nearly 50% of a company's manufacturing engineering staff and drives all downstream functions. It is usually based on the experience of a few critical people and its results are inconsistent.

The John Deere Computer Aided Process Planning System (JD/PPS) is a logical extension of GT taking advantage of the similarity of parts and features to develop consistent and standard logic for planning their production. Designed as a knowledge-based system, JD/PPS captures the rules of expert planners. In addition to the part feature database in GT, CAPP uses similar databases about machines, tools and material.

The approach used in JD/PPS is to provide a generic structure for creating logic modules corresponding to various manufacturing processes and/or part families. A prototype system has been developed and put into production for sheet metal unitized punching and bending operations.

The system aids the planner in selecting a machine, selecting tooling, estimating part costs and generating the information to support manufacturing on the shop floor. Through comparisons of JD/PPS with expert manual process planning, JD/PPS provided better, more consistent plans in less time. Because of these results, the application of the system is being expanded and additional logic modules are being developed.

INTEGRATING CAD WITH CAM

Group technology and computer-aided process planning have provided valuable data and tools to improve communications among the design, manufacturing planning and manufacturing execution functions. A good example is the feedback on existing parts designers can receive through GT to avoid designing new ones. More fundamentally, the feature data for production parts defines the capability of manufacturing and allows design standardization on fewer selected features. Developing standard hole sizes and bend radii are just two examples where variability has been reduced and manufacturing operations simplified.

The language of CAD is primarily geometry-based with the results from the designer and draftsperson being stored in computer form as points and equations. These allow "lines," "arcs," and "circles" to be combined and displayed to represent a finished part. Downstream in CAM, however, features are the common language. Words like "hole," "notch," "slot," and "groove" have manufacturing meanings. Attributes about features are used in process planning and NC programming to make decisions and interpret the geometric drawing of a part created by the design engineer. One of the major challenges of CIM is to make the languages of CAD and CAM a common one by representing part features in a data structure that can be accessed and interpreted by any CAD or CAM application.

To provide the communication link between CAD and CAM, Deere is developing a logical extension to its GT database to provide a complete features-based part description in a neutral format. This is similar in concept to the Part Data Definition Interface (PDDI) activity within the Air Force's ICAM program. Prototype software is currently running on a graphics work station to interactvely tag geometric entities and other attributes on a CAD designed part. The database has been designed and the concept successfully demonstrated for families of relatively simple sheet metal parts. The result of the process is a full feature description of the part.

Another prototype system running on a graphics work station demonstrates the concept of designing parts by inserting parametrically defined features. Specifially developed for symmetrically turned parts, the system eliminates the need for construction geometry. By keying in data on bar length, radius and feature characteristics, the designer can insert turned diameters and various grooves, flanges, bores, etc. on the part. This approach encourages the use of standard features by making their choice by the designer easier than creating new ones. The result of this process is a CAD drawing of the part and its full feature description.

Just as there is leverage in grouping similar parts, basic advantages can be achieved in grouping similar features. Parametric data about features can replace raw geometry as the least common denominator for communicating between CAD and CAM.

CIM--ONE SLICE AT A TIME

Many of the successes of CIM to date have been achieved by focusing on very narrow families of parts. By leveraging on their similarities, computer programs have been written to allow parametric approaches to design, drafting, process planning and NC programming. Flexible Manufacturing Systems (FMS) are effective through similar leverage. There are many parts however, that fall outside the narrow families where CIM has been demonstrated and parametric approaches applied. A major challenge is to achieve CIM for the majority of parts.

While too narrow a focus limits the benefits of CIM, too broad a focus makes achieving CIM extremely difficult if not impossible. Integrating the diversity of computerized tools, systems and databases for a large existing factory, throughout the functions of product design and drafting, manufacturing planning and manufacturing execution is a monumental undertaking.

To make this task feasible, Deere is using pilot or prototype projects to implement CIM within the manufacturing cells discussed earlier. Each cell represents a vertical slice through a factory. The family of parts manufactured within the cell and the cell itself are treated as if they are a minifactory. All of the functions from conceptual design through physical manufacture can be understood more easily within the slice, and the computerized tools, systems and databases can be integrated to achieve CIM for this factory within a factory. By building the tools and systems to be modular and portable, they can be tailored and applied across multiple slices.

Such an approach is currently being applied at the John Deere Harvester Works. A pilot project underway is centered on a new manufacturing process for utilizing an NC turret punch with laser cutting capability for sheet metal. GT was used to develop cell concepts and to identify the family of parts to be manufactured. A full feature database has been developed for these parts and logic modules to plan their operations have been incorporated into JD/PPS. An automated dynamic nesting package is being interfaced with a graphics work station and MRP system to allow multiple part numbers to be manufactured on a sheet in a just-in-time mode. A Distributed Numerical Control (DNC) computer has been installed to allow finished NC programs for sheets to be stored and transmitted directly to the machine on the shop floor as they are required.

To provide communications among the various pieces of CIM, the pilot has incorporated a local area network (LAN) based on the General Motors Manufacturing Automation Protocol (GM MAP) specifications. A broadband cable backbone was installed in the Fall of 1984 and is one of the first production applications of MAP to become operational. Based on the success of this communications medium to date, the network is being expanded and additional NC machines are being connected.

This pilot project is providing Deere with a true computer-integrated manufacturing system for a family covering a large percentage of sheet metal parts. The pilot approach demonstrates the benefits of CIM and helps to identify the problems in achieving it. Most important, the pilot provides a vehicle to learn, to gain more experience and to develop generalized approaches, tools and systems which can be applied to other "slices" and other factories.

SUMMARY

Deere & Company considers the application of group technology and cellular manufacturing concepts as prerequisites to achieving CIM. This helps to simplify before integrating, and avoids misapplying computer technology to manage unnecessary complexity. Manufacturing cells based on families of parts with similar features provide focused slices for integrating the functions from conceptual design to physical manufacture. Part features are being used not only to identify part families, but to provide a common language for achieving both functional and systems integration, CIM can be achieved in digestible bites by focusing pilot projects on manufacturing cells. Such an approach has allowed Deere to effectively incorporate rapidly changing technology into its manufacturing operations.

Index

L

Labor, 88, 172, 182, 183, 190, 192
Leadtime, 8
Learning curves, 190
Local area network, 200
Local storage, 61

M

Machine shop completion dates, 43
Machine utilization, 183
Machining centers, 46
Machining systems, 167
Management
   analysis systems, 172
   approaches, 100
   asset, 3
   commitment, 59
   configuration, 7
   consistency, 6
   data, 4, 6
   deterministic planning, 5
   direction, 24
   downstream, 166
   entrepreneurial, 48
   executive support, 10
   factory support, 10
   factory views, 98
   financial strategy, 181-186
   foxhole, 10
   information systems, 26
   integration, 7, 15
   levels of, 33
   need for, 9
   objectives, 185
   in the organization, 10
   planning, 5
   policy, 9-16
   project, 7, 25, 56
   reporting systems, 61
   reports, 41,
   standards, 4
   systems, 6
   tools, 161
   top, 10, 11, 15, 33, 59
Management information systems, 47
Manufacturing Automation Protocol,
   6, 66, 70, 71, 137, 145, 200
Manufacturing control, 61, 99
Manufacturing planning, 44
Manufacturing Resource Planning,
   40, 47, 54
Market demand, 5
Marketing, 11, 13, 15
Master plans, 25
Master schedules, 40, 41
Material handling, 49, 99, 187
Metal cutting, 40
Microprocessors, 57
Milling, 42
Mind integration, 7
Modular distributed system, 61

Monolithic systems, 41
Mylar tracings, 41

N

Needs Analysis, 25, 26, 28, 30, 101
Needs matrix, 182
Nodal networks, 15
Numerical control
   benefits of, 175
   and CIM, 164
   cutter paths for, 179
   history, 42, 161
   machines, 42, 57, 175
   using minicomputers, 62
   opportunities, 39
   programming, 39-40, 41-42
   verification, 91

O

Operational control, 5
Order entry, 164
Organizational architectures, 14
Overseas supplier, 192

P

Pallets, 46
Parametric design, 14
Part numbers, 12
Part recognition codes, 54, 57
Parts storage, 41
Payback periods, 170
Performance tuning, 104
Personnel, 47
Planning, 5, 39, 164
Plant design, 60
Plant layout, 91
Plotting, 91
Prioritizing, 29
Process automation, 164
Process flexibility, 15
Process planning, 41
Product Data Definition Interface,
   13
Product Data Exchange Standard, 13
Product engineering system, 62
Production control, 62
Production planning, 41
Production sequencing, 98
Product life cycles, 193
Product planning cycles, 39
Product reliability, 15
Program control structure, 7
Programming, 4, 6, 39
Program structure, 4-6
Project economics, 32
Project initiation, 26
Project justification, 4
Project management plan, 26
Project organization, 26
Project selection, 5, 6, 7
Prototypes, 38, 174

Prototyping, 117-124
Published resources, 151-160
Purchasing, 41, 43

Q
Quality, 3, 4, 14, 38, 174, 176
Quality control, 42, 45, 47, 173

R
Raw part supplies, 191
Realistic expectations, 90
Reculturing, 17-23
Return on investment, 51, 101, 187
Richmond host computer, 65
Risk, 31, 179, 180
Robots, 13, 175
Router cutter paths, 62
Routing, 41, 62

S
Safety, 3, 7
Scrap, 27, 174, 182, 183
Security, 40, 43
Sensitivity analysis, 192
Setup time, 174
Sheet metal, 197-199
Shipping dates, 43
Shop floor, 58, 64
Shop floor control, 10, 58
Shop status system, 63
Simulation, 11, 164
Single product definition, 14
Software
  capital investment strategy, 27
  collision, 42
  conceptual description, 38
  design of, 47
  documentation, 102
  in-house, 61
  as an investment, 169
  modules, 38-39
  overall system of, 12
  planning, 5
  sets of, 102
  systems, 12
Solid modeling, 163
Speed, 179
Stages, 19-20
Standards
  changing, 4
  control, 100
  corporate, 70
  costs, 7

  data, 6, 7
  defacto, 70
  industry-specific, 71
  industry-universal, 71
  internal, 15, 70
  as a key to CIM, 4
  maximum, 61
  need for, 9
  planning, 4
  product, 70
  setting, 7
  technical 5, 6
  timeliness, 4
  use of, 4
Statistical process control, 14
Storage, 46-49
Strategic business plans, 25
Subassembly, 186
Subsystem level testing, 103
Subsystem views, 99
Surveys, 169
Synergies, 170
System engineering models, 100

T
Tactical planning, 102
Tech groups, 183
Technical and Office Protocol, 66, 67
Testing, 164
Throughput time, 183
Tolerances, 177
Tool control system, 61
Tool design, 164
Tooling, 27, 38
Tool inventory, 48
Top-down manufacturing, 182
Tracking, 41
Training, 27

V
Value Centered Manufacturing, 11
Vendors, 12

W
Warehouses, 186
Wash stations, 47
Welding line, 32
Wordprocessing, 164
Work-in-process status, 179

Z
Zero defects, 3, 7